THE TWO KOREAS
AND THE
UNITED STATES

THE TWO KOREAS AND THE UNITED STATES

Issues of
Peace,
Security, and
Economic Cooperation

Wonmo Dong
Editor

An East Gate Book

M.E. Sharpe
Armonk, New York
London, England

An East Gate Book

Library of Congress Cataloging-in-Publication Data

The two Koreas and the United States : issues of peace, security, and
  economic cooperation / edited by Wonmo Dong.
    p.   cm,
"An east gate book."
Includes bibliographical references and index.
ISBN 0-7656-0533-3 (alk. paper). — ISBN 0-7656-0534-1 (pbk. :
alk. paper)
    1. United States—Foreign relations—Korea (North) Congresses.
    2. United States—Foreign relations—Korea (South) Congresses.
    3. Korea (North)—Foreign relations—United States Congresses.
    4. Korea (South)—Foreign relations—United States Congresses.
    5. United States—Foreign relations—1989–   Congresses.   I. Dong,
Wonmo.
E183.8.K6T95   1999   99-37183
327.730519—dc21   CIP

Printed in the United States of America

BM (c) 10   9   8   7   6   5   4   3   2   1
BM (p) 10   9   8   7   6   5   4   3   2   1

Dedicated to Raymond Francis Johnson, the godfather of the
SMU–Dallas Forum on Asian Studies

Contents

Acknowledgments

The seventeen essays presented in this volume are based on the annual symposium of the SMU–Dallas Forum on Asian Affairs on the topic of "The Two Koreas and the United States: Issues of Peace, Security and Economic Cooperation." The symposium was held at Southern Methodist University, March 20–21, 1997, and was convened and organized by Wonmo Dong, Executive Director of the SMU–Dallas Forum.

The Forum is grateful for generous financial support from the Caltex Petroleum Corporation, which made possible the 1997 symposium as well as the 1996 symposium on "Post-Deng China and U.S.-China Relations" and the 1998 symposium on "India at the Crossroads: Challenges and Prospect." I am particularly indebted to Mr. David Law-Smith, former Chairman and Chief Executive Officer of Caltex, and to his predecessor at the corporation, Dr. Raymond Francis Johnson, for their steadfast moral and financial support of the SMU–Dallas Forum from its planning stages to the publication of this volume.

The SMU–Dallas Forum on Asian Studies is a joint project of SMU's Dedman College of Arts and Sciences and its Asian Studies Program. The symposia, which were held annually from 1996 to 1998, sought to focus on important domestic political and economic developments in China, the two Koreas and India, and their relationships with the United States, in the late 1990s. The three annual symposia highlighted events in these three countries of vital economic, political, and strategic importance for the post-Cold War global order and their relationships to the post-Cold War policy of the United States in the Asia-Pacific region.

The editor wishes to express his profound gratitude to the three recent deans of Dedman College—Dr. James F. Jones, Former Dean, Dr. U. Narayan Bhat, Acting Dean (1996–97), Dr. Jasper Neel, Dean of the College since 1997—and the Asian Studies Advisory Board at SMU and especially its chairman, Dr. Charles Ku, for their commitment to and interests in promoting Asian studies at SMU and in the greater Dallas community and for providing invaluable assistance in support of the three symposia in 1996–98. The editor also owes much gratitude to the staff of the dean's office for their endeavors to help organize and present the 1997 symposium as well as the two other symposia of 1996 and 1998. For preparation of the manuscript of this book, I am very appreciative of the splendid editing and word-processing assistance that Ms. Noëlle McAlpine of SMU's Tower Center for Political Studies has kindly rendered. The editor of this volume also wants to acknowledge the immense patience and excellent editorial assistance of Mr. Doug Merwin, Executive Editor of M.E. Sharpe, Inc., without which the publication of this book would have been further delayed. Last but not least, I wish to offer my heartfelt thanks to each panelist in the 1997 Korean symposium for his spirited participation in the symposium and for preparing an excellent, timely essay for the publication of this book.

Editor's Note

Given the passage of time since the SMU–Dallas conference in 1997, the chapters appearing in this volume are obviously less current now than they were two years ago. But it it quite remarkable—and indeed very surprising—to what extent that many, if not most, of the prognoses and predictions that a large majority of the contributors to this book made two years ago remain relevant and valid at the time of this publication. The new century is only several months away, but the end of the disturbing Cold War situation in the Korean peninsula is nowhere in sight. The change of government in Seoul in 1997, and the continuing pursuit of engagement policy with North Korea of the Clinton administration that the Kim Dae Jung government fully supports, have hardly changed the rigidities and basic characters of the Stalinist regime in the North. The unstable and unpredictable nature of North Korea's relationship with South Korea, the United States, and other major powers has not abated.

The proposed removal of economic sanctions against the North and normalization of U.S.–DPRK relations in 1999 notwithstanding, the complex issues of DPRK's nuclear arms and missile developments in U.S.–DPRK relations are yet to be resolved. In a fundamental sense, North Korea's dire economic situation and great uncertainties surrounding the regime stability in North Korea have never really dissipated. For these reasons the perceptive and penetrating analyses and findings presented in this volume will significantly contribute to the deeper understanding of the continuing crisis situation in the Korean peninsula that is spilling over into the twenty-first century.

Wonmo Dong
October 30, 1999

Introduction

Wonmo Dong

The Demilitarized Zone in Korea is "the scariest place on earth."

—*President Bill Clinton*

The Cold War has practically receded into history everywhere—except in Korea. While the rest of the world is rapidly progressing into the post–Cold War political order of ever evanescent ideological conflict, the two dangerously armed and hostile states of the Korean peninsula continue to confront one another across a narrow stretch of land called the Demilitarized Zone (DMZ). Korea continues to be a pivotal crossroads of Northeast Asia where the strategic interests of the four major powers (U.S., China, Japan, and Russia) persistently converge with the intermittence of heightened tension and unstable peace. In essence, the problem of inter-Korea relations and interactions among the Big Powers surrounding the two Koreas has become seemingly more complicated and intricate in the 1990s than in the relatively stable pre-1990 period of bipolar international order. Korea has emerged as a most difficult problem in the foreign policy of the United States in the 1990s. In this regard, Korea has been no less challenging a problem for the security and strategic interests of China, Japan, and Russia, the three other major powers having vital interests in the affairs of the Korean peninsula.

The two Koreas could never be more contrasting and different. But the Korean states cannot be more complementary. South Korea (ROK) has been known for its high-growth economy of the past three decades. Since 1987, it has been undergoing the stressful process of democratic consolidation under the civilian regimes of presidents Kim Young Sam and Kim Dae Jung. It is ranked the world's eleventh largest economy and its gross domestic product per capita in excess of $10,000 is twenty times as large as that of the communist north. The severe financial meltdown since late 1997 notwithstanding, the ROK is economically dynamic and prosperous and politically vibrant. But it is also the world's most densely populated country with a population of 45 million inhabiting a territory that is equivalent to the size of Indiana. South Korea clearly lacks land space and manpower for further economic growth. In contrast, the north's 23 million people living in an area that is slightly larger than South Korea are yet to benefit from linkage with the expanding economy of the Asia-Pacific region, let alone that of South Korea. Socialist market socialism of China, the only significant Marxist fraternal state for the Democratic People's Republic of Korea (DPRK), has not yet made an inroad into North Korea.

The sudden collapse of the former Soviet Union and its satellite states, which together with China were the principal ideological, trading, and military partners of DPRK, has cornered North Korea into the world's most isolated and heavily fortified state. Since the early 1990s, North Korea's real gross domestic product has declined by one-fourth of its value. North Korea's worsening economic difficulty is attributed to the poor management of the economy by the monolithic regime and several years of drought and flood, which have reportedly resulted in the deaths of several million people from famine during the past three years. The heavy burden of excessive military expenditures account for more than one-fourth of the country's dormant economy. To compound the already difficult situation, with the death in 1994 of President Kim Il Sung, the world's longest reigning chief of state, North Korea has gone into a period of apparent leadership crisis. The emergence of enigmatic Kim Jong Il, Kim Il Sung's son, as a *de facto* leader of the communist regime, has ushered in a period of uncertainty and further mystery in North Korea.

Subsequent to Kim Il Sung's death, the explosive issue of DPRK's nuclear arms and missile developments was brought under control by the Geneva Agreed Framework, a bilateral accord between North Korea and the United States. Some important achievements in direct U.S.–DPRK talks notwithstanding, however, there are a myriad of difficult and complex issues that need to be resolved successfully if the stubborn persistence of the Cold War situation in Korea, sometimes referred to as

East Asia's "most dangerous flash point," is to be brought to an end.

The seventeen essays presented in this volume are divided into the five topical groups, the last group dealing with future prospects of the Korean situation. The contributors to the joint undertaking of this book were invited to focus on the following questions, *inter alia:*

- What is really happening in the post–Kim Il Sung North Korea? Who is in control of this unstable, unpredictable, and isolated regime? What are the principal domestic and foreign policy initiatives of the DPRK, and how can they be explained? What are the causes of sometimes erratic behaviors of the DPRK regime in its dealings with the ROK, the United States, and other major powers? What are the new opportunities of economic cooperation between DPRK and other countries, especially the United States?

- How would the progress of the current democratic consolidation process under President Kim Young Sam's civilian government in South Korea (1993–98) be assessed? What is the essence of South Korea's policy on North Korea? What are its major pitfalls, and what can be realistically done about a significant improvement of inter-Korea relations? Will the structure of U.S.-ROK cooperation continue to suffer from the constraints of occasional and sometimes fundamental policy differences? Can the United States further promote its important economic ties with South Korea while creating a new structure of peace and security on the Korean peninsula?

- Is the current Korea policy of the Clinton administration sound and balanced? What are the main strengths and weaknesses of the U.S. policy toward DPRK and ROK? Is the American concept of a soft landing of post–Cold War DPRK much different from that of South Korea and other countries? What are the main components of Korea policies of China, Russia, and Japan? Do they have much in common with the U.S. policy toward the two Koreas? How can the United States and other major powers cooperate more effectively for the stabilization of the fragile Korean situation that directly impinges upon the regional peace and security of Northeast Asia and the Asia-Pacific region?

The authors of the chapters in this volume are some of the most distinguished scholars, diplomats, and public commentators who have been examining the subjects of the two Koreas and the United States, as well as related issues in recent years. The contributors are representative of several contrasting, if not conflicting, observations and opinions on the main topics of discussion.

North Korea: The Politics of Muddling Through?

The first three essays by Dae-Sook Suh, Marcus Noland, and Samuel Kim concern the unpredictable dynamics and the murky reality of North Korea's domestic politics and economy in the period after the death of Kim Il Sung, that is, since 1994. The essays deal with the three important aspects of the recent developments in North Korea: the viability and durability of political leadership in the post-1994 period (Dae-Sook Suh's chapter); the unraveling reality of North Korea's *juche* (self-reliance) economy (Marcus Noland's chapter); and the sustainability or the survival of the North Korean communist system. In addressing these issues, each author seeks to ascertain the patterns of both changes and continuity of the Marxist-Leninist—or the Stalinist-Confucian system, if you will—of the DPRK. It is rather striking that the two political scientists, Suh and Kim, have arrived at almost the same conclusion as Noland, an economist, with reference to not only the current situation but also the future—near-, mid-, and long-term—of the North Korean regime.

In his lead article based on his ongoing analyses of the North Korean polity, Suh pinpoints several major problems that the North Korean political system has been beset with in recent years. Foremost among them is a sudden change in early 1997 of several top leaders of the DPRK, such as the defection of Hwang Chang-yop, chief ideologue; the death of Ch'oe Kwang, minister of People's Armed Forces; and the resignation of Kang Song-san, premier of the Administrative Council. Suh cites available evidence that suggests "a discord among the top leaders of North Korea." Listing other debilitating problems such as the sorry state of the North Korean economy, the catastrophic flood of 1995 and 1996, and the subsequent mass starvation of the civilian populations, Suh agrees with other scholars of North Korean affairs, but maintains that "North Korean crisis is *real*, but it is erroneous to link it with the collapse of regime." It is noteworthy, however, this long-time student of North Korean affairs argues, that in spite of the fact that Kim Jong Il, Kim Il Sung's son and heir apparent is still "an unknown and unproved leader," the junior Kim is likely to inherit the Great Leader's mantle. According to Suh, the reasons for this conclusion include: (1) there is no credible opposition leader or group that can effectively challenge Kim Jong Il's supremacy; (2) North Koreans have been too ideologically indoctrinated; and (3) North Korea's communist system is so institutionally entrenched that the current crisis will not lead to the system's collapse.

Marcus Noland offers his careful, cogent analysis of the current economic crisis of North Korea, which he describes as "an archetypal CPE (Central Planning Economy)" under extraordinary strains. At its peak in 1990, DPRK's per capita income was somewhere between $1,300 and $3,800 purchasing-power-adjusted dollars per year, with a central estimate of $2,284, which would have put North Korea contemporaneously in the same league with Indonesia and the Philippines. Citing the Bank of Korea and other sources, Noland estimates the North Korean economy suffered a cumulative decline of roughly 25 percent through 1995. The ratio of South to North Korean incomes was about 4:1 in 1990, 6:1 in 1995, and will be roughly 12:1 by the year 2000. While making note of a continuing shrinkage of North Korea's economy caused by an annual grain shortfall of about 2 million tons and a severe shortage of energy, however, Noland observes that "The North Korean regime could survive a prolonged period of economic decay." The two principal reasons cited for the unlikelihood of the imminent collapse of the political regime in North Korea are: (1) North Korea has succeeded in "fusing *juche* (self reliance) ideology to [North] Korean nationalism and (2) the absence of "institutions capable of channeling mass discontent . . . into effective political action." Noland sums up his appraisal of the North Korean situation by saying that North Korea is "more likely to *muddle through*, supported by China (and possibly by Japan and South Korea, who would like to avoid its collapse."

Samuel Kim makes a convincing case for his forecast of North Korea's middle-range future, the time horizons of which the author designates as the future of the North Korean communist system in 2002–2004. Arguing that this longer-term scenario is "ultimately more important than the issue of the recent past and the immediate future" Kim lists and compares a spectrum of alternative scenarios—"futuribles (possible futures)"—system collapsing, system decaying, system maintenance, system reforming, and system transforming. Kim argues that in the context of North Korea, the system-decaying-cum-system-collapsing scenario is not "sustainable" because it is fallacious to equate economic collapse with system collapse, and the collapse of the Kim Jong Il regime with the North Korean regime. According to Kim, several powerful factors that gravitate against the system collapse scenario are: (1) the opposition of Beijing, a balancer in Korean affairs, to remove North Korea ("the junior socialist ally in the strategic buffer zone"); (2) North Korea is not a "Fourth World banana republic that would collapse quietly without a big fight or without creating the huge mess that no outside neighboring powers can or want to clean up"; and (3) both Pyongyang and Seoul do not want "the clear and present danger of German style hegemonic unification." In tune with Suh and Noland, Kim concludes that by far the most likely and viable is the system-maintaining scenario, that is, the survival of the North Korean state through the middle-range future of 2002–04.

South Korea: Democratization and Inter-Korea Relations

By 1997, it had been a full decade since South Korea's democratic consolidation process got underway in 1987. Kim Young Sam—a former dissident politician who in 1990 formed a grand coalition party with General-turned-President Rho Tae Woo and Kim Jong Pil, a principal coup planner of the 1961 military coup and former director of the Korean Central Intelligence Agency (KCIA)—became the president in 1993. Enjoying impressive support of the general populace, President Kim made great strides during the first two years of his five-year term (1993–98). His economic reform programs were thoroughgoing and sensational, especially the real-name bank account system and the forced revelation of the personal wealth of high public officials. Likewise, his purge of "political generals" was no less aggressive. How did he perform in the foreign policy arena, particularly in ameliorating the hard inter-Korea relations? Did U.S.–South Korea relations improve, or at least remain stable, during the tenure of the Kim Young Sam government? Kwang Woong Kim, Victor Cha, and David Steinberg present penetrating, cogent analyses of South Korea's domestic political economy and its linkage with the external relations with North Korea and the United States.

Each author looks at the internal politics of South Korea and its effects on foreign policy behavior.

The North Korea policy of Kim Young Sam's civilian government, according to Kim, showed "no clear strategy of how to influence events in the North." During his five-year term in 1993–97, President Kim interacted with North Korea with an inconsistent policy—from assuming a conciliatory posture during the first three months of his administration in 1993, to taking a hard-line position in June 1993, and reverting to a more accommodating one in January 1994. However, after Kim Il Sung's death in July 1994, Kim Young Sam reverted to a confrontational policy toward the northern regime. In essence, South Korea in 1993–97 carried out an ambivalent policy between a soft landing and an abrupt collapse (a hard landing) of North Korea. In his chapter, Kim attributes the failure of South Korea's policy toward North Korea to three important elements: (1) lack of leadership—the failure to lead both the people and government functionaries; (2) lack of capacity to help build a consensus among the people for an effective northern policy; and (3) lack, or obvious inadequacy, of policy coordination between the four government agencies that were involved in North Korean affairs. The Kim administration did not arrive at a set of principles, and it did not provide an environment in which productive policy discussion was encouraged. Lacking both policy initiatives and directions, South Korea grudgingly followed U.S. engagement policy toward North Korea. The author states that toward the end of his presidential term, Kim became more concerned about "his own soft landing" after leaving the office than that of the Pyongyang regime. By keeping, and wooing, the powerful security apparatus and the military on his side, President Kim in essence carried out—or wanted to appear to follow—"a tough line against Pyongyang." In addition to North Korea's intransigence, some notorious domestic scandals—especially the multibillion-dollar Hanbo Incident and the corruption case of Hyon Chol Kim, the president's son—severely constrained Kim Young Sam's ability to launch an effective North Korea policy during the last two years of his administration.

Victor Cha's essay examines a key policy dilemma of South Korea toward the North—engagement strategy. Cha notes that a prevailing view among the policymakers in South Korea's current regime (the Kim Young Sam government) is that North Korea does not want to be engaged and that South Korea's engagement strategy toward North Korea does not in fact constitute engagement in a generic or genuine sense. There are two reasons for a wide gap between the rhetoric and public statement of engagement and the reality or absence of engagement strategy in South Korea, according to Cha. First, South Korean policymakers continue to suffer from "an inability to transcend the zero-sum mentality of the Cold War." The mainstream of the policy community in South Korea tends to equate genuine engagement with North Korea with appeasement and weakness. It claims that only the weaker of the two states on the Korean peninsula should employ this strategy. Second, South Korea follows "a fundamentally narrow notion of security." In the Cold War-mindset of Korean policymakers, genuine security is derived from deterrence and superior military balance. Security cannot be achieved through engagement and accommodation. Since 1993, the United States has pursued a genuine engagement policy toward North Korea. This post–Cold War policy was based on an assessment that South Korea is the stronger of the two Korean states and engaging the weaker, less stable, and less privileged of the two, that is, engaging North Korea is "the safer and cheaper way of enhancing the security of the stronger half (the ROK)." Cha points out that the engagement strategy of South Korea during the Kim Young Sam administration did not espouse an explicit engagement. South Korea's reluctant and half-hearted engagement—or failure to attempt genuine engagement—came from no less than the persistent cognitive underpinning of the concept of engagement, a notion that engagement is a policy option of the weaker actors. Lack of South Korea's engagement mentality, Cha notes, can be based on its failure to see "the potential benefits from a token transmission of condolences for Kim Il Sung's death in 1994" and South Korea's intermittent lack of cooperation with the U.S.–North Korea Agreed Framework. Clearly lacking an element of explicit engagement, the South Korean concept of engagement—be it economic engagement or political give-and-take—is boiled down to simply "a vision for unification" but not an effective strategy of the stronger actor(s).

In his assessment of the current state of the U.S.–South Korea alliance system, David Steinberg contends that looking from the vantage point of South Korea's domestic politics there are several discernible, troubling trends and forces that deeply constrain the bilateral structural relationship between South Korea and the United States. Steinberg finds that some of these problems are quite new and that they are both internal as well as external to South Korea. Given the depth and persistent nature of these problems, the author is of the opinion that by the spring of 1997, the two alliance partners had gone into an era of growing disquiet and distrust. It is futile, he warns, to replicate "old patterns and traditional criteria" in resolving the new issues of bilateral relations between the two countries. The new approaches are needed if the damages already done are to be controlled and the long-term national interests are to be promoted. By far the most disturbing to a great many South Koreans—especially to leaders of the Kim Young Sam government—is the U.S. engagement policy with North Korea since 1993 that sometimes contradicts South Korea's ambivalent North Korea policy. As Kim and Cha show in their essays, the main thrust of Korean policies in response to North Korea's hard-line and often unpredictable position has been largely the policy of *quid pro quo* and continued Cold War–style vigilance. With reference to the successful Geneva Agreed Framework between the United States and North Korea, the South Korean government was effectively kept out of the negotiating process. This was how it was perceived by most of the South Korean leaders and general public. At various times, South Korea expressed its displeasure by arguing that the Geneva Accord—and for that matter, its engagement strategy—were "naïve and counter-productive." Steinberg also points to the issue of anti-American feelings in South Korea, and notes that the sentiment is "essentially inherent in the continuously unbalanced relationship between South Korea and the United States since liberation in 1945." It is generally agreed that the direct negotiation of the United States with North Korea—with a nominal consultation with Seoul—further widened the gap between the Kim Young Sam government and the Clinton administration. On this delicate subject, Steinberg writes: "American preoccupation with nuclear proliferation, at the expense, in Korean terms, of South Korean interests reflects a division in priorities [between South Korea and the United States] that is important that Americans understand, even if it does not want to change their policies." An important dimension of anti-American sentiment in South Korea is the dichotomy of the politically conservative public and the *minjung* (mass or people's) movement. These two groups are pessimistic against anything foreign, especially American. Another constraint, Steinberg suggests, is a worsening trade imbalance between the United States and Korea, especially the latter's trade deficits, that is caused by not only the rising level of agricultural products, but also many luxury goods. Labor relations, in general, and the acceptance of more militant alternative labor organizations, in particular, also contributed to the fragility of social instability in South Korea. Steinberg notes that South Koreans have become increasingly proud of their nation, thanks to the reputation of their "miracle economy" and South Korea's entry into the Organization for Economic Cooperation and Development (OECD), an exclusive club of rich nations. But they also became aware of their growing vulnerability in the post–Cold War environment both on the Korean Peninsula and in the more open and global economic relationships with other market economies, especially the United States. This essay concludes that given the severe erosion of trust, fundamentally new post–Cold War approaches are called for in strengthening the relationship between the two alliance partners.

Korea and Korea's Asian Neighbors

In the next three essays Masao Okonogi, Quangsheng Zhao, and Evgeniy P. Bazhanov discuss the changing dynamics of bilateral relations between each of the two Koreas, on one hand, and Japan, China, and Russia, on the other. The authors focus particularly on new policy issues that have emerged in recent years—especially since the death of Kim Il Sung in 1994. Zhao and Bazhanov provide a brief examination of the evolution of China and Russia's relations with the two Koreas during and following the end of the Cold War. Each author dwells on new opportunities that the two Koreas and the major powers—including the United States—may explore to reduce the high level of tension on the Korean peninsula.

Rejecting the notion that the future of the North Korean regime has already been set, Okonogi carefully explores and compares several possible scenarios on the fate of the DPRK. This includes (1) North Korea's invasion of the South; (2) the implosion and internal collapse of the Kim Jong Il regime, caused largely by worsening economic difficulty; and (3) peaceful resolution and unification with the South. According to Okonogi, the worst-case scenario is that the DPRK decides to resort to a second Korean War if the food crisis in North Korea worsens; the October 1994 U.S.-DPRK Agreed Framework and the KEDO implementation are abandoned; and Kim Jong Il fails to achieve his supreme leadership, possibly necessitating a brinkmanship for his political survival. The most optimistic scenario, this author suggests, would follow a major breakthrough in DPRK-ROK relations after the December 1997 Presidential Election in South Korea and the successful resolution of North Korea's food and economic crisis given DPRK's possible option of phased opening of DPRK and PRC-style market economy with a Leninist political system. This scenario is more plausible if Kim Jong Il succeeds in achieving the supreme leadership (*suryong*), Okonogi contends. It is worth noting, however, this author is not optimistic on the phased opening and economic reform of the DPRK. His concern is that the present political structure that is based on "a trinity of the supreme leader, the political system and the state (DPRK)" might not tolerate the eventuality of a *collapse by stages,* which would be incumbent upon the opening of the country to the global economy. Okonogi emphasizes that Japan has an important role to play, especially to promote the opening and reform in North Korea. In this regard, this scholar concludes that it behooves Japan—and South Korea, the United States, and China—to develop simultaneously the policies of promoting North Korea's opening through economic exchange and preparing also for a sudden internal collapse.

Quansheng Zhao begins his essay with a comprehensive analysis of China's changing priorities of foreign policy from the Maoist era (1949–76) to the Deng Xiaoping era (1978–97). During the latter period, Zhao notes, the principal objectives of China's "post-revolutionary state" shifted to pragmatic considerations of national interests. Its first priority was economic development and modernization, not "a single-minded preoccupation with world revolution" of the Mao Zedong era. Since the late 1970s the People's Republic of China (PRC) has sought to pursue a determined, balancing policy toward the two Koreas, or what Zhao refers to as "a triangular relationship among Beijing, Seoul and Pyongyang." China essentially wants to maintain an optimum triangular relationship with both North and South Korea. In the words of a U.S. official, "[h]aving good relations with both [Koreas] puts China in the best possible situation." China's situational, unambiguous tilting toward one of the two Korean states is based on China's top-priority policy objective of the regional stability of Northeast Asia and its considerations of pragmatic national interests, which emphasizes China's economic development and modernization. Zhao provides a cogent analysis of how China's flexible two Korea policy of the Deng Xiaoping era has shifted back and forth between pro–North Korea and pro–South Korea. China has intermittently supported the DPRK as the latter's single most important fraternal state and trading nation, but it has also disappointed North Korea with its objection to North Korea's nuclear arms development under a nuclear-free Korean peninsula formula. In the same vein, China's support of North Korea as a fellow communist state turned out to be quite limited when in May 1991 China threatened to approve South Korea's entry into the United Nations, thus practically effecting the simultaneous entry of both Koreas into the world organization. Since China normalized its diplomatic and economic relations with South Korea, an enemy state of the DPRK, in 1992, the two-way trade between South Korea and China reached US$15 billion by 1995—a four-fold increase since 1990. In 1994 China–South Korea trade was almost nineteen times as much as the volume of China–North Korea trade. The heads of state of China and South Korea have already visited the other capital. In spite of such important economic relations between South Korea and China, however, the latter has objected to economic sanctions against North Korea. China's balancing acts toward Korea are very adroit, if not unpredictable. Zhao concludes his essay by stating that: "The ground for cooperation [between China and each of the two Koreas] will . . . be much greater than for conflict. Each side . . . may regard the other as a counterweight to the increasing economic and military strength of Japan."

Evgeniy Bazhanov's article, which is largely based on Russian sources and his personal involvement in the foreign policy process in Russia, provides a detailed analysis of the evolution of increasingly intricate bilateral relations between the former Soviet Union and its successor state, the Russian Federation, on one hand, and the DPRK and the ROK, on the other. This study looks into the major policy changes—underlying causes, policy processes and consequences—in two distinct periods: (1) the Gorbachev period of 1985–91; and (2) the period of the Russian Federation (1991–97).

When Gorbachev came to power in 1985, he denounced inequality among socialist states and was openly sympathetic to the desires of smaller socialist states for greater political autonomy and less economic dependence on the Soviet Union. Concerned keenly about a trilateral Washington-Tokyo-Seoul military networking system, Gorbachev offered to help the DPRK, militarily, politically and morally, which pleased the DPRK leadership, particularly Kim Il Sung. However, the honeymoon between the new *glasnost/perestroika* regime of the Soviet Union and the DPRK was very short-lived as Pyongyang soon became extremely agitated with the Soviet new thinking (political opening and economic restructuring), which it renounced as heretical and dangerous. The North Korean leadership was shocked by the political liberalizing trends in Eastern Europe and the democratization of Soviet society. A definite turning point in post-Gorbachev USSR-DPRK relations was the Seoul Olympics of 1988, during which many influential Soviet citizens visiting South Korea were genuinely impressed by the high-growth economy of the ROK. North Korea boycotted the Seoul Olympics, and, in the eyes of the reformist regime of the Soviet Union, the isolated North Korea was clearly out of sync with the rising trends of opening and reform in most of the Marxist countries. As early as May 1986, the Politburo in Moscow had recognized South Korea as "a factor of global military-strategic alliance" and called for a closer relationship with it, at the same time promoting a more independent posture of South Korea toward both Washington and Tokyo. Bazhanov's essay examines important policy initiatives in Moscow and Seoul, leading up to the May 1990 Summit Meeting in San Francisco of Gorbachev and South Korea's president, Roh Tae Woo. In the rest of his study, Bazhanov discusses how since 1992 Yeltsin continued an increasingly close economic relationship with South Korea at the expense of the fraternal relationship with its former ally, the DPRK. This essay points out that the new economically oriented bilateral relations between the Russian Federation and South Korea were marred by several new problems—the downing of a Korean Airlines jet (KAL 007) in 1983 by a Soviet fighter plane, for which Russia expressed regret, and the controversial disposal of nuclear wastes in the Far Eastern seas, for which South Korea joined Japan to criticize Russia's irresponsible practices. The Russian Federation made repeated attempts to put Russia–North Korea relations back on track, but without much success. This chapter concludes that, while enjoying continuing, albeit occasionally uncomfortable, relations with South Korea, the Russian Federation has recently been making "slight improvement" in Russia–DPRK relations. By 1994 Russia's share of North Korean imports declined to 10 percent of the total from 60 percent in 1988. It is worth noting in this study that the DPRK has been seeking to use "a Russian card" in its determined efforts to maximize its negotiating position in all-important DPRK–U.S. bilateral relations, which is North Korea's top-priority foreign policy initiative in the 1990s.

The United States and Its Korea Policy

The six chapters on the United States and the two Koreas examine the Korea policy of the United States government. The chapters are authored by two former ambassadors (Donald P. Gregg and Robert L. Gallucci), a former Korea desk officer of the State Department (David E. Brown), the two think-thank scholars (Selig S. Harrison and William J. Taylor, Jr.) and a program officer of an independent U.S. government agency (Scott Snyder). These authors were invited to participate in our Korea symposium and to contribute to the present publication because of their intimate knowledge of and their actual involvement in both the development and implementation of the United States government policies toward the two Koreas. The six essays collectively and individually shed significant light not only on the complexity of the issues of the U.S. Korea policy but also on the reasoning, concerns, and assumptions of those who were on the cutting edge of the policy process, and the actual negotiations with North Korean diplomatic functionaries and officials of the South Korean government.

Rejecting the Huntington thesis that it is in the best interest of the United States in the post–Cold War era to pursue "an Atlanticist policy of close cooperation with its European partners" at the expense of strategic relations with the countries of Asia and other regions of the world, Gregg presents a cogent argument for the use of "force and diplomacy" to help accomplish the goal of a balanced foreign policy toward Asia and especially the Korean Peninsula. Gregg shares his assessment of the sources of Kim Il Sung's anxiety and frustration (such as post–Cold War isolation and lack of respect from the United States), and supports the logic and the efficacy of the prudent engagement policy toward the DPRK, while objecting to the withdrawal of the United States ground forces from South Korea.

Robert L. Gallucci, presently dean of the Walsh School of Foreign Services at Georgetown University, was the chief negotiator with North Koreans of the United States Government in 1993–94 that resulted in the conclusion of the U.S.–DPRK Agreed Framework. Gallucci was most instrumental in articulating the underlying assumptions and the basic objectives of the U.S. policy toward North Korea—and, for that matter, the whole Korea—from the explosive, if not panicky, spring of 1993 detection and imminent threat of DPRK's nuclear weapons program leading to the successful U.S.–DPRK Agreed Framework in October 1994. He explains the urgency and the goal-directed nature of the U.S. policy toward North Korea whereby North Korea's nuclear weapons program, with its grave global implications for the future of the Nuclear Nonproliferation Treaty, was brought under effective control while engaging the isolated, Stalinist regime of North Korea for the specific strategic goal of the United States in Northeast Asia. Gallucci maintains that the U.S.–DPRK Agreed Framework, which resulted in the immediate moratorium of DPRK's nuclear weapons program with the building of the two light-water reactors under the management of the Korea Energy Development Organization (KEDO)—was intended to contain the immediacy of the nuclear issue while lowering the level of isolation and consequential paranoia of the DPRK regime. It is worth noting that this experienced diplomat and his policy was against an all-out resistance from South Korea. He says that despite the considerable mutuality of national interests that stem from the implementation of the Agreed Framework, a high level of anxiety in South Korea over the outcome of the Geneva accord was caused in no small measure by the very nature of the alliance system between the United States (a superpower and the stronger of the two partners) and the Republic of Korea (objectively the less powerful of the alliance partners). He notes that he has experienced a similar problem in his dealings with West European alliance partners.

David E. Brown's essay is very instructive in terms of understanding the delicate nature of the triangular U.S.–DPRK–ROK relations. He writes that the "American tie with South Korea needs constant tending; there is no such thing as *too much* assurance of American fidelity," and observes that all things considered, "the most volatile leg" of the triangular relations is U.S.–ROK relations. According to Brown, this is because South Korea is basically ambivalent in adhering to the goal of North Korea's "soft landing," which both the Bush and Clinton administrations have promoted with an ostensible endorsement of South Korea.

In implementing the soft landing objective, Washington often loses sight of the fact that "while South Korean *heads* drew them in one direction—toward peaceful reconciliation, their *hearts* too often drew them in another—toward retribution, or at least away from extending the long-time foe a hand in time of need." Given this emotional dimension and the incongruence between what *heads* and *hearts* dictate, South Koreans sometimes resent what they consider "semi-independent U.S. relations with the DPRK."

Regarding the successful conclusion of the Agreed Framework at Geneva, Brown notes that Robert Gallucci's pivotal role in the mid-November 1993–October 21, 1994, negotiations with North Koreans marked a happy compromise between the "core objectives" of the nonproliferation policy community and those of the "Asia hands" in Washington. The author adds that the timely intervention of former president Carter further provided a momentum for the attainment of a realistic policy to deal with the nuclear crisis. Brown concludes by saying that in implementing the goal of the Agreed Framework, "American leverage depends on strict U.S. performance of its own commitments." In this regard, Brown is concerned that the U.S. government has failed badly.

Selig S. Harrison notes that the United States' Korea policy has, for most of the post–Cold War era, become "a hostage to entrenched and right-wing military and political leaders" in South Korea. He argues that the DPRK is not likely to implode or explode in the foreseeable future and that the most prudent and realistic U.S. policy toward North Korea is the one that is calculated to induce a soft landing—but not a sudden breakdown or the "contained collapse"—of the North Korean system. To accomplish the objective of this *engagement* policy in a productive manner, Harrison recommends the removal of economic sanctions and the grant of food and other aid by the United States (and South Korea and Japan) that would be made conditional on the progress of economic reform policies in North Korea. Such a measured policy would cause the DPRK to gradually emerge from the cocoon of isolation, and move toward the Chinese-style Leninist market economy.

William J. Taylor, Jr. maintains that, given the extreme rigidity ("the anthropocentric nature") of North Korea's *juche* ideology that perpetuates the dictatorship of the Supreme Leader (*suryong*), Kim Jong Il, it is very unlikely that the DPRK will follow a "a gradualist reform strategy" that has been implemented in China and Vietnam. Taylor argues that there is no need to worry about the threat of North Korea's military adventurism, given the dire straits of the North Korean economy and the absolute military superiority of the combined forces of the United States and South Korea. Saying that to engage the DPRK is "akin to hugging a rattlesnake," Taylor argues that the policy of *constructive engagement* will simply, and unnecessarily, prolong the precarious life of the bankrupt and dangerous regime of North Korea. It would not contribute to a soft landing of North Korea. According to Taylor, North Korea's implosion is practically inevitable. Therefore, the most Washington and Seoul can do under the circumstances is to wait for North Korea to move toward "a train wreck," suffering the ultimate end of its Stalinist system.

In his essay on the management of U.S. policy toward Korea, Scott Snyder begins his analysis by correctly noting that the crisis situation has become a normal state of affairs on the Korean peninsula and that in the Korean context, "the instigation and escalation of 'crisis'" has become a basic element in the process of managing and resolving the conflicts among all actors—particularly between the DPRK and ROK. Snyder points out that the DPRK has been very successful in using "crisis diplomacy" (the threatened nuclear withdrawal from the Non-Proliferation Treaty and the IAEA) to bring about direct negotiations with the United States. The crisis diplomacy has played no less an important role in the difficult management and sometimes virtual breakdown of U.S.–South Korean relations. Snyder notes that policy coordination between the United States and the Republic of Korea has been complicated by a combination of "unresolvable internal differences within the South Korean policy community," the fluctuating North Korea policy and profound and persistent South Korean fears that the United States may cut a deal with the DPRK. He concludes his study by suggesting that policy coordination between the two alliance partners may be better secured on a long-term and proactive basis, rather than by pursuing short-term reactions to "crisis diplomacy," for which the DPRK has proven to be remarkably adroit and effective.

The Two Koreas and the Twenty-First Century

The two last chapters of this volume are by P.H. Koo, a leader of the business community in South Korea, and Professor Robert A. Scalapino of the University of California. Their essays seek to provide some prospects for the future of the two Koreas and their relationships with other countries—especially the United States.

First, explaining that in Chinese the word "crisis" is comprised of the two words, *wei* (danger) and *ji* (opportunity), Koo admits that there is a crisis on the Korean Peninsula at the threshold of a new century, but the situation is not hopeless but lends itself to new opportunities in the future. Koo notes that the DPRK's recent willingness to engage the United States and other countries may be attributed to "hunger-driven pragmatism" that reflects a change in North Korea's current thinking, indicating that there is "some hope that disaster may be averted." South Korea and the United States should strive toward "a soft collapse" of North Korea should "a soft landing" prove to be unattainable. The main thrust of Koo's thesis is that, buttressed by a strong market economy, the business community in the two countries should not play the role of a passive partner but take a proactive lead in "prodding" their respective government to turn a current crisis into a new opportunity to help gradually bring the DPRK into the orbit of the international market economy.

Robert A. Scalapino begins his essay by noting that in Korea the United States was often regarded as "a distant power" that can counterbalance the hegemony and intrusion of the neighboring powers. Whether exploring trilateral talks (United States, ROK, and DPRK), quadrilateral talks (United States, PRC, and the two Koreas) or another formula that involves Japan and the Russian Federation, the United States should seek "carefully phased relaxations" of the DPRK with the full cooperation with South Korea. Scalapino lists and compares five scenarios for the future of North Korea: (1) "the early, rapid collapse of the DPRK government"; (2) the "gradual disintegration of the North over time"; (3) a DPRK attack on South Korea as "a product of desperation"; (4) the "hunkering down" scenario (e.g., Soviet-era Albania), which is along the thesis of William Taylor; and (5) a "soft landing" (the gradual transformation of DPRK).

The current Korea policies of the United States and South Korea are based on the fifth scenario, which Scalapino is willing to support but with a caveat that "any answer that posits a single definitive outcome is unwise." While he clearly supports the soft-landing scenario, Scalapino notes that "it would be unwise to abandon all 'sticks' and rely wholly upon 'carrots.'"

Given the fluidity of the situation on the Korean peninsula, Scalapino suggests, the most appropriate near-term policies of the United States and the Republic of Korea should include, among others, continued U.S.–ROK bilateral consultation between the alliance partners; resumption of the meaningful DPRK–ROK dialogue as an integral part of the normalization of the U.S.–DPRK relations, especially after Kim Jong Il's anticipated assumption of the presidency of the DPRK government and an election of a new president in South Korea in December 1997; and the support and implementation of the Agreed Framework and the KEDO project. Looking to the new century, he concludes that the U.S.–ROK alliance—including the issue of the continued presence of the U.S. ground forces in South Korea—can be reconsidered, given the great change taking place in military technology. But he says the *timing* of policy change toward the rollback of the U.S. military force is vital. In fact, he says "now is not the time."

As the global political order rapidly approaches the onset of the twenty-first century, the Korean peninsula remains as one of the most dangerous flashpoints in the world. The explosive situation in Korea continues to upset the peace and security of Northeast Asia and the rest of the world. It is deeply worrisome to the policy and academic communities, and all watchers of contemporary East Asian affairs, that most of the problems under study in this volume show no sign of abating. The fragility of the political, economic and military balance within the two Koreas and in Northeast Asia stubbornly persists.

The essays presented in this volume represent divergent views on the topic on which each author was asked to focus. Each writer has provided an in-depth analysis of the principal underlying factors that give rise to the continuing Cold War situation on the Korean peninsula. To a significant extent, they have successfully unraveled many aspects of the complicated domestic political and economic dynamics of the two Koreas and the patterns of relationship between the two rival states of Korea, as well as their changing relationships with the United States and other major powers.

Part I
North Korea's Domestic Politics and Economy in the Post–Kim Il Sung Era: Patterns of Change and Continuity

1
Crisis Management by New Leaders in North Korea

Dae-Sook Suh

Since the death of their supreme leader, Kim Il Sung, in July 1994, the North Korean people have suffered considerable setbacks in all aspects of their social and political life. Their economic difficulties are so severe that the Flood Damage and Rehabilitation Committee of North Korea made an international appeal for support for food, an unimaginable campaign from a country that prides itself on the widely publicized idea of self-reliance. North Korea claims with some justification that its economic difficulties are due in part to natural calamities caused by the floods of 1995 and 1996, but the difficulties are not confined to economic problems.

In February 1997, four serious political setbacks were reported. First was the defection of the top ideologue, Hwang Jang Yop, a most significant indication of discord among the top leaders of North Korea.[1] More important than the defection of Hwang was the resignation of Kang Song-San. North Korea announced that Kang, premier of the Administration Council, had resigned because of illness and was replaced by an acting premier, Hong Song Nam. Kang was ranked third behind Kim Jong Il and O Chin U at the time of the death of Kim Il Sung, and he had been premier since December 1992. He is the architect of North Korean economic reforms, which included the introduction of the Joint Venture Laws, the Tumen River Project, and the creation of the Rajin-Sonbong special economic zone in North Korea.[2] His loss to the North Korean government has far greater impact on North Korea than the loss of Hwang. This is not all. North Korea lost its two top military leaders: Ch'oe Kwang, the minister of People's Armed Forces, and Kim Kwang Jin, the deputy minister of People's Armed Forces, within a week. These events will have far-reaching impact on North Korea.

The North Korean press has been hinting that the North Korean people are making an "arduous march" similar to the one made by Kim Il Sung during his struggle for Korean independence. The joint New Year Editorial that replaced the familiar annual New Year Address by Kim Il Sung proclaimed that 1997 is the final year of the march that will end in victory.[3] The joint editorial of three newspapers *(Nodongsinmun, Chosoninmin'gun, and Chongnyon chonwi)* represents the position of the three most powerful organizations in North Korea: the Workers' Party of Korea, the Korean People's Army, and the Kim Il Sung Socialist Youth League. From reading this editorial, one can surmise that North Koreans consider the transitional period—the three-year self-imposed mourning period—is over, and their "arduous march" will come to an end in 1997.

The "arduous march" refers to the agonizing march that Kim Il Sung and his revolutionaries were supposed to have made during their anti-Japanese guerrilla days in Manchuria. This march, commonly referred to as the "march in distress," *konanui haenggun,* was made in the winter of 1938. Because of the Japanese expeditionary force that was commissioned specifically to suppress the Chinese and Korean guerrillas in Manchuria, Kim Il Sung's revolutionary forces left a small town called Namp'aeja in Menjiang prefecture in the northeastern part of Manchuria in December 1938 to escape Japanese expeditionary force attack. They marched toward the southeastern part of Manchuria for five months until April 1939, when they reached a wooded area near the town of Puktaejongja in Changpai prefecture on the Sino-Korean border. They often marched without food for three or four days, fighting the pursuing Japanese expeditionary force, and enduring the bitter cold of Manchurian winter without adequate clothing and shelter. They suffered the consequence of defecting comrades, but their revolution persisted. They even claim that the agonizing march had reinforced their resolve to fight the Japanese to the end for Korean independence, and they instilled anti-Japanese spirit to the village people along the route of their march.[4]

The new leadership in North Korea compares the current difficulties with the experience of this "march in distress." The march was completed shortly before the Japanese expeditionary forces completely crushed the guerrillas of the Northeast Anti-Japanese United Army, and many leaders were either killed or they fled Manchuria to the Russian maritime province. It is at times compared with the "long march" of the Chinese Communist movement, and it is used to distinguish the loyal from the disloyal. It is also used to measure the endurance and to test the commitment of the guerrillas to the cause of revolution. If the "march in distress" of 1938–39 was the agonizing march for Kim Il Sung, North Korea seems to claim that the three-year transitional period of 1994–97 is the arduous march for Kim Jong Il. There are many front-page stories of *Nodong sinmun* that claim increased production in factories because the people are working with the spirit of the march.[5]

Frequent reference to the hard times that North Korea had endured in the past and the description of how heroically its people and revolutionaries had solved the problems signify that the regime is appealing to its people to make super-human sacrifices to solve current difficulties. Similarly, frequent reference to the march also signifies that North Korea is undergoing a difficult time today. Some argue that it may not overcome the current economic crisis, and others contend that its political regime, as we understand it, may not survive the crisis. North Koreans, however, have faced trouble before, and their diagnosis of the current difficulties is vastly different from our analysis of their situation.

The reason for seriousness of our concern this time is the fact that the supreme leader of North Korea, Kim Il Sung, who solved the problems for the people in the past, is no longer there to take care of the crisis. His successor, Kim Jong Il, is an unknown and unproven leader who may or may not be able to manage the crisis to a successful conclusion. This short essay is an effort to identify major problems that North Korea confronts today after the death of Kim Il Sung and to assess whether it is feasible for new political leaders to successfully manage the current crisis. It should be pointed out at the outset that this is not a frivolous exercise in predicting doom for North Korea, nor is it an effort to discount the seriousness of difficulties it faces after the death of Kim Il Sung. North Korea's crisis is real, but it is erroneous to link the crisis with the collapse of the regime. North Korea's problems are complex, but they were not created by the new leader, Kim Jong Il; rather, he inherited many of his father's problems. Crisis management in this essay refers to a long-term solution to the problems.

Problems of North Korea

Except for natural calamities, such as the floods of 1995 and 1996, the problems of North Korea are not short-term difficulties that can be solved quickly. Kim Il Sung's demise had been anticipated by North Koreans, and Kim Il Sung prepared himself for a successor for more than two decades. North Korea has initiated a campaign for the people to be loyal to Kim Il Sung generation after generation. Many problems emanate not from political or social disturbances but from the long and uncompromising rule of Kim Il Sung, who governed the people with an idea of his own that was not in step with the time of his son's generation.

Four major long-term problems at the time of the death of Kim Il Sung in July 1994 are identified. First is the domestic problem related to the political succession that was not completed. Kim Il Sung succeeded in appointing his son commander-in-chief of the armed forces, but Kim Jong Il was not elected general secretary of the party or president of the republic. Thus, Kim Il Sung's sudden death created an abnormal and uneasy political state where a military commander, not the head of the state, had to rule the country. The second problem is in the conduct of its foreign policy. North Korea needed to find its place in the community of nations after the collapse of the Soviet Union and its satellite countries in Eastern Europe. It condemned the failure of socialism in the Soviet Union and justified its own style of society but it failed to adapt itself to the new international political environment and seek new friends and allies in capitalist countries.

The third problem is the debilitated state of North Korean economy. Contrary to common understanding, North Korean economy did not decline abruptly after the death of Kim Il Sung; it had been in serious trouble since the middle of the third seven-year economic plan in the late 1980s. Although the floods of 1995 and 1996 revealed the seriousness of the problem, the economic problem had existed for nearly a decade. The fourth and the most serious problem is related to military and security issues. North Korea was heavily dependent on the Soviet Union and China for its security, but both countries concluded diplomatic relations with South Korea when the Soviet Union collapsed and China became busy dealing with capitalist countries to improve its economy. For the survival and security of their country, North Korea ventured into developing nuclear weapons, but it immediately confronted opposition from friends and foe alike. Their nuclear program signified that North Korea can no longer compete with the South in the modernization of conventional weapons.

Other problems remain, such as North Korean relations with South Korea. North Korea has always considered South Korea its adversary, and inter-Korean relations have fluctuated according to the political vicissitudes of both sides, but they have never been cordial. Various political, economic, social, and humanitarian negotiations were conducted, and they even signed the Agreement of Reconciliation, Nonaggression, and Exchanges and Cooperation between the North and the South in February 1992, but none of the provisions was implemented.[6] Shortly before his death, Kim Il Sung even agreed to a summit meeting with the South Korean president in an effort to break the South Korean barrier to establish meaningful relations with the United States and Japan, but his untimely death eliminated all possibilities. South Korea's handling of Kim's death further aggravated the tense situation, and inter-Korean relations gradually deteriorated. Today, new leaders of the North refuse to deal with the government of Kim Young Sam, and they seem to avoid any direct contact with the current regime in the South. Even when international appeals for food are made, North Korea refuses to deal with the South, seemingly waiting for a new leader and a new regime to emerge in the South.

Management of the Problems

The four problems cited above are important to Kim Jong Il and require immediate attention by the new leaders. Unsuccessful resolution of any one of the four may lead North Korea into a state of acute crisis detrimental to its survival as a political regime. It is important to briefly state the nature of the problems and examine how the new leaders can manage the crisis at hand.

1. The Domestic Political Front

While Kim Il Sung's eccentricities were often endured by the people, his political leadership was admired. When he chose his son to be his successor in the face of opposition, he succeeded either by persuasion or by coercion to have his decision accepted. His careful handling of the selection process prevented domestic political unrest, but the process took an inordinate amount of time—twenty years from the time when he first introduced his son as successor in 1974 to the time when Kim Jong Il managed the affairs of the party and the state in 1994. Because the succession process was not completed, the regime was in disarray. Three years after the death of Kim Il Sung, the government has not chosen the president of the republic and the ruling party still lacks a general secretary. The Workers' Party of Korea has not convened in seventeen years, and the Supreme People's Assembly has not held a regular session for the past seven years. Because Kim Il Sung has not observed the party bylaws or the constitutional provisions to convene the sessions on time, it is not unusual for the party and the legislature to delay convocation of their sessions. It is unusual, however, that the position of general secretary of the ruling party and the office of the president of the republic are left vacant for nearly three years. [7]

North Korea seems to be governed by an ad hoc council headed by Kim Jong Il. The council may consist of party, government, and military leaders selected by Kim representing both his father's generation as well as his own. The temporary rule by the council does not constitute crisis in the administration of government and party operations because the North Korean political scene after the death of Kim Il Sung appears to be calm and stable. The more important question on the domestic political front is how Kim Jong Il will reconstitute the new government and the party. The 1992 constitutional amendments gave rise to the speculation that the new state institution under Kim Jong Il may entertain the notion of collective leadership.[8]

It is speculated that Kim Jong Il will most likely assume the general secretary position of the party at its Seventh Party Congress, and he may yield the presidency of the republic to another leader. He will remain as the head of the National Defense Commission to control the North Korean armed forces as commander-in-chief. The constitution stripped away the power of the president of the republic to act as the supreme commander, and gave control of the military to the chairman of the National Defense Commission. In order to prove his political prowess, Kim Jong Il may assume all three positions—as head of the armed forces, the party, and the government in 1997—but the chance of relinquishing the presidency within a few years is a distinct possibility. Since the government carries out the policies set out by the party, as general secretary Kim Jong Il would control the operation of the government as well as appoint or remove the president of the republic.

Political leadership under Kim Jong Il may consist of a mixture of old leaders of the Kim Il Sung generation and young leaders of the new generation. It is most likely that at the time of the Seventh Party Congress, a number of old-generation leaders will remain in the position of power, but a majority of the members of the Central Committee will be leaders from the younger generation. Kim Jong Il will eventually replace the old with new leaders who will take over the North Korean political scene. At the time of the Ninth Supreme People's Assembly in May 1990, for example, it was claimed that nearly 60 percent of the 687 representatives to the North Korean legislative body consisted of men and women younger than 55 years of age.[9] It is important to point out that all leaders, old and new, are in full support of Kim Jong Il and his leadership.

2. North Korean Foreign Relations

Kim Il Sung proclaimed that North Korean foreign policy goals were threefold: independence, friendship, and peace.[10] He observed the goals effectively and became independent from heavy Sino-Soviet influence over North Korean relations with other countries. Although it remained in the Socialist camp, North Korea actively sought to enter into the nonaligned movement, ultimately becoming a member of the conference of nonaligned nations in 1968. During the tenure of Ho Tarn as foreign minister, 1970–83, North Korea expanded its horizon and concluded diplomatic relations with seventy-five countries. It also established a North Korean Permanent Observer Mission in the United Nations, and Ho brought about great progress in North Korean foreign relations in the 1980s. However, Kim Yong Nam, his successor who took over the foreign ministry in 1983, failed to change the direction of North Korean foreign policy to adapt to the new political environment of the world in the 1990s.

Although Kim Yong Nam survived the transition from Kim Il Sung to Kim Jong Il and still serves as foreign minister, it was during his tenure as chief foreign policy maker that North Korea suffered setbacks. He failed to counter the aggressive South Korean foreign policy to normalize diplomatic relations with the Soviet Union and China and made no efforts to seek new friends and allies in capitalist countries. For example, North Korea joined the United Nations as a member not because it wanted to change direction from its past practices and join the community of nations, but because it feared exclusion if South Korea were to represent the Korean peninsula in the United Nations. And no new foreign policy initiatives were made to explore the possibilities of expanding economic relations that may lead to the normalization of diplomatic relations with the technologically advanced and industrialized countries of the West.

Kim Yong-Nam made little effort to improve North Korea's image in the world. Western industrialized countries, for example, did not consider North Korea important enough, politically or economically, to establish meaningful political or commercial relations. In general North Korea was considered a dogmatic, and at times a fanatic, subscriber to a peculiar brand of communism that often engaged in state-supported international terrorism. Kim Yong-Nam spent an inordinate amount of time disseminating Kim Il Sung's ideas to third-world countries.

Such campaigns were costly, and while they may have impressed the leaders of African and Latin American countries, they have done nothing to improve North Korea's image in industrially advanced countries. The image suffered further when North Korea engaged in terrorist activities shortly before the 1988 summer Olympics in Seoul.

Kim Yong-Nam failed to make adjustments for the collapse of fraternal socialist countries, and he was not able to counter the South Korean initiative to take away North Korea's major allies. Negotiations under his direction to conclude diplomatic relations with Japan and the United States also failed, and his policy toward the United Nations and the IAEA aroused suspicion among the capitalist countries about North Korea's true intention to promote peace in the international community.

To manage the policy setbacks, Kim Jong Il must find a new foreign minister who can more effectively implement the three foreign policy goals. The most important task for the new foreign minister is to improve the image of North Korea in the new world. It is also imperative that North Korea establish diplomatic relations with the technologically advanced and industrialized countries of the world, particularly with the G-7 countries.

To achieve this objective, it is contended that North Korea's immediate task is to negotiate successfully with Japan rather than with the United States.[11] Japan is geographically nearer to North Korea, and it has greater interest and involvement in North Korea than does the United States. Cultural affinity does exist between Japan and Korea, and North Korea has its front organization, Chosoren, in Japan. North Korea is in a position to receive considerable reparations when and if it succeeds in establishing diplomatic relations with Japan. North Korean foreign policy in the second half of the 1990s should be flexible enough to engage Japan in a renewed negotiation.

The current North Korean policy of dealing with the United States to solve its problems with South Korea and Japan should be reevaluated. North Korean relations with the United States are marked by South Korean interference and American military presence in South Korea. A peace treaty between the United States and North Korea without South Korean participation may be a difficult task. The United States may not be willing to make any meaningful concessions to North Korea at the expense of its traditional ally, South Korea. Although the United States may support the idea of North Korea's "soft landing" in the community of nations, it may be wise for North Korea to consider the option of establishing formal diplomatic relations with South Korea as two separate governments in the Korean peninsula.

3. North Korean Economy

The difficulties related to the state of North Korean economy need immediate attention. North Korea's economy suffered from three major problems: (1) the inadequacies in the basic concept of economic development, (2) the structural deficiencies domestically and changes in its external economic relations, and (3) the heavy burden of supporting the military. Kim Il Sung's basic concept of economic affluence was to fulfill the basic human necessities. Remembering the hard times he had suffered during his revolutionary days in Manchuria, Kim's idea of economic affluence was for the people to have three meals a day, a roof over their heads, and enough clothing to fend off the cold. Even when North Korea's economy improved somewhat, his idea of an affluent lifestyle was to have meals of rice and meat, to have tile-covered roofs, and to wear clothes made of silk. His idea was to build an affluent agrarian society, and he did not strive hard for an advanced industrial society. In this regard, Kim Jong Il had a completely different upbringing from his father. Although he grew up under the watchful eye of his powerful father, he had an affluent childhood compared to that of his father. He and his new political leadership will undoubtedly change the goals of economic development from those of his father's generation.

Kim Jong Il realized that what he inherited is an economy that cannot provide even the basic necessities of life to the people. The change, therefore, must come from the basic concept of what constitutes affluence in economic life. Catherine Bertini, the executive director of the World Food Program, visited North Korea in March 1997 to discuss an estimated food deficit of 2.36 million metric tons. Nongovernmental organizations made new appeals for food to meet immediate needs, but these are short-term solutions to the problems. While it is important to address the short-term problems and ease the immediate sufferings of the people, it is more important to rethink long-term economic goals.

The North Korean economy is centrally planned; the first one-year and two-year economic plans began even before the Korean War. After a five-year economic plan was concluded successfully, the first seven-year economic plan was launched at the time of the Fourth Party Congress in 1961, but it soon ran into difficulties and was extended for three more years in 1966 at the time of the Second Party Conference. It was completed in 1970, making it a ten-year plan. Similar to the first seven-year economic plan, the latest plan, the third seven-year economic plan, was also extended an additional three years to complete in 1996. Although North Korean officials claim success in meeting the goals set by these often extended economic plans, it is obvious that North Korea suffered from the usual problems associated with centrally planned economies.

The second problem lies in the many structural problems with centrally planned economies. In an effort to meet the quota assigned to each unit, party cadres, instead of government officials in charge of economic work, directed production. Campaigns to mobilize the labor force were devised to maximize output, but the problems were more fundamental and not because of the lack of industry on the part of the labor. North Korea suffers from overemphasis on heavy industry at the expense of consumer goods, misallocation of capital, lack of advanced technologies, and other chronic structural difficulties prevalent in centrally planned economies.[12] It needs to increase production, but it also needs to have proper distribution of what has been produced. Kim Jong Il and the new political leaders must pay close attention to the needs of consumers.

North Korea's economy also suffered significantly from the collapse of the Soviet Union and from the changes in trade practices of both Russia and China. It has suffered negative economic growth for the past six years, and there is no relief in sight. In its own inefficient way, North Korea, however, tried to venture into new economic initiative and change, and this effort is nowhere more clearly exemplified than in the rise and fall of its chief economic planner and prime minister, Kang Song-san, who just resigned. During his tenure as prime minister in 1984–86, North Korea adopted the first Joint Venture Laws to attract foreign investments, but when Kang was unable to induce substantial foreign investment under this venture, he was relieved and sent to the Hamgyong-pukto regional party committee. Kang continued to promote international economic cooperation, and developed the Tumen River Project, which involved China, Japan, Russia, South Korea, and the United Nations. At the Twentieth Plenum of the Central Committee, he was recalled from the province to head the Administration Council as prime minister in December 1992.

Recalling Kang to head the Administration Council was interpreted as an earnest effort on the part of the new generation of political leaders to improve the economy by increasing trade and commercial relations with other countries. Under his leadership, North Korea began to promote the Rajin and Sonbong free trade zones to attract foreign investments, and it has held several investment forums in the United States, Japan, and North Korea to induce foreign investments. Although the progress is slow, Kang's effort to develop North Korean economy by inducing foreign investments is a step toward the right direction. [13]

The third and most important cause of North Korean economic problems is the burden it carries to support a large military force. The North Korean defense outlay exceeds 20 percent of the national budget annually, and it is the root cause of economic setbacks. Furthermore, it seems that North Korea's military economy exists independent of the central plan. From the basic supply of farm goods for military consumption to the export of missiles to foreign countries, North Korea's military maintains a separate economic operation from the centrally planned economy. It seems to have special access to goods and supplies, and soldiers seem to participate in North Korean construction as laborers.

Kim Jong Il and his new leaders must find the means to lessen the burden of the North Korean military. The impact of military outlay to its economy is a problem that requires both political and economic solutions. They must reduce the armed forces, find new and reliable allies that can replace the former Soviet Union, or negotiate with powerful neighbors to satisfy security concerns.

4. Military and Security Problems

Because of the need to sustain its political system to compete with the South, North Korea has always maintained unusually large armed forces.

With the support from the Soviet Union and China, it competed for several decades, at times successfully, with South Korea on matters related to military preparedness. But when the Soviet Union collapsed and China ended diplomatic relations with South Korea, the North had to solve the problem of national security on its own. By the early 1990s North Korea found itself isolated. North Korea's economy was so far behind that it was not able to compete with South Korea; nor was it able to purchase fuel and supplies in international markets to modernize the military. Kim Il Sung began to indoctrinate North Korean soldiers with patriotism and prepared them to fight with inferior weapons and equipment. He emphasized that it is the human spirit, not the quality of weapons, that determines the outcome of any conflict. Such rhetoric was hardly convincing, and he had to find new weapons to satisfy his national security concerns.

The path it chose was to develop nuclear weapons—not so much to launch an attack on any particular military target or country, but to safeguard its survival. Such a move to develop nuclear weapons in North Korea coincided with an effort on the part of the United States to dismantle nuclear weapons throughout the world after the collapse of the Soviet Union. It also threatened existing security arrangements in East Asia. After prolonged negotiations, threats, and inspections of nuclear facilities by the IAEA, North Korea decided to enter into an agreement with the United States to suspend its development of nuclear weapons.[14]

The agreement, the so-called Agreed Framework, was signed between the United States and North Korea on October 21, 1994, ostensibly to provide North Korea with light-water reactor power plants to generate electricity.[15] It also stated that the agreement was an effort on the part of the United States and North Korea to achieve peace and security in the *nuclear free* Korean peninsula. Arrangements were made subsequently among the United States, Japan, and South Korea to provide North Korea with the light-water reactor (LWR) under the direction of the Korean Peninsula Energy Development Organization.

A fundamental problem exists with this arrangement. The Agreed Framework may have satisfied U.S. objectives to prevent North Korea from developing nuclear weapons in the Korean peninsula, but it has not solved North Korea's problem of national security. This problem is due in part to North Korea's insistence that its purpose in developing a nuclear program was not to develop nuclear weapons but to generate power.

But as is well known to all parties concerned, the real purpose in

North Korea's effort to develop nuclear weapon capability was to en-hance its military and security, not simply to generate power. North Koreans will accept the LWR, but until their security needs are satisfied, they will always entertain the option of developing nuclear weapons.

Mishandling of this problem will indeed lead North Korea into mili-tary and security crisis. Kim Jong Il seems to use, at times appease, the military to support his position at home, but if he creates a situation where national security is threatened, North Korean military leaders may challenge him. The military is the only group that is capable of success-fully challenging his leadership; when it does, North Korea will indeed be faced with a crisis.

To satisfy military leaders, Kim Jong Il must find a way to establish a meaningful relationship with the United States by concluding a peace treaty to replace the truce accord reached at the end of the Korean War. He also has to find a way to convince the leaders of the military that South Korean armed forces and American troops stationed in the South do not constitute threats to North Korean security. The suspension of the joint military exercises, such as the Team Spirit, would be a good sign. Although American troop withdrawal from the Korean peninsula in the near future is hardly a possibility, there are growing concerns in the United States to reconsider "permanent" deployment of American troops in Korea.[16] In short, Kim Jong Il must make headway in his negotiations with the United States on military and security matters.

Conclusion

Kim Jong Il may have received blessings from his father to take over the country, but he does not seem to have the "mandate of heaven." He suffered many political and economic setbacks from the sudden and untimely death of his father and from the natural calamities of 1995 and 1996 floods that devastated the countryside, putting the North Korean economy into chaos. He took over a government that could not feed its own hardworking people. His traditional allies have either collapsed or changed their direction away from North Korea, and his military is hope-lessly outmoded. His efforts to develop nuclear capabilities were effec-tively curtailed by his adversary in the South and by the United States. What he inherited from his father was not a socialist "paradise" on earth as was advertised, but a failing regime with major problems.

However, Kim Jong Il inherited a stable and resilient government that his father so laboriously built over the past five decades. Either coerced or persuaded, the people in the North are in full support of their government. Except for the defection of Hwang Chang-yop, there is no credible opposition leader or group that professes to challenge the regime. Instead, the people are ideologically trained or indoctrinated to be loyal to their country, filial to their parents, and love one another in building toward a permanently socialist organic community. Kim Jong Il may have major economic problems, but he does not have anyone challenging his political leadership at home. The resignation of Premier Kang Song San is a major setback, but Kim has already found a new leader, Hong Song-san, to replace him. The death of two top military leaders, Ch'oe Kwang and Kim Kwang Yop, is also a setback, but they were old generals of the Kim Il Sung era. More leaders of that generation will die in the near future, but they can be replaced by the leaders from the new generations. Of the 247 top leaders who constituted the funeral committee at the time of the death of Kim Il Sung in 1994, 22 have died.[17] Even Hwang Chang-yop in his defection message predicted that the North Korean regime will not collapse. It is contended here that Kim Jong Il and his new leaders will be able to manage the problems toward a successful conclusion.

Current North Korean difficulties are long-term problems that will not be solved quickly. While the North Korean people seem to give their new leaders ample time and extended opportunity to solve them, this does not mean that the people will remain permanently obedient. If and when the people are convinced that Kim Jong Il and his new leaders are unable to solve their problems, they may indeed change their leader. However, this does not signal a collapse of the North Korean system. Still other leaders will emerge to maintain and improve the system. In order for the North Korean system to collapse, an anti-Communist and anti-Kim Il Sung revolution must take place. It is unrealistic to expect such revolutionary change within this century. The problems North Korea confronts today should not be confused with the crisis that will lead to the system's collapse. This may be Kim Jong Il's "march in distress," but like his father in 1938, he may endure the hardship and emerge as a leader who would carry out the legacy of his father.

Notes

1. Hwang Chang-Yop was secretary of the Workers' Party of Korea and chairman of the Foreign Affairs Committee of the Supreme People's Assembly. He

served as chairman of the Supreme People's Assembly and president of Kim Il Sung University for more than fourteen years. He is widely known as the ideologue who developed the idea of self-reliance in North Korea.

2. Kang Song-San was elected premier at the Third Session of the Seventh Supreme People's Assembly in January 1984, but was dismissed because his idea for joint ventures failed to attract foreign investors. He was sent to the Northeastern regional party committee, where he developed the idea of the Tumen River Project. He was recalled from the provincial committee and reappointed premier in December 1992 at the twentieth Central Committee meeting of the Sixth Workers' Party of Korea.

3. *Nodong sinmun*, January 1, 1997.

4. There are many accounts of this march. See the latest account in Kim Il Sung's memoirs. Kim Il Sung, *Segiwa toburo* [With the Century], Vol. 7 (Pyongyang: Choson nodongdang ch'ulp'ansa, 1996), pp. 147-181.

5. See, for example, the story of the Sangnong silver mines and how the workers increased production in *Nodong sinmun,* August 22, 1996.

6. A comprehensive agreement was reached by the delegates at their fifth meeting in Seoul on December 13, 1991. The agreement was signed and ratified at the sixth meeting held on February 19, 1992. See text of the agreement in *Korea and World Affairs* (Vol. 16, no. 1, Spring 1992), pp. 145-148.

7. The sixth party congress of the Workers' Party of Korea was held in October 1980, and the latest, the Ninth, Supreme People's Assembly was convened in May 1990. The last time the Central Committee convened its plenum was in December 1993. *Nodong sinmun,* December 9, 1993. The most recent Supreme People's Assembly session, the seventh, was held in April 1994. *Nodong sinmun,* April 7, 1994.

8. See the report on the amendment of the constitution in *Nodong sinmun,* April 9, 1992. The text of the amended constitution was not immediately released.

9. Kim Chung Nin reported on the findings of the Credential Committee. He said that out of 687 representatives, 2.9 percent was 35 years old or younger, 56.8 percent was between 36-55 years old and 40.3 percent was 56 years or older. See his report in *Nodong sinmun,* May 25, 1990.

10. Kim Il Sung, *Report to the Sixth Congress of the Worker's Party of Korea on the Works of the Central Committee* (Pyongyang: Foreign Languages Publishing House, 1980), pp. 82-97.

11. See the argument in more detail in my essay, "North Korean Foreign Policy of the 1990s," in *Democracy and Communism. Theory, Reality and Future,* The KAIS International Conference Series, 3 (Seoul: KAIS, 1995), pp. 657-670.

12. For a good assessment of North Korean economy, see Marcus Noland, "The North Korean Economy," *Joint U.S.–Korean Academic Studies* (Washington, D.C.: Korean Economic Institute of America, 1996), and Eui-Gak Hwang, *The Korean Economies* (Oxford: Clarendon Press, 1993).

13. The Twentieth Plenum also promoted Kim Tal Hyon and Kim Yong-Sun to the Politburo as alternate members. Kim Tal Hyon is chairman of the State Planning Commission and Kim Yong Sun has been active in diplomatic negotiations both in Japan and the United States. For the changes in the twentieth Plenum, see Dae-Sook Suh, "Prospect for Change in North Korea," *Korea and World Affairs,* vol. 17, no. 1 (Spring 1993), pp. 5-20.

14. There are many studies on nuclear negotiations, such as Michael Mazarr, *North Korea and the Bomb. A Case Study in Nonproliferation* (New York: St. Martin's Press, 1995).

15. See the text of the "Framework Agreement on the Nuclear Issue Signed between the United States and North Korea" in *Korea Times,* October 22, 1994. See also the North Korean announcement of the text in *Pyongyang Times,* October 22, 1994.

16. See, for example, a study by Doug Bandow, *Tripwire: Korea and U.S. Policy in a Changed World* (Washington, D.C.: Cato Institute, 1996).

17. From the top fifty leaders, only three (O Chin U, Ch'oe Kwang and Kang Hwi-Won) died, and from the top 100 leaders, only ten died. In addition to the above three, they are Ch'oe Pok Yon, Kim Ch'ang Ho, Yi Sok, Paek Pom Su, Kim Pong Yul, Kim Kwang I'm, and Paek Ch'ang Sik.

2

The Economic Situation in North Korea

Marcus Noland

"Anyone who tells you that they are an expert on
North Korea is either a liar or a fool."

—*Walter Mondale, former vice president
and ambassador to Japan*

Introduction

I make no claim to be an expert on North Korea. Rather, I am a conventionally trained American economist interested in the situation in North Korea. As for the other labels—well, read on and you can decide.

The Korean peninsula was colonized by Japan at the beginning of this century; Korea began its industrialization during this period of Japanese occupation. Nearly two-thirds of industry was located in the northern portion of the peninsula, which was blessed with considerable mineral wealth, while the South was the breadbasket, producing agricultural products for Japan and the more industrialized North.

Japanese rule ended in 1945 with partition of the peninsula into zones of U.S. and Soviet occupation. Most of the Japanese colonists returned to Japan, while at the same time the peninsula experienced an influx of returnees from various parts of the defeated Japanese empire. Economic statistics from the immediate post-war period show that the Koreans were able to maintain local production of manufactures in every identi-

fiable industrial category, indicating that while the Japanese had dominated economic life in the colony, local residents had acquired and developed a considerable amount of economically relevant skills.

The United States and the USSR were unable to reach a successful
resolution of their stand-off, and in 1948 independent states, the U.S.-
allied Republic of Korea (ROK) in the south, and the Soviet-backed
Democratic Peoples' Republic of Korea (DPRK) in the north, were declared in the respective zones of occupation. Under Soviet tutelage, the
North Koreans undertook a land reform and began constructing a So-
viet-style centrally planned economy (CPE), building on the industrial
legacy left by the Japanese.

In 1950 North Korea invaded South Korea. Under the auspices of the
United Nations, a U.S.-led multinational force entered the war on the
Southern side, while China eventually intervened in support of the North.
A truce agreement signed in 1953 left the original borders more-or-less
intact, but the seesaw character of the war, with both armies traversing
the length of the peninsula, left both countries economically devastated.

In the North, central planning and the collectivization of agriculture
were intensified in the aftermath of the conflict. The familiar institutions of a market economy—money, prices, and private property rights—
were thoroughly suppressed and replaced by bureaucratic control by the
central planning apparatus.

The system worked, at least on its own terms, at the outset. The planners, following the Stalinist emphasis on heavy industry and the military, were able to mobilize resources, building on the industrial legacy
of the colonial period. The share of population employed in industry
rose steadily, and the British economist Joan Robinson wrote that "all
the economic miracles of the [post–World War II] world are put in the
shade by these achievements" and concluded that "as the North continues to develop and the South degenerate, sooner or later the curtain of
lies must surely begin to tear."[1] Conventional wisdom holds that the
South did not overtake the North in terms of per capita income until the
1970s, and one prominent academic specialist dates it as recently as
1986.[2]

While adhering to Stalinist orthodoxy internally, under the *juche* (self-
reliance) philosophy proclaimed by founding leader Kim Il-Sung in 1956,
North Korea claimed nominal independence in external affairs, timing,
for example, its central plans to frustrate linkage with other CPEs, and
declining to join the socialist Council of Mutual Economic Assistance.

(Although given North Korean dependence on economic assistance from both China and the USSR, this was self-reliance of an idiosyncratic sort.)

The system began to falter in the 1970s, however, when the North Korean system was unable to successfully make the transition from extensive development through the mobilization of resources to intensive development through raising the productivity of those resources employed. Pyongyang's initial response was to borrow from abroad to maintain the growth of domestic spending, and they found willing partners in Western bankers eager to recycle petrodollars. Unable to generate sufficient hard currency revenues to service the loans and unwilling to compress domestic spending to free up the resources necessary to pay off the creditors, North Korea defaulted on its foreign debt in the mid-1970s and found itself effectively cut off from Western capital and technology.

Soon even the USSR had soured on the North, reducing economic assistance and demanding repayment of North Korea's accumulated debt. By 1987 net transfers had turned negative—resources were flowing from North Korea to the USSR. This drag on the economy was compounded in 1989, when the DPRK suffered an enormous trade shock when the political and economic upheavals in the East bloc disrupted North Korean trade with its traditional trade partners. At the dawn of the new decade North Korea found itself without money—or friends, and in 1990 the North Korean economy began its slow collapse.

The Current Crisis

Economists are fetishists for numbers, and if there were a list of cardinal sins for economists, spurious precision would surely be among them. One of the reasons that the North Korean economy is so little examined is that, in conventional terms, there is little to study. The only economic information that the government has regularly released has been the state budget, and even this has not been announced for several years. Mundane data such as the volume and composition of international trade is treated as a state secret.

Nature abhors a vacuum, and the South Korean authorities have stepped into the breach. Unfortunately, much of what they produce appears nearly as unreliable as the propaganda pronouncements emanating from Pyongyang. The sad result is that the public discussion of the North Korean economic situation often resembles the proverbial blind men examining an elephant. The admission of North

Korea into the United Nations has helped in some respects, with the DPRK authorities releasing data of little apparent strategic value to various U.N. organizations as part of these agencies' routine international data compilation work. So, for example, demographic data released to the United Nations by the North Koreans has been analyzed by Western demographers, who found no obvious internal inconsistencies or evidence of tampering or falsification.[3]

So what can be determined about the current state of the North Korean economy? At its peak in 1990, North Korean per capita income was probably something on the order of $1,339 to $3,897 purchasing power adjusted dollars per year, with a central estimate of $2,284.[4] This would have put North Korea contemporaneously in the same league with Indonesia and the Philippines, among the Asian countries, and Romania among the CPEs, although educational attainment rates, literacy, and other indicators of social development look a little higher than would be expected on the basis of the income figures alone. Yet these figures should be taken with large grains of salt—the practical and conceptual leaps necessary to arrive at them are daunting, and the mapping between national income and household welfare is highly uncertain in CPEs, especially those devoting huge sums to the military.

Since 1990, however, the economy has undoubtedly shrunk. The Bank of Korea (BOK), the South Korean central bank, estimates a cumulative fall in output at roughly 25 percent through 1995, a figure privately confirmed by DPRK officials (Figure 2.1). (This figure should not be taken at face value either—the methodology used by the BOK in arriving at this figure is questionable on a number of grounds, and the figure itself is said to be subject to interministerial bargaining within the South Korean government. Likewise, it is unclear if the North Koreans truly accept this figure or were simply citing the familiar BOK number in an attempt to establish credibility with a Western audience.) If this figure is correct (and again there are serious conceptual issues of how one values the output of CPEs) it would imply a large, although not unprecedented, fall in income. (Some of the former Soviet republics have experienced 50–80 percent declines in output.) If the BOK figures are applied to the previous estimates of per capita income, they imply that the ratio of South to North Korean incomes was around four to one in 1990, six to one in 1995, and if current trends continue, will be twelve to one by the year 2000. (In comparison, the ratio of West to East German per capita income was between two and three to one in 1989.)

Figure 2.1 **North Korean GDP Growth Rates**

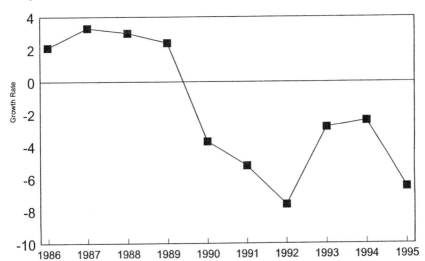

These income estimates are subject to enormous uncertainty. Perhaps the best statistical indicator of the state of the North Korean economy is its declining volumes of international trade (Figure 2.2). A healthy economy located in booming Northeast Asia should exhibit strong increases in trade volumes. In the case of North Korea, international trade, which can probably be estimated more reliably than income, is falling. Moreover, North Korea runs chronic balance of trade deficits on the order of hundreds of millions of dollars. Cut off from international capital markets, it depends on remittances from ethnic Koreans in Japan and nontraditional sources of foreign exchange, such as counterfeiting, drug trafficking, and arms sales, to cover its financing gap.

The impression one gets is of an archetypal CPE: overcentralized, overindustrialized, plagued by inefficiency and environmental degradation, able to achieve basic needs relatively quickly, but unable to develop beyond this, and now subject to substantial negative external shocks. The real question, however, is whether this economic decay threatens the regime's political stability, and by extension, the interests of other states that would partly bear the burden of an economic and political collapse in North Korea.

Unfortunately we do not have reliable theories to connect economic distress and political change. It may well be that given North Korea's isolation, the state's instruments of social control, and the lack of any

Figure 2.2 **International Trade**

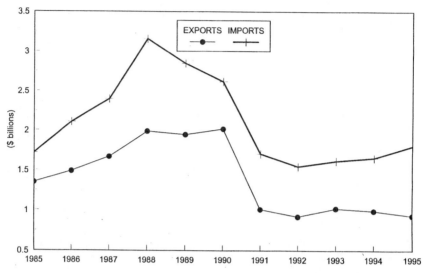

civil society capable of channeling mass discontent (to the extent that it exists), the regime could survive a prolonged period of economic decay. As a consequence, it might be worth reframing the issue in terms of what it would take economically to insure the biological survival of the population.

Indeed, it is against this backdrop of secular economic decline that North Korea experienced several years of bad weather that culminated in international appeals for food aid in 1995–97. While flooding may have precipitated the immediate crisis, its origins lie in decades of mismanagement, starting with the pursuit of food self-sufficiency that was both wrongheaded and unsustainable: the bureaucratic collectivist nature of North Korean agriculture is surely inefficient, and has involved bringing inappropriate land into cultivation and inappropriate application of chemical fertilizers. The denudation of hillsides has contributed to soil erosion and exacerbated the flooding. The environmental damage will take decades to repair.

A number of organizations and individuals have analyzed the food situation in North Korea, and the consensus is that North Korea is experiencing an annual grain shortfall of roughly 2 million tons.[5] (Again, these estimates are constructed in a variety of ways based on little systematic observation of conditions on the ground and may be subject to substantial error.) Although the shortfall is partly due to bad weather and flooding, at base it is structural in character, and provision of food aid is only a short-run palliative in the absence of more fundamental economic reforms. North Korea should be exporting mineral products and manufactures and importing food—not chasing the chimera of self-sufficiency.

The situation with regard to energy is similarly clouded by a lack of information. North Korea is reliant on imported oil to generate fuels and fertilizer for use in transportation and agriculture. Oil imports have been squeezed by foreign exchange shortages and the reduction in subsidized supplies from Russia and China (although recently there have been increased reports of arms-for-oil deals in the Middle East). Electricity is mainly generated using coal and hydropower. Electricity generation is hampered by difficulties in extracting increasingly inaccessible and low quality domestic coal reserves. Beyond the problem of lack of energy inputs, the power grid (largely underground for security purposes) is said to suffer from extraordinarily large transmission losses.

Energy problems will be partly addressed through the U.S.–North Korea Agreed Framework, which provides for provision of fuel oil during the construction of light-water nuclear reactors and the rehabilitation of the electrical grid. Nevertheless, North Korea will need additional energy inputs beyond those specified in the Framework Agreement if it is to reattain its peak level of electrical consumption.

This is not a very pretty picture. However, if the Framework Agreement is faithfully implemented and the consensus estimates with regard to the food situation prove correct, the actual cost of purchasing the estimated shortfalls in grain and energy inputs would not be very large—on the order of hundreds of millions of dollars. Indeed, the sums of money required to maintain population survival appear to be within the margin of error of what we think we know about the North Korean economy. It may well be that North Korea can survive (in a biological sense) without any (or with relatively modest) external assistance. In the short-run China, Japan, or South Korea could keep North Korea afloat (in this narrow sense). Indeed, both Japan and China at present appear to have surplus government grain stocks that could be used to make up the North Korean shortfall with minimal expenditures.

At the same time, it must be underlined that this analysis is based on incomplete and fragmentary information. It is not outside the realm of reason that a "silent famine" similar to what took place in China during the Great Leap Forward is unfolding in North Korea. Indeed, U.S. government sources estimate the number of deaths due to the food shortage in the thousands. It is worth noting that among the worst (and least understood) famines in this century took place in socialist countries in which governments were to a greater or lesser extent successfully able to restrict the flows of information to people both internally and externally.[6] North Koreans have been conditioned by nearly two generations of extreme regimentation. It is not implausible, given the terrain and the instruments of social control at the disposal of the current regime, that it could prevent the mass population movements observed during famines in Africa or the Indian subcontinent. If a famine were to occur in North Korea, the killers would be cholera and tuberculosis, not kwashiorkor, and we might learn of its full magnitude reading a graduate student's dissertation, not watching CNN. If such a famine does materialize, its roots will be in political decisions made in Pyongyang, not material resource constraints.

The North Korean Response

The obvious question then is what are the capabilities and interests of the North Korean government? Neither question can be answered definitively. Since the death of Kim Il-sung, the state has seemed to be on a kind of extraconstitutional autopilot: political (and biological) heir Kim Jong-il has not formally assumed his late father's offices, the national assembly has not met and the terms of the sitting members have lapsed, and the government budget, the sole piece of economic information that the government regularly announced, has not been released for several years.

At the same time, the regime has managed to pull off some achievements. The Agreed Framework was successfully concluded with the United States, a trade and investment conference in the special economic zone of Rajin-Sonbong attracted hundreds of foreign participants, and critical institutions such as the public food distribution system appear to be functioning. While there have been indications of system fraying (the defection of Hwang Jang Yop and the erection of internal barriers to trade in food and energy as local political and military leaders attempt to satisfy the needs of their constituencies) the overall impression one gets is that the government is performing at a reasonably high level of coherency and efficiency, given the strains of the current crisis.

The question then becomes what are the interests of the regime? Here

Table 2.1

Distribution of Labor Force in Selected CPEs at Onset of Reform

Country	Agriculture	Industry	Other
		Sector	
Czech Republic (1989)	11[a]	39	50
Slovakia (1989)	15[a]	34	51
Poland (1989)	7[a]	37	56
Hungary (1990)	15[a]	36	49
USSR (1987)	19[a]	38[b]	43
Ukraine (1990)	20	40	40
Belarus (1990)	20	42	38
Romania (1990)	28[a]	38	34
Bulgaria (1989)	19[a]	47	34
North Korea (1987)	25[c]	57[b]	18
China (1978)	71	15	14
Vietnam (1989)	71	12	17

Source: Marcus Noland, "External Economic Relations of the DPRK and Prospects for Reform," paper presented at the conference on "North Korean Foreign Policy in the Post-Cold War Era," Columbia University 31 May–1 June 1996, Table 5.

Notes: a = agriculture and forestry; b = industry and construction; c = farmers; d = workers

the analysis of the situation must by its nature be highly speculative, and frankly outside my area of comparative advantage. Nevertheless, one can imagine a variety of generic strategies that the government might pursue in addressing its economic problems.

First, the government might pursue policies of fundamental economic reform. This would involve decisively liberalizing and marketizing the economy. In this regard, the experiences of China and Vietnam may be misleading. At the time of their reforms, these economies were far more agrarian than North Korea (Table 2.1) and their ability to shift extremely low productivity labor out of agriculture and into the emerging non-state-owned light industrial sector has been the key to their success thus far. Successful reform of a more industrialized economy such as North Korea is likely to be far more difficult in purely technical terms, and imply tremendous change for the North Korean economy. Moreover, policymakers in China and Vietnam were able to undertake reform under relatively secure political and military conditions. The existence of a prosperous and democratic South Korea poses enormous ideological challenge for the North—while reformers in China and Vietnam were able to construct tortured rationalizations for why marketization really was what Marx had in mind, reform in North Korea could call into question the regime's whole raison d'être: why be a second-rate transitional economy when you can join South Korea?

Reform would therefore be a high-risk, big-payoff strategy. The economy is so distorted that one recent study concluded that the gains to national income resulting from successful liberalization and reform could be on the order of 50 percent.[7] The share of international trade in national income could rise fivefold, and much of this trade would be with Japan and South Korea—two states with which North Korea has highly problematical relations. Moreover, this transformation would involve hundreds of thousands of people moving from the countryside to the cities, and literally millions of people changing jobs. Change on this scale would likely unleash political changes that the regime would find destabilizing, and it is highly doubtful whether the current regime has either the skill or the guts to go this route.

More likely the regime will temporize, making a set of ad hoc adjustments as problems arise. A good example is the Rajin-Sonbong free trade and economic zone. Established in 1984 following Kim Il-Sung's 1982 and 1983 visits to China, it has attracted only a fraction of the foreign investment originally envisioned. The zone is plagued by its extreme isolation, lack of infrastructure, bureaucratic interference and ineptitude, and high costs. If the zone is to succeed in any meaningful way, it is likely to be (at least initially) as an entrepôt port for China's booming Jilin province.[8]

Moreover, by establishing the special economic zone in such an isolated region the regime has hamstrung further efforts at reform: to attract investment the government must insist that no broader reforms will be undertaken so as to convince foreign investors that Rajin-Sonbong is the only venue available. Otherwise, potential investors will just wait for more desirable locations to be opened to foreign investment. Indeed, it could suit the authorities for the zone to remain, in effect, an isolated island generating desperately needed foreign exchange, quarantined from infecting the rest of the economy (and the population at large) with any of its spiritual pollution.

The problem with such a minimalist strategy is that it risks collapse (defined as the inability of the economy to sustain the population biologically) if future events develop in a way less inimical to the regime than policymakers had anticipated. In other words, miscalculation could result in even greater havoc than the regime appears to be willing to absorb. What could prevent such an outcome?

The internal political response could take the form of an explicit regime-preserving coup, such as occurred in Romania in 1989, or an implicit coup in which some group or institution assumed the powers currently thought to reside with Kim Jong Il, while maintaining the putative leader as a figurehead or puppet. The responses of external powers could be critical in this regard, especially if the worst-case scenario were to emerge: civil war accompanied by an appeal by some group or faction for external intervention.

The Role of Foreign Powers

The experiences of other transitional economies suggest that a period of *ad hoc* muddling through could last years before a more permanent turn toward reform or chaos, especially if external powers find this outcome to be in their interests.

Indeed, it may well be the case that China, Japan, Russia, and arguably even South Korea, would prefer a muddling, domesticated, North Korea to a unified, capitalist, and possibly nuclear-armed state on the Korean peninsula. China (and for similar reasons Russia and Japan) may prefer continued economic engagement with South Korea, and would be willing to expend some resources to maintain North Korea as an allied buffer state. China has begun to pick up some of the slack left by Russia, North Korea's former patron, although the extent to which current Chinese exports of food and other essentials are on concessional terms is not known. Nor is it known what kind of economic or foreign policy conditions (if any) are being attached to these flows. Indeed, its dual goals of continued support for the North and enhanced economic engagement with the South present Beijing with a delicate diplomatic conundrum.

Unification along the lines of the German model would complicate the strategic planning of China and Japan, and would further reduce Russian influence in the region. At least in the short- to medium-run, one can envision China providing North Korea with aid and technical assistance, South Korea engaging China (and possibly North Korea) economically while protected by the American security umbrella, and concerns of a Sino-Japanese military imbalance submerged by the American counterweight.

In contrast, the United States would bear little of the unification's direct costs, and unification would hold forth the promise of eliminating the direct threat posed by North Korea to U.S. troops currently stationed in Northeast Asia, as well as the prospect of ending North Korean proliferation of weapons of mass destruction. While there may be some benefit to the United States in helping prop up the North, long-run U.S. interests are surely better served by unification, and in this regard the United States may be unique.

In the end China is key. With South Korea effectively paralyzed by fundamental policy disagreements internally over unification strategy, which are unlikely to abate in the foreseeable future, China emerges as the one power with the interest, resources, and possibly credibility with Pyongyang, to keep the sinking North Korean ship afloat.

Conclusion

The North Korean economy is in bad shape, but so little hard information is available that assessing the extent of economic distress with any degree of precision is hazardous. It appears that minimum biological survival requirements can be maintained with little, if any, external support. At the same time, however, the existence of a small-scale "silent famine" in regards to particular locales, or with respect to particular socioeconomic groups, is reportedly underway.

The regime is making cautious, hesitant steps toward reform that will neither alter the fundamental character of the economy, nor reverse its secular deterioration. Fundamental reforms could have huge pay-offs, but are politically and economically risky and are unlikely to be adopted. Yet it is difficult to make the case for an imminent collapse of the political regime. The Kim regime appears to have been largely successful in fusing its *juche* ideology to Korean nationalism, and unlike the countries of Central Europe, North Korea has no institutions capable of channeling mass discontent (to the extent that it exists) into effective political action. At the same time, an implicit or explicit regime preserving change in political leadership cannot be ruled out, however.

In light of its domestic politics and geopolitical position, North Korea is more likely to muddle through, supported by China (and possibly Japan and South Korea), who would like to avoid its collapse. Ironically, the reduction of North Korea to a dependency would represent the inversion of the ideology of its founder, Kim Il Sung, and a restoration of the status quo of much of the last millennium.

Notes

1. Joan Robinson, "Korea, 1964: Economic Miracle," in *Collected Work.* Oxford: Basil Blackwell, 1965. Originally published in the January 1965 issue of *Monthly Review.*

2. Eui-Gak Hwang, *The Korean Economies.* Oxford: Clarendon Press, 1993.

3. Nicholas Eberstadt and Judith Bannister, *The Population of North Korea.* Berkeley: Institute of East Asian Studies, 1992.

4. Marcus Noland, "The North Korean Economy," *Joint U.S.–Korean Academic Studies*, vol. 6, pp. 127–128.

5. Hong-Tack Chun, "Economic Conditions in North Korea and Prospects for Reform," in Jongryn Mo and Thomas H. Hendriksen, eds., *North Korea After Kim Il Sung: Continuity or Change?* Stanford: Hoover Institution Press, 1997.

6. Nicholas Eberstadt, "The D.P.R.K. As An Economy Under Multiple Severe Stresses: Analogies and Lessons from Past and Recent Historical Experience," undated manuscript.

7. Marcus Noland, Sherman Robinson, and Monica Scatasta, "Modeling North Korean Economic Reform," *Journal of Asian Economics*, vol. 8, no. 1, pp. 15–38.

8. Marcus Noland and L. Gordon Flake, "Opening Attempt: North Korea and the Rajin-Sonbong Free Economic and Trade Zone." Washington: Institute for International Economics, 1996, processed.

3

The Future of the Post–Kim Il Sung System in North Korea

Samuel Soonki Kim

For good or otherwise, North Korea—formally known as the Democratic People's Republic of Korea (DPRK)—is once again back in the news as East Asia's most dangerous crisis-in-waiting. Only a few years ago it was becoming quite trendy to say, especially in the wake of German reunification, that a divided Korea, too, was heading inexorably toward reunification. Then Pyongyang captured global prime time with its nuclear-weapons program as the first nuclear crisis of the post–Cold War era. More recently, the terms of debate have shifted from the nuclear issue to the question of whether North Korea has any future. Indeed, a dichotomist endgame debate on the future of the post–Kim Il Sung system—whether it will survive or collapse—has become a favorite sport that almost anyone, including North Korea's elite defectors, could play.[1]

In this essay I take as a point of departure that there are a variety of what Bertrand de Jouvenel calls "futuribles" (possible futures),[2] each of which seems compelling without being comprehensive from a particular perspective and that the either/or endism debate needs to be enriched by the appreciation that the future of the post–Kim Il Sung system is not providentially predetermined but rather a product of selective human behavior. To telegraph the main lines of inquiry, this chapter is organized (1) to suggest why prediction in social science is so difficult yet so important and necessary; (2) to construct a baseline for projecting several futuribles scenarios by delineating the temporal scope, the nature of the post–Kim Il Sung system, and the meaning, type, and direction of change as well as the key variables involved in a given scenario; (3) to identify and analyze three of the most plausible scenarios in terms of the initial assumptions and concomitant policies; and (4) to assess the policy implications as well as the relative desirability and feasibility of the three select scenarios in terms of securing a long peace on the Korean peninsula.

The Limitations and the Possibilities

Paradoxically, the possibilities of shaping a preferred future are embedded in the inherent difficulties of prediction in social science inquiry. There are many reasons why prediction is so problematic—and so often off the mark—in international relations.[3] To begin with, we should be wary of any scientistic claim for general laws in world politics as there are few laws that really command uncontested paradigmatic status and validity. Conceptual and methodological problems in establishing and validating general laws with predictive power abound: the unmanageably large number of known variables; the magnitude of the unknowns; the volatile nature of political phenomena; the resistance of available data to controlled laboratory experiment; the elusiveness of values and norms in quantitative analysis; and the complex and mysterious interaction between exogenous and endogenous factors. In short, state behavior is seldom determined by a single factor. Also, state learning can rise in politics, especially at a time of national security crisis, as an intervening variable providing "significant room for choice by publics and statesmen" in moving from here today to there tomorrow.[4] Microdecisions made today by leaders in Pyongyang or by foreign leaders elsewhere for or against North Korea can exert a progressively larger impact on the future North Korea will inherit.

Futuristic international-relations research is replete with examples of erroneous predictions and glaring failures to anticipate major events.[5] Most recently and tellingly, nobody predicted the demise of the Soviet Union as a superpower, the collapse of communism in Eastern Europe, German reunification, and the end of the Cold War. It is both surprising and revealing that structural realist theory, the most dominant international relations theory of the 1980s,[6] proved to be so wide of the mark, with so little predictive power for the macrostructural changes in the international system, including the end of the Cold War and the demise of tripolarity and bipolarity.[7]

Predicting the future of the post–Kim Il Sung system, always hazardous, has never been more so than today, when North Korea is experiencing a profound domestic social, economic, and ecological crisis even as the global system to which it is now uneasily connected undergoes a structural and political transformation as well. History has not ended, as Francis Fukuyama would have us believe,[8] it has been accelerating, even overheating and often making a mockery of our expectations and predictions. Of course, at a time of such rapid and unpredictable change, it is easy to succumb to the fallacy of premature optimism and pessimism on the changing relationship between the future of North Korea and the future of regional and global politics. Recent momentous global changes are unprecedented in their nature, scope, and rapidity. As Robert Jervis reminds us, past generalizations can no longer provide a sure guide for the future if they are themselves no longer valid. To a significant degree, the flow of world politics has become contingent or path-dependent, since particular unexpected events can easily force world politics along quite different trajectories.[9] In other words, "past experience"— whatever this may mean and even if not forgotten—can no longer serve as a reliable guide for the future.

The difficulties of predicting the future shape of world politics are directly connected to the challenge of prognosticating on the future of the post–Kim Il Sung system in North Korea, since any country's future, especially that of such a small state as North Korea sandwiched in the strategic crossroads in Northeast Asia where the United States, China, Russia, and Japan uneasily meet and interact, will be significantly affected by the structures of regional and global politics that prevail. Whether the future of post–Cold War world politics is dominated by state actors (realism); by a multiplicity of diverse actors (pluralism); by a single, integrated global system (globalism); or by sovereignty-bound and sovereignty-free actors in a multicentric two-worlds system (bifurcationism) will greatly influence the possible scenarios for the future of North Korea. Each of these competing theoretical perspectives starts from different sets of premises and suggests different sets of opportunities and constraints, with different degrees of pressure upon North Korea for systemic change and systemic continuity.

To predict the exact shape of things to come in post–Kim Il Sung North Korea is inherently problematic. It is like predicting the terminal point of a moving target on a turbulent trajectory subject to the competing and often contradictory domestic and external pressures that are characteristic of any state in an increasingly interdependent and interactive world. To predict the future of North Korea is also difficult because we cannot be certain about the relative weight of the key variables in Pyongyang's informal politics and decision-making process in the post–Kim Il Sung era.[10]

All that said, however, we may proceed from the premise that the way in which the outside world, especially Beijing, Moscow, Seoul, Tokyo, and Washington, responds to Pyongyang is closely keyed to the way in which North Korea responds to the outside world. To say North Korea's future is unpredictable is to say its future is malleable, not predetermined. Herein lies the potential of external factors in the reshaping of North Korea's future in a preferred direction. Such a nondeterministic image of the future of the post–Kim Il Sung system opens up some space for the outside world to use whatever leverage it might have to help North Korean leaders to opt for one futurible scenario or another in the coming years.

Still, the method we need to rely on in minimizing the problems and difficulties of prediction and in clarifying the gap between the actual (or the probable) and the preferable (or the potential) is *forecasting*, not *prediction*. As Nazli Choucri put it, "A prediction is generally made in terms of a point or event; a forecast is made in terms of alternatives. A prediction focuses upon one outcome, a forecast involves contingencies."[11] A forecast can help to foster a better understanding of the dynamics of the post–Kim Il Sung system by charting out a range of alternative futurible scenarios. We have little choice but to project a series of plausible scenarios, if only to learn from possible egregious errors and then return to the drawing board to ascertain where and why they were made. All the same, we should be wary of committing the fallacy of premature optimism or pessimism on the shape of things to come in post–Kim Il Sung North Korea. To capture the dialectics of extrapolative forecasting and normative forecasting we need to steer clear between the Scylla of utopian idealism and the Charybdis of conservative realism. As Johan Galtung put it, "Man is somewhere between God and termite, and the future of human society takes shape according to principles somewhere between those underlying the Act of Genesis and termite society."[12]

Establishing the Baseline

Analytically, we can identify at least five scenarios spanning the whole spectrum of the possible from one extreme pole to the other extreme pole—system-collapsing, system-decaying, system-maintaining, system-reforming, and system-transforming. In this chapter we will focus on three of the most plausible futurible scenarios—system-maintaining, system-reforming, and system-decaying. To pursue this line of inquiry further, we need to clarify briefly the temporal scope, the nature of the North Korean political system today as the baseline for assessing any change or continuity, and the key variables involved in each scenario.

First of all, the future of North Korea may be divided into three time horizons: (1) the immediate future, viewed here as a one-year temporal horizon of immediate concern and focus (e.g., academic year, fiscal year, etc.); (2) the middle-range future, a five- to seven-year horizon of a longer-term project (e.g., a four-year college career, five-year electoral cycles in many democratic societies, or seven-year economic plans in socialist countries including North Korea); and (3) the long-term futures, thirty- to fifty-year horizons of dreamers, revolutionaries, and designers of world system transformation. The fifty-year boom-to-burst cycle known as the Kondratieff economic wave, often used in world-system literature, belongs to the outer reach of the long-term future. As Harry Harding points out, most American analysis of North Korea in recent years has focused on the recent past and the immediate future, but it is North Korea's "longer-term future" that is ultimately more important than the issues of the recent past and the immediate future.[13] Harding does not define the temporal scope of "longer-term future," but in the present essay, the main focus is on the middle-range future—that is, the future of the post–Kim Il Sung system in 2002 or 2004.

Second, the nature of the North Korean political system Kim Jong Il inherited and seemingly determined to maintain in the post–Kim Il Sung era—officially touted as "our style socialism"—is a hybrid of modern Stalinism[14] and traditional Korean feudalism; indeed, the first-ever socialist dynastic political system. As Hwang Jang Yop, chief architect of *juche* ideology and the highest ranking official yet to defect from North Korea, put it, "The confrontation between North and South Korea is not a confrontation between socialism and capitalism but that of capitalism and feudalism."[15] The single defining and differentiating feature of the North Korean political system is a totalistic, mind-numbing, and resource-depleting *suryong* (Great Leader) system. In the megalomania of the leadership cult, North Korea is beyond compare. No state in our times has expended as much scarce human and natural resources in building so many monuments (as many as 50,000 of them by one Japanese estimate) and such a huge military and industrial complex. North Korea displays all the trappings of theocracy in an age of expanding democratization—the third wave of global democratization.[16] The North Korean theocracy proved to be extremely expensive and cost-ineffective as both state and society were gradually drained and exhausted by the protracted leadership cult and the father-to-son succession process, spawning swollen garrison state and spent society. In April 1992, for instance, despite being hobbled by the deepening economic crisis with a negative GNP growth of –7.6 percent for the year, North Korea managed to spend no less than $US 1 billion for the eightieth birthday celebration of the Great Leader (Kim Il Sung).[17]

It is a swollen garrison state fielding the fifth-largest army in the world (after China, India, Russia, and the United States) with its ratio of troops to total population being by far the highest for any country in the post–Cold War era. By 1993, North Korea's military manpower has grown to 1.2 million, and at 53.0 troops per 1,000 population the world's highest troop-to-population ratio. Measured in terms of defense spending as a percentage of GDP, North Korea, with its defense expenditure estimated at 25.2% of its GDP, became the world's third-largest defense spender (after Bosnia and Angola).[18] When its 1.2 million active military personnel are combined with a total of 5.9 million in active reserve, security, and paramilitary forces, a whopping 29 percent of the population make up a swollen garrison state. North Korea is beyond compare in this respect as well, as no state in our time has placed its economy on such an extreme and prolonged war footing with the constant drain of scarce resources into military-related industries over such a long period of time. According to the estimates of the Institute of Contemporary International Problems in Moscow, up to 50 percent of the DPRK's national income is now spent, in one way or another, on military needs, reducing its capacity to meet basic human needs.[19] While the security challenge from the South was a contributing factor, the chief catalyst was largely political. Indeed, the father-to-son succession process and a new wave of rapid militarization developed in tandem in a mutually complementary way.

Even without going nuclear North Korea commands massive and forward-based forces deployed aggressively along the northern side of the so-called demilitarized zone (DMZ) on the Korean peninsula. By the early 1990s, North Korea was testing its *Rodong* missiles with a range estimated at 600–800 miles that would bring within reach not only the southern half of the Korean peninsula but also such major population centers as Kyoto, Beijing, and Khaborovsk. Currently, it is developing the *Taepodong* class of Intercontinental Ballistic Missiles (ICBM), which when perfected would have a range of up to 6,200 miles. Moreover, North Korea has capabilities for producing chemical weapons, including nerve gas; it is reported to have the world's third-largest inventory of these chemical weapons.[20]

By any reckoning the most serious weakness of the post–Kim Il Sung system is the ailing economy. Various collapse scenarios of the post–Kim Il Sung system are based on and proceed from the premise that the economic crisis has already reached a system-breaking point and that the onset of this crisis has further accentuated the structural contradictions within the system, with far-reaching consequences for political stability and regime survival. The North Korean economy suffers from the structural problems that have plagued all late state-led socialist economies, to be sure, but it is a combination of domestic and external factors that has caused the economy to fall behind its Southern rival in both relative and absolute terms.

By the early 1990s, the cumulative and closely interrelated multiple effects of the sudden demise of Soviet aid; the collapse of the socialist world market; the structural problems of the command economy with little material incentives; the overallocation of resources to heavy industry and military spending; the inordinate misappropriation of human and natural resources dedicated to the deification of the Great Leader (as in ancient Egypt of the Pharaohs); and several bad harvests have all reflected and effected a succession of negative GNP growth: –3.7 percent in 1990, –5.2 percent in 1991, –7.6 percent in 1992, –8.5 percent in 1993, –2.0 percent in 1994, and –5.0 percent in 1995 (according to Russian estimates). In short, the North Korean economy contracted by over a fourth in 1990–95. By 1993, continuing food shortages led the government to launch a "let's eat two meals a day" drive. In December 1993, the government for the first time admitted the failure of the Third Seven-Year Plan, and in his last (1994) New Year message, Kim Il Sung himself set the next three years (1994–96) as a period of "adjustment" in socialist economic reconstruction, endorsing "agriculture-first, light industry-first, and foreign trade-first" policies. The three-year stopgap adjustment plan has come and gone with few tangible gains in any of the three priority sectors.

It is worth stepping back a little to better appreciate the present economic crisis in historical perspective. In early 1962 the Great Leader promised that the working people in North Korea would soon be able to "lead a rich life, living in tile-roofed houses, eating rice and meat, and wearing fine clothes." Thirty years later, tellingly enough, the Great Leader was reiterating, as a "long-cherished desire" of the people and a "goal in socialist construction," that people should be able to "eat white rice and meat soup regularly, wear silk clothes and live in a house with a tiled roof."[21] Two years later, in May 1995, the proud and putatively self-reliant North Korea made an unprecedented request to Japanese "reactionaries" and South Korean "puppets" for rice aid and received some 650,000 tons of rice without breathing a word to its own people. After major floods in July and August 1995 North Korea, for the first time in its international life launched a global campaign crying out for help from the United Nations and its related agencies and foreign governments. Today, the North Korean economy is in a shambles, suffering from three critical shortages (food, energy, and hard currency) with an increasing number of people moving dangerously close to the brink of stealth famine and some 70 percent of factories halting their operation. Facing a critical summer desperately short of food between June and September 1997, the government sounded the alarm on its food situation on February 3, 1997, saying that it had only half the grain needed to feed its people and that grain shortages would soon reach a "pre-disaster level" in the near future.[22] At the same time, the government began to make an unprecedented request to foreign investors interested in various projects in the Rajin-Sonbong Free Economic and Trade Zone to make their down payments on land with gasoline, flour, or soybeans.[23]

Third, change as made manifest in North Korean state behavior can be conceptualized as of two kinds—tactical policy change and fundamental paradigm change. One of the most important findings to emerge from a multiauthored collaborative project on "learning" in Soviet and American foreign policy is that policy change often takes place in the absence of a prior change in beliefs (paradigm change), when governments pragmatically redefine their self-interests with little or no reassessment of basic beliefs and goals.[24] All the same, policy change—especially when sweeping and sustained—and paradigm change can become mutually interpenetrable and interdependent, producing progressively greater systemic ramifications. As Alexander Wendt argues in rebutting structural realism in international relations theory—and the argument may be no less relevant in parsing various alternative futurible scenarios of the post–Kim Il Sung system—"agents and structures are produced or reproduced by what actors *do*."[25] The key independent variables likely to exert the greatest impact upon the shaping of one futurible scenario or another are both Pyongyang's own policies and the policies of key external actors.

As for the direction of change, it has several possible trajectories. The system-maintaining scenario, for instance, may continue unchanged in its current trajectory, or it may shift toward the system-reforming or system-degenerating trajectory. The three futurible scenarios should not be viewed as mutually exclusive, as one can flow into another or vice versa.

The System-Maintaining Scenario

This scenario envisions a high degree of continuity with the recent past, with the Kim Jong Il regime commanding firm control of ideology and policy. The main objective remains defensive as he seeks to prevent the breakdown of the Kim Il Sung system despite being constrained by economic difficulties. The formal politics of everyday life remains chock-full of trumpery about the omnipotence of *juche* (self-reliance) ideology as the motive force "leading our country toward the strongest position in the world." As ideology decides all things in the course of human history, we are told, North Korea is indeed the one and only "ideological superpower" and "the most powerful country" in the world.[26] In none of the writings in recent years has Kim Jong Il expressed anything positive about reform and restructuring. On the contrary he has argued that it was the "collusion between the imperialists and counter-revolutionary forces" and the "penetration of imperialist ideology and culture," (i.e., *perestroika* and *glasnost*) that had accelerated the demise of the socialist world.[27] As if to provide more evidence of such commitment to the system-maintaining approach, Kim Jong Il is depicted as having captured the high ideological/theoretical ground as a savior of world socialism in trouble. The crumbling of socialism in various countries today has nothing to do with the failure of socialism as a science, but has everything to do with "the renegades of socialism" who carry out "reforms" with the "material-is-almighty doctrine and the economy-is-almighty doctrine" in order to restore capitalism. The *juche*-oriented theory of socialism makes it possible to promote the cause of socialism victoriously under any circumstances by giving absolute precedence to the superstructure (ideological struggle) over the material base (the founders of Marxism are criticized for putting the main stress on material and economic conditions).[28]

Kim Jong Il's pronounced commitment to the system-maintaining approach would not stand in the way of demonstrating tactical (policy) flexibility in a situation-specific way. Projecting this system-maintaining scenario toward 2002 or 2004, the leadership would stretch the outer limits of the three-year economic readjustment plan (1993–96) of giving priority to agriculture, light industry and foreign trade while at the same time tightening socio-political control. More specifically, this scenario would entail further "adjustment" measures such as:

- A more vigorous promotion of the Rajin-Sonbong Free Economic and Trade Zone (RSFETZ).
- A greater toleration of informal (black) markets cropping up all over the country and production of above-quota output for the market but not decollectivization of the land.
- Greater access of international aid workers to on-site inspection and monitoring.
- A more vigorous pursuit of aid diplomacy.
- Selling access to nuclear waste dumping sites in North Korea for cash payment.
- Trafficking in everything from small arms to missiles with some of the world's rogue regimes.
- Seeking closer links with the capitalist economies of the West as a way of attracting more foreign direct investment (FDI) and taking a slice of the global market.[29]

This scenario would not involve any relaxation of socio-political control, let alone political reform, other than the more frequent reshuffling of officials on the basis of performance as well as political loyalty.

The viability of the system-maintaining scenario depends largely on the extent to which the post–Kim Il Sung leadership can ride out the current economic difficulties. This will in turn hinge to a large extent on the policies and actions of Washington, Tokyo, Seoul, Beijing, and Moscow. Much of Pyongyang's diplomatic time and capital has been expended and will continue to be expended in developing and exploiting the American connection. This is not surprising as Washington is now believed to be holding the master key to all of Pyongyang's positive and negative foreign policy objectives in the post–Cold War era. Just as the nuclear weapons program was made to be a cost-effective strategic equalizer in its competition with the South and as a bargaining chip for brinkmanship diplomacy in 1990–94, the Agreed Framework of 1994 has been turned into an all-purpose fungible and endlessly negotiable instrument of foreign policy, applicable to almost any situation in Pyongyang's international relations. Yet the smooth implementation of the nuclear deal has become hostage to charged and unpredictable domestic politics in Washington and Seoul. More recently, North Korea seems to be giving signals that it would join the four-party peace talks if the price is right.

Despite all the booby traps on the long road to peace, it is not too far-fetched to imagine that the post–Kim Il Sung leadership will be able to navigate the state on the system-maintaining trajectory to 2002 or 2004. This would require a virtuous circle of mutually reinforcing positive policies from Pyongyang, Washington, Tokyo, and Seoul. Pyongyang continues to follow its nuclear obligations, not overreacting to congressional politics in Washington, even as it demonstrates greater tactical flexibility in its foreign economic policy. The three-year adjustment period was extended on January 1, 1997.[30] The Clinton Administration overcomes by veto or otherwise an unbelievably shortsighted Republican opposition politics to meet America's part of the bargain on the nuclear deal (the 500,000 tons of fuel oil gratis as promised in the Agreed Framework), even as it accelerates the pace of normalization process with Pyongyang. In addition, the extant sanctions and economic barriers are removed at a greater speed. Tokyo, always seeking an equidistance between Seoul's and Washington's North Korea policy so as not to lag too far behind Washington and not to surge too far ahead of Seoul, shifts its gears to accelerate its normalization process. As a result, full-fledged diplomatic relations are established with Tokyo providing a compensation package of $12 billion (a ball park figure that takes into account Tokyo's aid package of $800 million in 1965 now adjusting for differences in population, accrued interest, changes in the price level, and appreciation of the yen since 1965).[31] North-South economic relations resume and continue unabated despite the lack of a major breakthrough in political relationship.[32] In 1995, Seoul emerged as Pyongyang's third-largest trade partner after Japan and China, as North-South trade, most of it still made through third countries, increased 48 percent from 1994 to $287 million. It is worth noting in this connection that South Korea has become a major source of trade surplus (about $177 million in 1994) and as such a major source of hard currency. In effect, South Korea's trade with North Korea is aid in disguise. Taken together, Washington, Tokyo, and Seoul can help the Kim Jong Il regime ride out the current economic difficulties. By such cautiously optimistic assessment the future of North Korea 2002 or 2004 will resemble the North Korea of 1976–80 when it registered an annual economic growth rate of 4.1 percent or even higher.

The System-Reforming Scenario

Under this system-reforming scenario North Korea would follow the post-Mao Chinese model of gradual but extensive reform and opening to the global political economy. There is of course good reason for North Korea to be impressed by this model of development which managed to establish an all-time global record in doubling per capita output in the shortest period (1977–87).[33] According to the World Bank's purchasing-power-parity (PPP) estimates, China became the world's largest economy, after the United States and Japan by 1992 and, tellingly enough, the world's largest recipient of the World Bank's multilateral aid and Japan's bilateral aid! It has been projected that if recent growth rates persist China could overtake the United States as the world's largest economy in a decade or two (between 2003 and 2020), with almost incalculable consequences for the political economy of China, East Asia, and the world. Yet the rise-of-China thesis is far more problematic than the aggregate economic numbers would suggest. Domestic problems and obstacles in Beijing's long march to the promised land of superpowerdom are becoming legion.[34]

Still, the system-reforming approach could come about as the result of either deepening systemic crisis or growing self-confidence. The deepening system crisis may finally serve as a teacher of the reality principle for the Kim Jong Il or his successor/replacement regime, that more thoroughgoing reform and restructuring would be essential to arrest further economic decline and even system collapse. Alternatively, such a change of course may reflect growing confidence stemming from the modest success of the system-maintaining approach that a more extensive reform would not necessarily give rise to political and social instability. In any case, the system-reforming scenario would require such concomitant policies as:

- Thorough restructuring of the ownership system and the system of economic decision-making in Pyongyang, major agricultural reform coupled with the family-owning system (decollectivization).

- Gradual expansion and extension of a free trade and economic zone from the Rajin-Sonbong area to other eastern and western coastal cities, even some political reform measures keyed to the functional requirements of a market-oriented but still state-led economy.
- Extensive opening to the global economic system with Pyongyang joining (or allowed to join) all the keystone international economic institutions (e.g., APEC, Asian Development Bank, IMF, the World Bank, and WTO).
- Full normalization of relations with Washington accompanied by removal of all the existing economic sanctions and barriers.
- Full normalization of relations with Tokyo with a compensation package of about $12 billion in several categories (e.g., grants-in-aid, soft loans, and credits).
- Return to North-South dialogue and detente, if not a peace treaty, accompanied by considerable aid and great expansion of inter-Korean economic cooperation.
- Select and gradual demobilization of the Korean People's Army (KPA) to generate more labor force needed to fuel North Korea's modernization of agriculture, light industry, and science and technology.
- Sending students to—and inviting foreign experts from—Japan, the United States, and Europe for advance training, as post-Mao reformers have done since 1979.

Despite the impressive aggregate performance indicators of the Chinese reform model, a simple reality check suggests that post–Kim Il Sung North Korea is no post-Mao China. The initial conditions of post-Mao China do not apply to and are not readily reproducible in post–Kim Il Sung North Korea. Obviously, North Korea modeled its RSFETZ (established in December 1991) on post-Mao China's four special economic zones (SEZs) in Shenzhen, Shantou, Xiamen and Zhuhai. In September 1993 Kim Il Sung reportedly told a visiting Chinese delegation that he admired China "for having achieved brilliant reforms and openness" while continuing simultaneously to build "socialism with Chinese characteristics," and that the Chinese experience would become "an encouraging factor for us, Koreans."[35]

Beyond this, however, the major differences between the two are far too many. First, there is an important difference in global geopolitical timing. Post-Mao China's reform and opening came about during the heyday of the Cold War when anti-Soviet China enjoyed and exercised its maximum realpolitik leverage, as made evident in Beijing's easy entry into the World Bank and IMF in May 1980. Second, North Korea does not have "the ten calamitous years of the Great Proletariat Cultural Revolution" from which to break away. In making a public declaration of the open-door policy as "another turning point in Chinese history," Deng Xiaoping first aptly attributed China's backwardness and the slow pace of modernization to its "international isolation from the middle of the Ming dynasty through the Opium War, and from the Sino-Soviet split of the late 1950s through the Cultural Revolution."[36] He then summed up the logic of breaking away from Maoist self-reliance: "To accelerate China's modernization we must not only make use of other countries' experience. We must also avail ourselves of foreign funding. In past years international conditions worked against us. Later, when the international climate was favorable, we did not take advantage of it. It is now time to use our opportunities."[37] In other words, with the ascendancy of Deng Xiaoping as the new paramount leader in December 1978 (after purging the Gang of Four and Mao's designated heir apparent Huo Guofeng), post-Mao China had a fortuitous combination of favorable domestic and external factors as a powerful magnet fueling the born-again modernization-cum-status drive. Third, unlike post-Mao China, post–Kim Il Sung North Korea does not have rich, famous, and enterprising overseas Koreans to generate the kind and amount of foreign direct investment (FDI) that post-Mao China had attracted. It is worth noting in this connection that post-Mao China quickly emerged as the Third World's largest recipient of FDI and that some 80 percent of FDI came from overseas Chinese in Hong Kong, Southeast Asia, and Taiwan. The closest functional equivalent of North Korea's "overseas Korean entrepreneurs" is the *chaebol* in South Korea whose freedom of economic movement is closely regulated by the ROK government and pro-Pyongyang Koreans in Japan associated with the Chosen Soren, whose membership and remittances to North Korea have registered negative growth rates in recent years.[38] In addition, post-Mao China in 1978–79 had no foreign debts to speak of while North Korea's foreign debts are estimated at about $US 10–11 billion with one of the highest country-risk ratings in the world. Fourth, the propitious initial economic conditions that enabled post-Mao reformers to launch reform in the agricultural sector to free up and channel surplus agricultural labor into the emerging nonstate or semiprivate light manufacturing and service sectors do not exist in the heavily industrialized North Korea. Moreover,

North Korea's reform and Chinese-style opening would still have to compete with China, Vietnam, and other Southeast Asian countries in the global marketplace while at the same time handicapped by its own high wages measured in terms of productivity; poor infrastructure; unstable energy supply; dismally low international credit rating; geographic and transportation isolation; ideological and bureaucratic constraints; and an uncertain future of the post–Kim Il Sung system.

Finally, but not least importantly, the Kim Jong Il regime cannot afford to ignore or forget the Tiananmen Massacre of 1989 and the sociopolitical consequences of post-Mao reform and opening to the capitalist world. The system-reforming scenario would almost inevitably expand the informal economy at the expense of the formal with a corresponding loss of state coherence and control. With a rapid rise of self-help unilateralism of all kinds and at all levels of the state (e.g., bartering, smuggling, stealing, bribing, and even defecting by bribery), the post–Kim Il Sung system is bound to encounter a dramatic increase in social unrest and political instability. In short, unlike post-Mao China in the 1970s, post–Kim Il Sung North Korea in the late 1990s may not command a combination of favorable domestic and external factors needed for the viability of the system-reforming approach.

That extensive system reform and restructuring is needed seemed beyond doubt. Lacking his father's charisma, authority, and power, Kim Jong Il has no choice but to shift decisively from charismatic or revolutionary legitimation to performance-based legitimation. Yet Kim Jong Il encounters here a systemic catch-22 dilemma—to save the *juche* system requires destroying important parts of it. To save the *juche* system also required considerable opening to and help from its bitter capitalist southern rival. And yet, to depart from the ideological continuity of the system the Great Leader Kim Il Sung ("the father of the nation") created, developed, and passed onto the son is viewed not as a necessity for survival but an ultimate betrayal of *raison d'état*. What accentuates Pyongyang's systemic dilemma and national identity angst with particular clarity is the "rise of South Korea" factor—the "illegitimate puppet" government in Seoul has almost won the unification game by surging so far ahead of the North in practically all dimensions of polity posing the clear and continuing danger of German-style hegemonic unification by absorption, a situation that neither post-Mao Chinese reformers nor Vietnamese reformers had to deal with. In short, to ask North Korea to follow the system-reforming trajectory is to ask North Korea to change its national identity until it becomes just like South Korea's!

Still, a shift to the system-reforming scenario does not necessarily require a new leadership or paradigm shift; it could be catalyzed by the Kim Jong Il regime's own assessment of either success or failure of the system-maintaining approach. There is a clear and present possibility that the system-reform scenario, when faced with rising political problems (such as China's democratic spring in 1989), may quickly shift back to the more comfortable system-maintaining track. Alternatively, there is also an extremely remote possibility that the system-reforming scenario may give rise to a Gorbachev-like leader shifting the gears more decisively from the system-reforming to the system-transforming direction. The rise of such a statesman taking a system-transforming and democratizing approach may be assigned to the realm of the improbable requiring no further discussion. As matters stand today the probability of the post–Kim Il Sung system shifting away from the current system-maintaining approach to the system-reforming approach is rather low.

The System-Decaying Scenario

This scenario starts from the premise that the North Korean political system is rigid in both theory and practice, possessing no self-correcting and self-learning mechanisms for redressing structural problems of the economy. In this scenario the Kim Jong Il regime continues the policies of the recent past—that is, muddling through—except that the economic decline continues unabated at the recent annual minus growth rate of about 4 percent. What Jervis said about the last dying days of the former Soviet Union in the context of bipolarity in world politics applies also to North Korea on the system-decaying trajectory in terms of North-South relations—that "the enormous domestic failure [of the Soviet Union] is the equivalent of a major military defeat" but that "this is a war without another country or coalition that acts like a winner, ready to move into the power vacuum and structure a new set of rules," and yet the Soviet Union still remained "the only country that could destroy the United States."[39]

Under this system-decaying-cum-system-collapsing scenario, there occur sporadic food riots in many cities as the country moves perilously close to the brink of economic collapse. Relative deprivation—social actors' perceived discrepancy between their expectations and capabili-

ties—is generally accepted as constituting the necessary, if not sufficient, condition for violent civil conflict, but its likelihood and magnitude of resulting in overt civil violence depend on the availability of
mediating societal and institutional mechanisms.[40] Whether this theory
of relative deprivation applies to the North Korean case is open to debate. As it is, the description that best captures the mood of the people in
North Korea is not one of a rising sense of deprivation ready to explode
but a quiet alienation and combat fatigue, but under the system-decaying scenarios things could change and change rapidly to bring about
violent civil conflict. In any case, this system-decaying scenario sliding
into system collapse is not likely to come about simply because of pov-
erty and repression; it is more likely to come about (1) when the state's
control mechanisms break down with the trickle of elite defectors, especially the police and the armed forces, becoming a flood; (2) when an
initial reform period of greater economic rejuvenation comes to a sudden halt and rising expectations of continued progress are suddenly
dashed; and (3) when the policy of studied aggressive moves against the
South go seriously awry.

All the same, Pyongyang asks for more and more international aid to
get less and less. International humanitarian aid trickles in to feed starving people but serves as a first-aid bandage for the country that is on a
tenuous external life-support system. Pyongyang launches another round
of brinkmanship diplomacy and threatens to go nuclear and expels KEDO
technical personnel and IAEA inspectors, only to bring upon itself economic sanctions in the United Nations Security Council (with China
abstaining or not participating in the vote). The tensions on the DMZ
rise with a North-South exchange of charges and counter charges. For
all its devotion to *juche* ideology and "socialism of our style," the symp-
toms of system pathology become progressively obvious: the state's increasing involvement in criminal money-making and money-laundry
activities; public executions of "criminals, traitors, and spies"; and a
flurry of elite defections and even massive refugee exodus.

The system-decaying scenario is not sustainable. It opens up two alternative possibilities—a system collapse or a system-rescuing approach
by signing a peace treaty with South Korea that is guaranteed by Washington, Beijing, Tokyo, and Moscow accompanied by two comprehensive aid packages from Seoul and Tokyo and one comprehensive
multilateral aid package promised by Washington to push through the
World Bank. The system-decaying scenario is a multi-stage process—a

system-collapsing process in slow motion. If not rectified, what starts as system decay in an early stage can end as system collapse in an advanced stage. Indeed, such a system-decaying-cum-system-collapsing process has happened in Eastern Europe. But the situation-specific conflation of domestic and external factors in Eastern Europe—the vibrant civil society and the external serendipity (Gorbachev) factor—is not present nor readily reproducible in the North Korean case to warn against such a scenario unfolding there.

Most system collapse scenarios commit the fallacy of premature economic reductionism based on the misleading equation of economic collapse and system collapse, and even the collapse of the Kim Jong Il regime with the collapse of the North Korean state. It is also widely—and wrongly—assumed that, given the ready alternative of absorption of North Korea into a prosperous and democratic South Korea, the collapse of the North Korean regime would ipso facto bring about German-style reunification by absorption. But economic collapse is not the same as the collapse of a state. The much-touted collapse of the former Soviet Union is really no more or no less than the collapse of the Soviet Union as a superpower and as a system, not the collapse or disappearance of the Soviet Union-turned-into-Russia as a state. More tellingly, many extremely poor developing countries—the so-called Fourth World countries (about forty of them in the world)—inch along with sluggish or even negative rates of economic growth despite seriously being battered by rampant bureaucratic corruption, ineffective or divided leadership, and endemic social unrest and without having the kind of totalitarian control mechanisms that North Korea has. And yet, these countries do not collapse, let alone disappear, partly because basic human needs are met minimally with international humanitarian aid and partly because social unrest and political opposition do not overwhelm the repressive forces of the state. Despite the widely recognized arbitrariness of the African "national" boundaries established by European colonialists, for example, there has not been "one significant boundary change in Africa since the dawn of the independence era in the late 1950s, and not one separatist movement has succeeded in establishing a new state."[41] Even Hwang Jang Yop had to warn against the danger of reading too much into his defection as a sign that the post–Kim Il Sung system is near collapse: "The republic [North Korea] is in economic difficulty but it remains politically united and there's no danger of its collapse."[42]

The system collapse scenario, especially if it means the collapse of

North Korea as a separate state or system, not the collapse of the Kim Jong Il regime, is less likely for no other reason than the ineluctable fact that North Korea is no Fourth World banana republic that would collapse quietly without a big fight or without creating a huge mess that outside neighboring powers can or want to clean up. Despite the differences in tactics and strategies, China, Japan, Russia, and the United States are more or less united in their common desire for and commitment to peace and stability on the Korean peninsula—that is, the status quo of the two Korean states in peaceful coexistence. Fearing both ideological and geostrategic consequences of a united Korea, Beijing might intervene— the Gorbachev factor reversed, as it were—to rescue the post–Kim Il Sung system on the verge of collapse as a way of maintaining a strategic *cordon sanitaire* in the northern half of the Korean peninsula or as a way of arresting a massive exodus of refugees flowing into China's already unmanageable floating population of about 100 million.

With the balance of overall national strength having already shifted so decisively in favor of South Korea—and thus enhancing the daily prospects of Korean unification by absorption—maintaining a close strategic relationship with the weaker North has become one of Beijing's central security concerns. What heightens Beijing's security concerns and its opposition to the unification-by-absorption scenario is the perception of U.S. strategy on the Korean nuclear issue. "To put it bluntly," as one pro-PRC newspaper in Hong Kong writes, "the United States wants to use this chance to topple the DPRK, and this is a component of U.S. strategy to carry out peaceful evolution in the socialist countries." And the United States "will practice a strategy of destruction against North Korea—the last Stalinist regime in the world—with the aim of enabling South Korea to gobble up North Korea, like West Germany gobbling up East Germany." Such U.S. strategy poses not only an ideological challenge but more significantly a strategic threat as "China regards the Korean region as an important buffer zone between China and the United States."[43]

Herein lies the logic of Beijing's opposition to sanctions against North Korea in the United Nations Security Council in recent years. Apart from maximizing its leverage as a balancer, the greatest danger would occur if the junior socialist ally in the strategic buffer zone felt so cornered with no way to escape except through fighting back that it would trigger a second Korean War. An alternative scenario could hardly be more comforting—economic sanctions work so well as to produce another collapsing socialist regime on its northern borders, with all the political, economic and social consequences for China's own stability. In short, in Beijing's eyes sanctions are a no-win proposition as they would bring about the worst of two possible outcomes—they would be ineffective in controlling nuclear proliferation as it can only strengthen the determination of the North Korean leadership to go nuclear and/or they will be effective in destabilizing the North Korean regime that would dump many of its ill-fed fleeing refugees on China's northeastern provinces.

The single greatest variable working against system collapse leading to Korean reunification is that neither Pyongyang nor Seoul wants this to happen. We should not ignore the unparalleled resilience of this "crazy state" in turbulent world politics, as it is the longest-surviving communist regime in the world today, a year older than the PRC. In the post–Cold War era, it has become Pyongyang's turn of misfortune to feel threatened by the clear and present danger of German-style hegemonic unification. "If the stark realities existing in north and south are disregarded and reunification through unification of the systems is advocated," Prime Minister Yon Hyong-muk warned in Pyongyang's first "state of the world" address at the United Nations General Assembly on October 9, 1991, "it will inevitably increase mistrust and confrontation, not reunification, and will lead, furthermore, to the recurrence of the national scourge of conflict and fratricidal war."[44] Just as Pyongyang's calls for unification used to be seen by Seoul as a sure recipe for revolutionizing or communizing the South, it has now become Pyongyang's turn to feel threatened by Seoul's calls for inter-Korean dialogue, detente, and economic cooperation, which are perceived and acted upon as moves toward hegemonic intersystemic unification—a cooptive strategy of gobbling up the North by pieces—and, as such, a sure recipe for another fratricidal war. There is no doubt about Pyongyang's determination to fight, rather than to succumb to German-style hegemonic unification. Even if system collapse comes about, it is more likely to be a violent and bloody one, triggering a civil war within the Korean peninsula, rather than encouraging peaceful reunification with the South.

Fearing social, economic, political, and military costs of German-style immediate reunification by absorption, Seoul would rather intervene to set up a separate regime to defuse the refugee bombs from exploding in the nation's capital that threatens to destroy its fragile democracy. Seoul seems to have learned the hard way the lessons of German unification: (1) German unification came about by stealth and serendipity (i.e., the Gorbachev factor), not incrementally, naturally, or inevitably as envisioned in the functional theory of "peace by pieces," and as such not readily reproducible in the Korean case; (2) preunification euphoria quickly degenerated into postunification despair and recrimination as West Germany's subsidies for East Germany ballooned to $100 billion annually, only to bring about an unprecedented rise in unemployment, social alienation, and death and suicide rates among former East Germans; and (3) German national identity soon proved itself to be a slender reed, not a solid foundation, for the politics of national reconstruction.

Of course, the costs and problems of West Germany swallowing up East Germany would pale in comparison with what South Korea would have to bear in absorbing North Korea. In almost every dimension, South Korea is no West Germany and North Korea is no East Germany. The monetary cost alone of rescuing North Korea's collapsing economy is estimated to be between $200 billion (Gary Hufbauer of the Institute for International Economics in Washington) and $1.2 trillion (Hwang Eui-gak of Korea University in Seoul),[45] although such figures are still little more than shots in the dark, given the absence of reliable statistics on North Korea and the uncertainties of domestic and external factors involved in the total calculus of Korean reunification. The response of South Koreans to the question, "What in your opinion is the most desirable and feasible type of Korean reunification?" debunks the popular notion in the West that there exist in South Korea abiding primordial passions for national unification at any cost: 9.5 percent for immediate unification without any preconditions and irrespective of systemic differences; 78.5 percent for unification only after the recovery of "national homogeneity" (meaning it would probably take many years to bridge systemic differences between the two Koreas); 7.1 percent against reunification because it is neither needed nor wanted; and 5.3 percent for "don't know.[46] The views of fifty international experts on the prospects for Korean reunification are slightly more sanguine: 2.1 percent within one year (1996); 8.3 percent before 2000; 29.2 percent by 2001–05; 20.8 percent by 2006–10; 16.7 percent by 2011–15; and 16.3 percent after 2015.[47] For what it is worth, I would put myself in the "after 2015" projection category.

Also noteworthy is that South Korea, in striking contrast with West Germany during the preunification period, has been marked by social and political instability. It has had no less than six republics with nine constitutional revisions, two military coups, three student and popular uprisings, twelve declarations of martial law and emergency decrees and several thousand industrial strikes. There is a sense in which South Korea, chronically plagued by fratricidal regional factionalism and searing labor-management conflict, remains yet to be geographically, socially, and politically unified within its own borders. To add a collapsing North Korea with at least two million poverty-stricken North Korean refugees flooding the South seemed like a sure recipe for civil war and/or an end of fragile democracy. Barring the outbreak of an accidental war, the probability of the system-decaying scenario turning into national reunification via system collapse in the North is as low as the system-reforming scenario shifting its gears toward a system-transforming direction.

Concluding Remarks

The preceding analysis leads to several obvious and somewhat paradoxical conclusions. First, nothing is more uncertain than the future of the post–Kim Il Sung system because nothing is irreversible or inevitable in North Korean politics. To say that nothing is more uncertain than the future of North Korea is to perceive some hope and space for policy choices and actions in Washington, Seoul, Tokyo, Beijing, and Moscow to help the post–Kim Il Sung system change its course in a preferred direction.

Second, the most obvious question—how long the post–Kim Il Sung system will survive and in what shape or form—has no simple answer because the interplay of North Korea with the outside world, especially South Korea, the United States, and Japan, is highly complex, variegated, and even confusing. What complicates our understanding of the shape of things to come in North Korea is that all the countries involved (China, Russia, Japan, the United States, and North and South Korea) have become moving targets on turbulent trajectories of their respective highly charged domestic politics, subject to competing and often contradictory pressures and forces. Hence, the three main scenarios discussed above should not be regarded as mutually exclusive since one can easily shift to another or vice versa.

And third, the middle-range future will be more or less like the recent past. Of the three futuribles scenarios, the system-maintaining scenario is the most probable and desirable one for securing a long peace on the Korean peninsula. Herein lies the greatest irony of all—that the clear and continuing danger of system collapse in the North seemed to have served as a blessing in disguise for Pyongyang and as a great teacher of new security thinking in Washington, Seoul, Tokyo, Beijing, and Moscow— that is, the system-maintaining scenario is and becomes the worst-possible option, except there is no better alternative to replace it. UN membership; support of all the major powers involved who are more concerned with the maintenance of peace and stability (i.e., the two Koreas) than Korean reunification; Pyongyang's proximity to "the field of play"; and its "military card" and "refugee bomb card" —all of these factors combined will go some way in the international support and legitimation of the DPRK's status and security as a separate and sovereign, if not completely equal, state on the Korean peninsula. South Korea does not want and cannot afford to absorb system collapse. North Korea does not want to be absorbed by South Korea and will fight to the death to prevent such unification by absorption. The Clinton administration, too, has learned the hard way the core premise of Common Security 101; that any fair and effective security framework must address the legitimate concerns and interests of all its members and that, in the present Korean context, to enhance the security of the weaker, less-privileged half (the DPRK) is the safer and cheaper way of enhancing the security of the stronger half (the ROK).[48] A cornered and insecure North Korea is *ipso facto* an unpredictable and even dangerous North Korea that may feel compelled to launch a preemptive strike, igniting a major armed conflagration in the Korean peninsula and beyond. For geopolitical, geoeconomic, and other reasons, Beijing, Moscow, and Tokyo would be happier to see the peaceful coexistence of the two Korean states on the peninsula than to cope with the turmoil, chaos, and even massive exodus of refugees that system collapse would generate in its wake.

Notes

1. For a wide array of speculations and analyses on the future of post–Kim Il Sung North Korea, see Byung-Joon Ahn, "Korea's Future after Kim Il Sung," *Korea and World Affairs*, 18:3 (Fall 1994); Nicholas Eberstadt, "North Korea: Reform, Muddling Through, or Collapse?" *NBR Analysis*, 4:3 (1993): 5–16; idem, "Hastening Korean Reunification," *Foreign Affairs* 76:2 (Mar/Apr 1997): 77–92; Harry Harding, "The New Regime in North Korea and Its Future: Principal Scenarios," in *The Future of North Korea: Implications for the Korean Peninsula and Northeast Asia* (Seoul: The Institute of Foreign Affairs and National Security, 1995), pp. 21–37; Byung-Chul Koh, "Prospects for Change in North Korea," *Korean Journal of National Unification* 3 (1994); Choong-Nam Kim, "The Uncertain Future of

North Korea: Soft Landing or Crash Landing?" *Korea and World Affairs* 20:4 (Winter 1996): 623–636; Kyung-Won Kim, "No Way Out: North Korea's Impending Collapse," *Harvard International Review* 18:2 (Spring 1996): 22–25, 71; Lee Young-sun, "Is Korean Reunification Possible?" *Korea Focus* 3:3 (May-June 1995): 5–21; Gavan McCormack, "Kim Country: Hard Times in North Korea," *New Left Review*, no. 198 (March-April 1993): 21–48; Dae-sook Suh, "The Prospects for Change in North Korea," *Korea and World Affairs* 17:1 (Spring 1993): 5–20; *Kim Chong-il ch'eche ha ui pukhan* [North Korea under the Kim Jong Il System] (Seoul: T'ongil won, September 1996); and Robert Scalapino, "North Korea at a Crossroads," Essays in Public Policy No. 73 (Hoover Institution, Stanford University, 1997): 1–18.

2. Bertrand de Jourvenal, *The Art of Conjecture* (New York: Basic Books, 1967).

3. For further analysis and elaboration, see Nazli Choucri and Thomas Robinson, eds., *Forecasting in International Relations* (San Francisco: Freeman, 1978); Samuel S. Kim, *The Quest for a Just World Order* (Boulder, CO: Westview Press, 1984), chap. 8, pp. 301–42; Gabriel A. Almond and Stephen J. Genco, "Clouds, Clocks, and the Study of Politics," *World Politics* 29:4 (July 1977): 489–522; and Robert Jervis, "The Future of World Politics: Will It Resemble the Past?" *International Security* 16:3 (Winter 1991/92): 39–73.

4. Jervis, "The Future of World Politics," pp. 40–41.

5. For a list of erroneous predictions, see Kim, *The Quest for a Just World Order*, pp. 317–18.

6. There is general agreement in the field of international relations that Kenneth Waltz's *Theory of International Politics* (Reading, MA: Addison-Wesley, 1979) is the most dominant and influential theory, as it is said to have given classical realism the kind of theoretical rigor and parsimony that such classical realists as Morgenthau (1973) and others had long promised but never quite delivered. Waltz's structural realism emerged as the *Politics Among Nations* of the 1980s, as no other international relations theory has commanded as much success—and controversy—as his. According to one account, more than 350 scholarly articles in the field of international relations cited Waltz's *Theory of International Politics* in the period 1983–92, as counted in the *Social Science Citation Index*. See Nicholas G. Onuf and Thomas J. Johnson, "Peace in the Liberal World: Does Democracy Matter?" in Charles W. Kegley Jr., ed., *Controversies in International Relations Theory* (New York: St. Martin's Press, 1995), p. 180.

7. See Daniel Deudney and G. John Ikenberry, "Soviet Reform and the End of the Cold War: Explaining Large-Scale Historical Change," *Review of International Studies* 17 (Summer 1991): 225–50; John Lewis Gaddis, "International Relations Theory and the End of the Cold War," *International Security* 17:3 (Winter 1992/93): 5–58; Charles W. Kegley Jr., "How Did the Cold War Die? Principles for an Autopsy," *Mershon International Studies Review* 38 (1994): 11–41; Friedrich Kratochwil, "The Embarrassment of Changes: Neo-Realism as the Science of Realpolitik without Politics," *Review of International Studies* 19 (1993): 63–80; Richard Ned Lebow, "The Long Peace, the End of the Cold War, and the Failure of Realism," *International Organization* 48 (Spring 1994): 249–78; and Sean Lynn-Jones and Steven Miller, eds., *The Cold War and After: Prospects for Peace* (Cambridge, MA: MIT Press, 1993).

8. See Francis Fukuyama, "The End of History?" *National Interest*, No. 16 (Summer 1989) and *The End of History and the Last Man* (New York: Free Press, 1992).

9. Jervis, "The Future of World Politics," pp. 42–45.

10. For a detailed analysis of North Korea's informal politics, see Samuel S. Kim, "Informal Politics in North Korea," in Lowell Dittmer, Haruhiro Fukui, and Peter N.S. Lee, eds., *Informal Politics in East Asia* (New York: Cambridge University Press, 1999), pp. 237–268.

11. Choucri, "Key Issues in International Relations Forecasting," in Choucri and Robinson, *Forecasting in International Relations*, p. 4.

12. Johan Galtung, "On the Future, Future Studies and Future Attitudes," in H. Ornauer, H. Wiberg, A. Sicinski, and J. Galtung, eds., *Images of the World in the Year 2000: A Comparative Ten Nation Study* (Atlantic Highlands, NJ: Humanities Press, 1976), p. 4.

13. Harding, "The New Regime in North Korea and Its Future: Principal Scenarios," pp. 21–22.

14. North Korea is perhaps the only country in the world today that still indulges in the cult of personality for the late Joseph Stalin. The Soviet revisionists are condemned for having branded "loyalty to Stalin as a personal idolatry. . . . The counter-revolutionary maneuvers perpetrated by those traitors, who debased Stalin who had fostered the young Soviet Union into a great power, blotting out all of his prestige and achievements, were the meanest act of betrayal which is beyond imagination." *Rodong sinmun* (Pyongyang), November 3, 1996.

15. Hwang's letter dated January 3, 1997, more than a month before actual defection, was passed onto Mr. X of South Korea and published in *Chosen ilbo* (Seoul), February 13, 1997, p. 3.

16. According to Huntington, between 1974 and 1990 35 countries shifted from authoritarian to democratic systems of government causing "the third wave of democratization in the modern era." In eleven countries, including South Korea, democratization came about through "transplacement"—that is, joint action by government and opposition groups. See Samuel P. Huntington, "How Countries Democratize," *Political Science Quarterly* 106:4 (Winter 1991–92): 579–616.

17. McCormack, "Kim Country," pp. 35–36.

18. "Defense Technology Survey," *Economist* (London), June 10, 1995, p. 7.

19. "The DPRK Report (September–October 1996)" prepared by the Center for Nonproliferation Studies (Monterey Institute of International Studies, Monterey, CA) and the Center for Contemporary International Problems (located at the Diplomatic Academy, Moscow) as transmitted by Northwest Asia Peace and Security Network Daily Report.

20. Eberstadt, "Hastening Korean Reunification," p. 85.

21. Kim Il Sung's New Year Address, in *Rodong sinmun*, January 1, 1992, pp. 1–2; quote on p. 2.

22. KCNA, February 3, 1997, on-line.

23. According to Ian Davies, a UN official advising the DPRK government on bringing in foreign investment, as reported in AP on-line, March 12, 1997.

24. Several chapter essays, especially the essay by Ernst Haas, "Collective Learning: Some Theoretical Speculations," in George W. Breslauer and Philip E. Tetlock,

eds., *Learning in U.S. and Soviet Foreign Policy* (Boulder, CO: Westview Press, 1991), pp. 62–99.

25. Alexander Wendt, "Collective Identity Formation and the International State," *American Political Science Review* 88:2 (June 1994): 390, emphasis in original.

26. FBIS-EAS, August 3, 1995, pp. 39–41.

27. See, for example, *Nodong sinmun*, May 27, 1991; February 4, 1992; October 10, 1992; and March 4, 1993.

28. "Sahoechui nun kwahak ita" ["Socialism Is a Science"], *Nodong sinmun*, November 4, 1994, pp. 1–3. This was officially released on November 1 but published in the November 4 edition of *Nodong sinmun*.

29. So Chol, a low-ranking diplomat at the North Korean UN mission in Geneva made a statement to this effect: "The global market has now changed and that means we have more opportunities in the West." See AP on-line, February 4, 1997.

30. "This year, too," North Korea pronounced through its New Year joint editorial, "we must strictly implement the policy of giving primary importance to agriculture, light industry and foreign trade, as demanded by the party's revolutionary economic strategy." Korean Central News Agency (hereafter cited as KCNA), January 1, 1997.

31. See Marcus Noland, "External Economic Relations of the DPRK and Prospects for Reform," in Samuel S. Kim, ed., *North Korean Foreign Policy in the Post–Cold War Era* (New York: Columbia University Press, 1998), pp. 187–211.

32. In late February 1997, South Korea's Daewoo returned to North Korea to resume its modest joint venture project in Nampo.

33. World Bank, *World Development Report 1991: The Challenge of Development* (New York: Oxford University Press, 1991), Figure 1.1, p. 12.

34. For a more detailed discussion and analysis, see Samuel S. Kim, "China's Pacific Policy: Reconciling the Irreconcilable," *International Journal* 50:3 (Summer 1995): pp. 461–487 and "The Dialectics of China's North Korea Policy in a Changing Post-Cold War World," *Asian Perspective* 18:2 (Fall–Winter 1994): 5–36.

35. *North Korean News*, No. 702 (September 27, 1993), p. 5.

36. Harry Harding, *China's Second Revolution: Reform After Mao* (Washington, D.C.: The Brookings Institution, 1987), p. 133.

37. Deng Xiaoping, "Why China Has Opened Its Door," in FBIS-China, February 12, 1980, p. L3. For the same point stressing this conjunction of favorable domestic and external conditions, see Deng Xiaoping, *Deng Xioaping wenxuan 1975–82* [Selected Works of Deng Xiaoping 1975–82] (Beijing: Renmin chubanshe, 1983), p. 122 and Commentator, "Youli yu shijie heping de zhongda shijian," [A Significant Event Favorable to World Peace] *Hongqi* [Red Flag], No. 1 (January 1979): 6.

38. Nicholas Eberstadt, "Pachinko Woes in North Korea," *Wall Street Journal*, May 2, 1996.

39. Jervis, "The Future of World Politics," p. 41.

40. See Ted Gurr, "Psychological Factors in Civil Violence," in Richard A. Falk and Samuel S. Kim, eds., *The War System: An Interdisplinary Approach* (Boulder, CO: Westview Press, 1980), pp. 248–81.

41. Jeffrey Herbst, "The Creation and Maintenance of National Boundaries in Africa," *International Organization* 43 (Autumn 1989): 675–76.

42. Cited in *Far Eastern Economic Review* (February 27, 1997), p. 15.

43. See *Hsin Pao* (Hong Kong), April 8, 1994, p. 24, in FBIS-China, April 12, 1994, pp. 13–15 and *Hsin Pao*, June 24, 1994, p. 25, and in FBIS-China, June 24, 1994, pp. 7–8; quotes respectively on p. 14 and p. 7.

44. For the text of Yon's speech, see UN Document A/46/PV 18 (October 9, 1991), pp. 61–78, quote on pp. 69–70.

45. See "Costs of Unifying Koreas Put at $200 billion to $2 trillion," *The Korea Herald* (Seoul), June 29, 1996, p. 1.

46. *'95 Kukmin uisik chosa* [Survey of National Consciousness, 1995] (Seoul: Sejong Institute, 1995), p. 70.

47. Lee, "Is Korean Reunification Possible?" p. 10.

48. James Laney, United States Ambassador to the ROK until recently, was a foremost advocate and spokesman for this view, openly calling for food aid and economic assistance to North Korea to guard against Pyongyang's collapse or desperate measures to starve off collapse, which he said is "manifestly not in our long-term interests." *The Korea Herald* (Seoul), June 29, 1996, p. 2.

Part II
South Korea and Inter-Korea Relations:
Domestic Political Economy
and the U.S.-ROK Alliance System

4
Two Scales:
Democratization and the North Korea Policy of the Kim Young Sam Government

Kwang Woong Kim
in collaboration with Junki Kim

Introduction

The ghosts of authoritarianism still linger in South Korea. The administration of President Kim Young Sam wound down to a disappointing end. This is in sharp contrast with the triumphant way that Kim, the country's first democratically elected civilian president in three decades, came into office in 1993. Kim dealt a damaging blow to South Korea's emerging democracy on December 30, 1996, when he ordered to rush through parliament an imperious new law giving wide-ranging powers to the country's National Security Planning Agency. At the same secretly convened, predawn parliamentary session, the administration also passed a controversial labor law that set off nationwide protests and paralyzed industries. What is most disturbing is the way in which these controversial laws came into existence and the process involved in passing them. This was staged with little or no debate either at the national or the parliamentary level. Further, these laws were passed without the presence of members of the opposition.[1] In addition, a scandal involving Hanbo Steel broke out in January that virtually crippled his government.[2] The Hanbo Steel scandal has severely damaged Kim's reputation as an honest politician because several of his close associates were implicated and subsequently arrested on charges of corruption.

By contrast, President Kim's first years in office were marked by bold democratic reforms. To fight corruption, he successfully introduced an ethics law, requiring ministers and officials to declare their assets. He also introduced a law that prohibits South Koreans from holding bank accounts and property under false names in an attempt to regulate financial and real estate transactions.[3] To spread democracy to provincial and local governments, governors, mayors, and county administrators were elected in June 1995 for the first time in thirty-four years. These elections, which were held for the 5,700 posts previously appointed by the president, were generally agreed to be among the fairest ever held in the country. Moreover, news media now have more freedom to criticize the government.

What went wrong with the Kim administration in a period of a little over three years? Many think it is unfortunate that such a promising administration has now fallen back into the authoritarian pattern of Korea's past. The purpose of this chapter is, thus, to examine the structure of democratic institutions in Korea and to review democratic development in conjunction with the implementation of its Northern policy under the present regime.

Striving for Democratization

The Hanbo Steel scandal is the toughest challenge to President Kim since he assumed office four years ago. Several close associates of the president have been arrested on charges of corruption and influence peddling, thereby severely crippling his government and tainting his own image as a "clean" president. The Hanbo Steel scandal not only provoked public skepticism over what Kim has achieved through his anticorruption campaign, but also nullified his efforts for the democratization of the country. With the embarrassing defeat in two by-elections for vacant parliamentary seats this March, a sense of crisis and panic is beginning to set in in the Kim government and the ruling party.

In his inaugural speech in 1993, President Kim diagnosed as "the Korean disease" the crisis of inefficiency and immorality that was precipitated by the past authoritarian regimes. He advocated the building of a new Korea through "changes and reform." He then proposed three major tasks: terminating corruption, revitalizing the economy, and establishing public discipline. Subsequently, President Kim has launched democratic reform programs in four successive waves.[4] Under these programs and in an attempt to make financial and real estate transactions less corrupt, he also introduced a law that eliminated rules allowing South Koreans to hold bank accounts and property under a false name.[5] To spread democracy to provincial and local governments, governors, mayors, and county administrators were elected in June 1995 for the first time in thirty-four years. In addition, the Election and Campaign Finance laws were amended to make way for "clean politics."

The fourth reform wave is currently underway "to rectify the past wrongs," or to restore Korean honor. It began on October 19, 1995, with the investigation of the political slush fund amassed by former President Roh Tae Woo, Kim's immediate predecessor. Public outcry about the scandal has forced Kim to declare a war on the old ruling triad of military generals, politicians, and *chaebols*. As a result, Korea's last two presidents have been arrested and indicted on numerous charges, including that of an illegal army mutiny in 1979 and ordering of the 1980 massacre of prodemocracy demonstrators in the city of Kwangju. Fourteen more generals have been arrested on charges related to the massacre. In addition, Roh Tae Woo and Chun Doo Whan have been indicted for amassing political slush funds over $650 million and $250 million, respectively, while in office. Chun's five close associates have also been indicted for taking bribes. More than thirty-four corporate leaders, including the heads of Korea's seven biggest *chaebols*, were investigated for offering bribes and kickbacks in return for business favors.[6]

The slush fund scandal has provided a timely opportunity for President Kim to remove the authoritarian enclave of the Minjung faction from the ruling Democratic Liberal Party. Linking the Chun government and its Liberal Justice Party to the corruption and brutality of the authoritarian past, he has been able to purge congressmen and party district heads who were associated with the Minjung faction and replace them with his loyal supporters. On December 6, 1995, Kim even changed the name of the governing party from the Democratic Liberal Party to the New Korea Party in an attempt to demonstrate a clean break with the authoritarian past.

In Kim's model of democratic consolidation, which contrasts sharply with Dahl's liberal notion that has served as a foundation for a minimal definition of democratic consolidation for decades,[7] the community's interests are placed ahead of its individual members. Kim chose to become a communitarian democrat subscribing to the notion that "democracy is partly a structure of laws and incentives by which less-than-perfect individuals are induced to act in the common good while pursuing their own goals."[8] By infusing democracy with a moral framework, President Kim finds it immoral and undemocratic to continue collaboration with former dictators who had previously seized power by military coups and oppressed people, and their supporters.[9] However, the institutionalization of these democratic procedures matters little unless primordial political habits and corrupt practices of the authoritarian past are transformed into communitarian, universal ones. To achieve such a democratic transformation, individual citizens would be made aware of all the illegal acts and injustices of the old military governments. Furthermore, they would also be encouraged to reorient themselves toward the community in which they live with others. Their elected officials should depart from an alliance with those responsible for the authoritarian ills. These officials and civil servants should also sever their collusive ties with the business community.

Initially, many observers, including a majority of Koreans, thought that the election of President Kim Young Sam signaled not only the end of decades of military and quasi-military rules, but also the termination of authoritarianism and its legacies. It appears that these optimists have been proven wrong. Even Kim's ardent supporters were dismayed when the democratically elected president had to rely on tear gas to control striking workers who took to the streets to demand union rights and denounce what they described as repression by the government. It is ironic that they were once championed by a long-time democracy proponent, Kim Young Sam.[10] More damaging is the criticism that President Kim has been accused of behaving like his predecessors. The president has retained undemocratic laws, intimidated newspapers with tax audits, and used a covert agency, the Agency for National Security Planning, to tamper with domestic politics. Although it may be too early to judge, there are obvious signs of government and leadership failures that seem to be multiplying in depth and magnitude.

We argue that the latest government scandals and subsequent social unrest are the results of three factors: the legacies of the past authoritarian regimes that fostered the regionalism which President Kim conveniently utilized; his reliance on his own secretariat and "backroom" politics that bypassed relevant ministries; and, most importantly, the lack of President Kim's commitment to adhere to democratic principles. We illustrate that the result has been the lack of public accountability and inconsistent policies.

Regionalism is the legacy from the Park Chung Hee regime. During his eighteen years of autocratic rule, Park depended on a set of "reliable" technocrats and politicians from his part of the country in order to prolong his regal presidency. This was necessitated by the nature of the autocratic regime which, for the sake of its own survival, had to prevent rule by a coalition of leaders from other parts of the country. Regionalism, in turn, fostered factionalism within the government as a way of preventing leakage of power. Kim was no exception to the rule of the past and has relied on "comrades from democracy campaigning days" (the Minju faction) and the "PK (Pusan and South Kyongsang) faction" for much of its internal policy making. This phenomenon has been particularly applicable in the presidential office, which is largely staffed by Kim's loyal supporters. Although the president's own secretariat carries out the important coordination function to aid policy consistency among different ministries, it has, in fact, exercised considerable authority and often has taken policy formulation away from ministers. The consequences of frequent intervention by the presidential office are twofold: first, the business of government was dominated by a chosen few and conducted in a "backroom" fashion,[11] and, second, the reliance on non-official channels created a public-accountability vacuum. It means that, as critical domestic and foreign policies were made in a non-public fashion, it was difficult to hold the official policy making hierarchy accountable for government policies. Furthermore, this has created not only a deep division in a country already torn apart by ideological conflicts from the earlier years, but also a mistrust of government policies.

Another fundamental problem facing the government is that most of the country's leaders have a lukewarm commitment to the new way of doing business, and the authoritarian mentality is still alive and striving. Kim does not welcome criticism within the government and shuffles his ministers about very frequently. In January 1994, the prime minister was fired in an unexpected rift in the leadership of President Kim. Kim may not be a general, but he behaves almost as imperiously as the military rulers before him. For instance, in March 1995 he tried to change the local election law that he himself sponsored in 1994. Fearing that his party would be humiliated at the polls, the president suggested that candidates should stand as independents rather than on a party ticket. It took violent protests to persuade him to back down.

President Kim has also intimidated former as well as current enemies by using various imperious and coercive tools, thereby creating further mistrust in government. A favorite technique of President Park and his successors was to use the internal revenue service against his opponents; Kim was also quick to utilize the tool. Hints of Park's aloofness to the public, his encouragement of "yes-men" and his habit of crushing potential rivals also surfaced in the Kim government. A case in point: Chung Ju Yung, the founder of the Hyundai conglomerate, the country's biggest *chaebol*, ran in the 1992 presidential election against Kim. Having said some unkind words about Kim, Chung received a suspended three-year prison sentence for supposedly infringing upon the often non-relevant campaign-finance laws, and his companies were refused permission to raise capital on the international bond market.

The long years of authoritarianism have bred arbitrary and imperious rules that have undermined the principles of equality and democratic accountability. It can be said that lukewarm commitment to democratic institutions and principles has undermined the development of Korea's emerging democracy and has, in turn, fostered resentment of government under the current administration. In other words, the administration is in danger of losing an important ally in the process, namely the people of Korea.

President Kim's recent handling of the introduction of a new labor law, which makes it easier for *chaebols* to lay off workers and hire temporary workers and allows replacement of striking workers, also reflects his leadership style and his lack of commitment to democratic principles. Although government officials claim that the new labor law, which was pushed through the parliament at a December 26, 1996 pre-dawn session without the presence of opposition, is crucial to improve international competitiveness and meet OECD requirements, this was done in a very authoritarian manner. With little or no debate, the government of President Kim passed the new law allowing layoffs for the first time, thus breaking the Korean tradition of jobs for life. Three weeks of labor protest ensued, frequently turning into violent confrontations between striking workers and riot police. The government denounced the strike as illegal and threatened the use of force to prevent the unrest.

While the focus of the confrontation may appear to be on the government's policies toward labor unions, there are also important implications for the way the Kim government conducts policy making. The incident shows that Kim is undemocratic in a broader sense. The recent handling of the passing of the new labor law lacks any forward-looking policy beyond austerity and belt-tightening, and also lacks any attempt to provide justification for the passing of the law. Not only was there little debate on the need to reform the labor market, which has shown some rigidities in recent years, but the law was passed in a secretly convened, predawn parliamentary session without the presence of opposition members. The subsequent public outcry has forced President Kim to revise the law, but Korean industries and labor unions are both unhappy with the compromised version of the law. As a result, the public is now focusing on President Kim's leadership style, and questions his commitment to the democratic institution and principles. Although this episode underscores South Korea's peculiar position at the crossroads of democracy and authoritarianism, it is President Kim who has undermined the democratic institution and principles. By taking an easier route to "political governance," President Kim is in danger of nullifying reform programs that were once effective at dismantling the remnants of the authoritarianism past. While the labor law has provoked the most protest, the new security law seems to be more troubling.

The security agency has survived largely intact despite the harsh military regimes of the 1970s and 1980s, which used domestic spying operations to muzzle peaceful political dissent. The intelligence services still wield vast power in Korea. In February 1995 it was discovered the intelligence services had plotted to subvert the local elections. The National Security law, a vaguely worded law that empowers the state to imprison anyone who says or does anything favorable about North Korea, remains on the statute books. That domestic political role was abolished with Mr. Kim's support in 1994.

The law is now being reinstated on the theory that between 30,000 to 50,000 people the government calls "hard-core leftists" have become a serious national security threat. Although South Korea has legitimate concerns about northern spying and infiltration (concerns that were heightened by the recent discovery of a North Korean commando submarine in South Korean waters), it is the timing of the reinstatement that is more troubling. Many suspect that the South Korean government has domestic reasons to fan the anti-North flames that were drummed up in support of the law. Both the Hwang defection in Beijing and the Lee shooting in Seoul have diverted attention from the embarrassing Hanbo corruption scandal.

Explanations for the continuing saga of President Kim's demise are complex, but they may have less to do with the specific issues that provoked the latest unrest in Seoul and more to do with the broad challenges of creating a democratic political culture. Many countries in Asia and around the world are wrestling with the difficulties of democratic transitions. Like these other countries, South Korea is finding that pluralism needs to be based on attitudes as well as on institutions. The creation of democratic institutions is relatively easy, but Kim has so far failed to adhere to a set of principles that would create a democratic process and political culture. It is indeed hard to change old habits. In the next section, we see how an inconsistent and undemocratic policy toward North Korea has created a deep division among the people and a rift with traditional allies including the United States.

Inconsistent Northern Policy

The current government's biggest failure seems to be in the area of its foreign and security policies and they became noticeably confused in the wake of the suspected nuclear weapons development in the North and with the Clinton administration's engagement policy toward the North. Kim has vacillated in his remarks on North Korea, and relevant government ministries and agencies have been at odds, fighting for Kim's influence. Ironically, however, Kim' government which was designed to reflect the popular will has caused a split in public opinion and is swaying over its foreign and security policies.

When Kim's policy toward the North is traced, it is difficult to find any consistency.[12] First, he started with a conciliatory posture toward the North in his inaugural speech in 1993 when he said that the allied nations could not overwhelm the Korean "ethnicity." However, he reversed himself in June of that year when the nuclear issue became serious and said he could not "shake hands" with the North if it had nuclear weapons. The following January, Kim said it was not certain that the North had nuclear weapons and his government would continue its effort to improve its relationship with the North. On the first anniversary of his presidency, at the end of February 1994, he reversed his position and said he would propose a summit meeting with Kim Il Sung if he contributed to the prevention of nuclear arms development. Other instances of the policy contradiction are not difficult to find: for example, the extraction of an apology from the North over the submarine incident in 1996. First, Kim declared that the South would freeze all contact and assistance to the North until the North apologized for the submarine incident. He went further, in an effort to appease the conservative voters in the South, by declaring the comprehensive review of all government policies on the North. His administration branded the North Korean intrusion a commando-style infiltration in preparation for wider military action and said it breached the terms of the armistice treaty. In another speech, Kim called the infiltration "an antinational provocation to the peaceful unification of the fatherland that should be punished in the name of the peace-loving people of the world." He added, "our armed forces must be fostered into crack units of strength capable of smashing any adventurism of the North, based on a firm superiority in power." Soon after, the government contradicted itself by saying that talks would be held before an apology was made, although its first task would be to obtain an apology.

The Kim government has also been accused of refusing to focus on what may happen in Pyongyang, where the food crisis has worsened amid signs of a leadership struggle under Kim Jong Il. With the North Korean economy severely damaged by years of bureaucratic central planning and three years of floods, the South has an unique opportunity to intervene in the process of the North's inevitable disintegration, which it has failed to utilize. There is no clear strategy of how to influence events in the North. The government is still undecided on whether it should actively guide the North to a "soft landing" with food aid and conciliatory offers, or take steps to lead to an abrupt collapse. An inconsistent policy toward North Korea has been attributed to several factors: failure of interagency coordination, failure of leadership and, most importantly, its failure to build a consensus among the people on its nordpolitik course.

Lack of interagency policy coordination is one aspect of the government problem. Four government organizations deal with North Korean affairs: the Unification Board, the National Security Planning Agency, the Defense Ministry and the Foreign Ministry; all are under the control of the presidential office. The National Security Planning Agency and the Defense Ministry traditionally have been hawkish and have not been on the same wavelength with the dovish Unification Board. Gaining a consensus on the North is not easy because of the struggle for leadership in government ministries and agencies, and frequent reshuffling of the cabinet.[13] The struggle has been accelerated by the appointment of scholars and technocrats from different spectrums of society. Kim's first unification minister was a "dovish" sociologist; his successor, the first of many, was a hard-line refugee from the north. Then came another scholar renowned for conciliatory approaches. The current man in charge, a former journalist, may be more susceptible to public criticism of his policy course.

On the leadership issue, Kim has shown the desire to lead all major policies and centralize the process. To unify security policies under one umbrella and to deal with the increasing criticism over the inconsistent northern policy, Kim began rebuilding his foreign and security policy team and even created a council in April 1994. Government disorder appeared to have settled down with the president himself giving policy guidelines through the chief presidential secretary. But Prime Minister Lee Hoi Chang balked at having been left out of the council's meeting and said council decisions needed his approval. This being regarded as a challenge to imperial presidential powers, Lee was subsequently fired. The creation of an "imperial presidency" has caused a concentration of power to those closely associated with the president and, hence, to the secretariat, bypassing the official policy channel. As these unofficial policy teams were not made accountable for policy failures, due to the difficulties in tracing the policy formulation process, they were frequently engaged in other undemocratic operations.

Furthermore, Kim has been accused of being more concerned about his own welfare after he steps down at the end of 1997 rather than the formulation of a coherent policy. He has been seeking a successor who will protect him by keeping the powerful security apparatus and army on his side, and taking a tough line against Pyongyang. Now, as his domestic troubles crowd in on him, President Kim's uncompromising stance toward the North wins him some popularity and pushes the scandals off the front pages. He is also using the North Korean threat to offset his critics.[14] After North Korea entered South Korea from a grounded submarine in September, Kim whipped up an anti-Communist frenzy, and all efforts at better relations were immediately frozen until North Korea apologized.

More importantly, the critical mistake the Kim government has made with respect to the design and implementation of security and unification policies has been its failure to lead and derive a consensus on the future course of the policy toward the North. It has relied, instead, on an undemocratic process, namely a "backroom" policy formulation process that does not build public consensus. A policy toward the North, in particular, requires close consultation with the Korean people as it involves monetary sacrifices on the part of the general public. Without a set of core policy directives or a clear negotiation strategy, the government has been a passive player in its relationship with the North. Kim's reliance on his own secretariat and other means of unofficial policy formulation processes has caused not only further division among his foreign policy team, but has also led to the pursuit of covert operations.

It is conceivable that while President Kim was concentrating on "righting the past wrongs," he himself lacked a clear vision of the structure of democratic governance. Although democratic leadership requires a commitment to a democratic institution and its principles, President Kim instead preferred a quasi-autocratic leadership style which often overrode other institutions in the name of national goals, a deviated version of communitarianism. Pluralism was considered detrimental to a newly emerging democracy and other criticism of the government's policies toward the North were pushed aside in the name of national security. Often the discussions of its nordpolitik policy were not encouraged as the government sought a unified approach in dealing with the North. To discourage opponents, critics of the government's policies were often being accused of sympathizing with North Korean policy directives and those that took further initiatives were investigated by its spy agencies. In other words, although he knew what went wrong with past authoritarian regimes, Kim failed to derive meaningful lessons for his administration.

To a certain extent, in dealing with North Korea, there is a need to come up with a united front and coherent policies. This, however, does not imply that policy design and formulation should be carried out undemocratically without deriving some form of consensus from the general public. It appears that the provision of an environment that is not fit for discussion and compromise has been the only consistent policy of Kim's government. In sum, President Kim's failure to adhere to a democratic institution, his encouragement of secretive "closed door" policy formulation, and his inability to arrive at a set of principles in dealing with North Korea has made the government particularly vulnerable to public criticism. This, in turn, has resulted in the government's tailoring of the North Korea policy to suit the public mood, which has been vacillating between a conciliatory stance during the floods in North Korea and the anti-Pyongyang posture since the submarine incident.

The government, paying far too much attention to the constantly changing public mood, has another important challenge: its relationship with the United States. Apart from domestic unrest involving violent student protests,[15] recent events threaten to deepen the friction between the two long-time allies. The current issue is whether efforts to make peace with and provide aid to economically desperate North Korea will be delayed or halted after the request by a high-ranking North Korean official for asylum in the South and the shooting of another North Korean defector in Seoul. While publicly in agreement on how to deal with North Korea, Washington and Seoul have been squabbling behind the scene for four years. At times it has seemed that the United States' relations with South Korea were worse than U.S.–North Korea relations. Although the United States has pursued a consistent policy of seeking to encourage North Korea to end its isolation and reduce the risk of a war, the Kim government has yet to take a clear position. It has only reiterated that it is naive of the United States to try to appease a Communist government that cannot be trusted. Kim's government also says that it believes that Pyongyang's economic woes provide leverage to drive a hard bargain with little policy guidelines.

Kim faces a grave situation because security and foreign policies can make or break a government in South Korea, where unification of the South and North is the ultimate aim of national policy. But President Kim has so far pursued short-term political goals that are based on undemocratic rules instead of tackling the real test of leadership for a South Korean president. The Kim administration's failure to build public consensus and its inability to design a consistent policy toward the North has not only increased public skepticism of its policy effectiveness but also caused the North to distance itself from the South. Even Roh Tae Woo was known for his patient "nordpolitik," which was evidenced in full diplomatic relations with the Soviet Union and China, as well as direct talks and formal agreements with North Korea.

Conclusions

There is no question that South Korea, despite its political gaffes, is a fully functioning democracy. Indeed, the vigor of the political debate shows that South Korea is becoming more open. To many outsiders, democracy in South Korea appears to have more healthy signs than in neighboring Japan—where candidates are not allowed to debate with each other in public during elections, and cannot put their names on their manifestos. None of this applies in South Korea, which is impressive given how recently it was known for repression.

South Korea, however, is still undergoing a painful transition from authoritarianism to democracy and faces the task of curing the "Korean disease"—rampant corruption, lawlessness, and lack of authority. After four years of reform under Kim Young Sam, however, the end of authoritarianism has yet to surface and may have even lost some ground. For example, South Koreans are increasingly apprehensive about their political, economic, and social troubles. As a result they are not only losing confidence but doubt that they will be able to achieve a full-fledged democracy. The creation of democratic institutions is relatively easy and this was largely done through the people's revolt against past authoritarian regimes. It is the responsibility of leaders to make democracy fully functional. Sadly, Mr. Kim has largely remained on the sideline for much of his tenure. A more damaging accusation relates to President Kim's failure to adhere to a set of principles to create a democratic process and political culture, as is evidenced in the lack of formal policies with the North.

President Kim faced an awkward dilemma, with most of his democratic endeavors refuted. Coming shortly after a serious debacle over the legislation of unpopular labor and national security bills, the Hanbo scandal accelerated Kim's steady decline in popularity A public opinion poll revealed that Kim's job approval rating fell from 90 percent to 10 percent towards the end of his administration. The diagnosis of what went wrong with Kim's administration is widely accepted. The cure, however, will have to contain the continuation of resolute reform and the change of leadership style towards a more democratic one. In order for the society to become more tolerant towards dissenting views, leadership has to accept pluralism and value democratic institutions and processes.

The future of South Korean democracy can neither be correlated with President Kim's popularity nor based on his tenure alone. The Korean people learned a valuable lesson during Kim's tenure; a lesson in which they began to appreciate the importance of the process and the role of the leadership. For this reason, the upcoming presidential election will pose an important test: a test of convergence in election and policies. In the meantime, however, it may be recorded in Korean history that President Kim, who was constrained by the characteristics of his transitional government, has paved a road to the full democratization of Korea.

Notes

1. The laws were eventually passed with a major rewriting in the parliament on March 10, 1997.

2. Some would argue that his reputation was already tainted through previous scandals that implicated several of his associates. The Chang Hak-ro incident is an example.

3. This was originally intended to broaden the tax base, as tax evasion was rampant among those holding assets under false names. However, Kim used it for the purpose of fighting corruption and some fear that because of the way it was introduced, involving only a limited number of academics and without building a support coalition or holding any substantive discussions, it led to many shortfalls. *Chosen Ilbo*, March 7, 1997, p.5

4. For the details on the first three waves, see Kihl (1993, 1995), D. Kim (1993), M. Kim, (1994), and Paik (1994).

5. In his 1996 New Year's speech to the nation, President Kim emphasized that "the campaign to rectify the distortions of Korean history is a signal for the birth of a new community which is ruled by law, justice, conscience and ethics." *The Korea Herald*, January 1, 1996, p. 1. He added that "we can no longer overlook in the name of national reconciliation, the acts and attitudes that disgraced the people and our history." Rather than leaving past misdeeds to the judgment of history, Kim decided to expose these activities and punish those responsible. What mattered more to him in building a democratic community was no longer national reconciliation or consensus; it was the purging of past wrongs.

6. K. C. Hwang, "The $650 Million Man." *Time,* November 6, 1995, p. 19.

7. See Robert A. Dahl, *Polyarchy: Participation and Competition.* New Haven, CT: Yale University Press, 1971.

8. See Pierre Manent, "On Modern Individualism." *Journal of Democracy,* 7, 1996, pp. 3–10.

9. Doh C. Shin and K. W. Kim, "President Kim Young Sam's Model to Consolidate Korean Democracy: Its Distinctive Features and Notable Consequences." Paper presented at the annual meeting of the Midwest Political Science Association in Chicago, April 18–20, 1996.

10. *The New York Times.* December 30, 1996.

11. Those close to the presidential office also lament the problem, saying that the people around the president took part in the prodemocracy struggle and do not have any administrative experience. In essence, they claim that the presidential office lacks talented personnel.

12. Previously, South Korea had provided rice and other relief goods since 1994, when the North was struck by hurricanes that ruined most of its crops. Under an unprecedented agreement in June 1994, South Korea supplied 150,000 tons of rice to the Stalinist North in a bid to lessen a chronic food shortage and to ease tensions between the two sides. In addition, it had shipped $1 million worth of powdered milk to ease child malnutrition while donating $2 million to the UN World Food Program to buy grain powder for North Koreans after a UN appeal for $43.6 million in flood-relief aid.

13. A study found that the average tenure of ministers in Kim's administration is 12.4 months. For details, see K. W. Kim's column in *Munwha Ilbo*, March 6, 1997, p.6.

14. Moreover, fear of North Korea is being kindled by articles appearing in newspapers about letters that Mr. Hwang, a former high-ranking official of the North Korean government, wrote or remarks he made in the months before he defected. He is said to have told South Korean officials that there are up to 50,000 North Korean agents in South Korea, including some highly placed in the government. In one letter, he is said to have written that the North's "fundamental policy

is national reunification through the invasion of South Korea" and that it "has no intention of dialogue." In all likelihood, the statements were leaked by South Korean intelligence officials to take advantage of the defection to offset the critics by trying to equate all opponents to the revised National Security Law to Northern sympathizers.

15. Another result of Kim's inconsistent policy toward the North has been student unrest. Indecision led to a violent campaign for reunification with North Korea by students, which president Kim crushed with the use of force.

References

Bedeski, Robert E. 1994. *The Transformation of South Korea: Reform and Reconstruction in the Sixth Republic under Roh Tae Woo*. Routledge.

Clifford, Mark L. 1994. *Troubled Tiger: Businessmen, Bureaucrats, and Generals in South Korea*. Armonk, NY: M.E. Sharpe.

Dahl, Robert A. 1971. *Polyarchy: Participation and Competition*. New Haven, CT: Yale University Press.

Hwang, K. C. 1995. "The $650 Million Man." *Time*, November 6, 1995, p. 19.

Kihl, Young Whan. 1994. *Korea and the World—Beyond the Cold War*. Boulder: Westview Press, 1994.

Manent, Pierre. 1996. "On Modern Individualism." *Journal of Democracy*, vol. 17, pp. 3–10.

Shin, Doh C. and K. W. Kim. 1996. "President Kim Young Sam's Model to Consolidate Korean Democracy: Its Distinctive Features and Notable Consequences." Paper presented at the annual meeting of the Midwest Political Science Association in Chicago, April 18–20.

5
Democracy and Unification:
The Dilemma of the ROK Engagement

Victor D. Cha

With increasing frequency, genuine concerns are being raised about the status quo that has existed on the Korean peninsula since 1953. The factors most often cited as jeopardizing this stability are internal to North Korea—negative growth rates, chronic agricultural and energy deficiencies, a growing number of defections at both the elite and mass levels, and the deaths of two top defense officials being the most salient in the first half of 1997. However, of equal importance to outcomes on the peninsula are the external pressures and/or inducements faced by the opaque North Korean regime. In this regard, one of the key policy dilemmas facing the Republic of Korea (ROK) is whether to engage its rival. A topic of intense debate in the South, the question of engagement is one of the few issues that substantively differentiates policies in a polity afflicted by more esoteric regional and personality-based issues.

The contours of this debate and the dilemma of ROK engagement are well-known to most. Arguments against engagement focus on its futility in the face of North Korean intransigence. In short, the regime in Pyongyang is still bent on subverting the South and will not change its objective. It does not respond positively to conciliatory gestures by Seoul; rather it perceives such gestures as signs of weakness, which in turn only reinforces the position of hardliners in Pyongyang. As a result, cooperative behavior is best elicited through containment policies that, in conjunction with the North's dire internal situation, will press the regime to capitulate. Pro-engagement arguments start from many of the same premises but reach different conclusions. The northern regime is in dire straits, but hard-line containment is likely to elicit rash and dangerous reactions rather than conciliatory ones. The primary obstacle to North-South dialogue is no longer the Cold War, but the legacies of this four-decade struggle manifest in deeply rooted mutual distrust and animosity. Conciliatory acts would help to dissipate these barriers and pave the way to confidence-building. Containment, on the other hand, only reinforces such barriers.

Rather than rehash this policy debate, this chapter seeks to approach the problem of ROK engagement from a slightly different perspective. The first cut at the issue is to understand what exactly we mean by "engagement." Discussions of ROK engagement thus far have seemed to miss this prior and critical question. The second cut is to assess the ROK's current policy initiatives toward the North in the context of this conceptual discussion. What emerges from this exercise is that current strategic thinking in Seoul on "engagement" is problematic, afflicted by certain fundamental cognitive biases about unification and security on the peninsula. Moreover, overcoming these biases is critical because in the medium- to long-term, the "default" policy for the peninsula is engagement. In other words, regardless of whether one is a "hawk" or "dove" the optimal policy for the ROK is one of engagement.

Three Ways of Understanding Engagement

Engagement refers to a process of strategic interaction in which a set of policies, noncoercive in nature, are designed to elicit cooperative behavior and establish norms of reciprocity with the target or adversary state.[1] The content and nature of these policies are polar opposites of those associated with containment (which focuses on deterrence based on the threat of force), and take three basic forms.

The first and most often assumed model of engagement is in the liberal/interdependent tradition.[2] This seeks to promote and cultivate a thick web of intergovernmental ties as the primary means of dealing with the problem state. These ties transverse a range of issues such as economics, the environment, politics, and culture to increase familiarity and transparency between the two sides and opening potential avenues for cooperation. Cooperation in one issue can have spillover effects in others; disagreements in one issue may be minimized because of positive ripple effects in others. The primary causal mechanism is that embedding the target state in a web of interdependent ties generally raises the costs of belligerent behavior.[3]

A second form of engagement is transnational. It is similar in process to (and often contemporaneous with) interdependent engagement but the locus of activity is more at the nongovernmental level. Encouraging the target state to embed itself in a web of international exchanges allows ties to develop between nongovernmental constituencies in the target state and those in other countries. With advances in communications and transportation technology (e.g., facsimiles, Internet), these groups can easily organize around common issues across national borders. These constituencies, once exposed and connected to nongovernmental groups outside their borders can pressure the government to change foreign policy and adhere to internationally accepted standards and norms of behavior.[4]

The third type is concert engagement. This seeks cooperation not by coercion nor by cultivating interdependent ties, but by adjusting one's own policies to accommodate the interests of the dissatisfied target state. It seeks to engage not by imposing rules on the adversary but by making the adversary part of the rule-making body. In this sense, the strategy accords the opponent's needs and interests (regardless of normative considerations) a degree of legitimacy by offering a place at the decision-making table. Classical engagement strategies are reminiscent of the balance of power politics and great power concert arrangements. Thus, cooperation is achieved through establishing a new status quo that accommodates the needs of both powers.[5]

Interdependent, transnational, and concert engagement represent three different modes of dealing with a problem state. Successful engagement strategies will often employ elements of all three. For the sake of argument, it was assumed that the objective of these strategies is cooperative behavior from the target state; however, in practice, the purposes of engagement can include a spectrum of desired outcomes. At the least ambitious end, engagement could be employed as a strategy to buy time and "muddle through" in contending with the target. It could also be used simply to increase transparency and gain more information about the target upon which to base later policies (which may not necessarily be of an engagement nature). In the middle-range of objectives, engagement could be used for the purpose of achieving mutual accommodation of policies. At the more ambitious end, it could serve to extract conciliatory behavior on a specific policy by increasing the interdependent costs of noncooperation. And at the most ambitious end, engagement could aim to effect a transformation in the overall interests and preferences of the target as the basis for cooperation.[6]

American and South Korean Engagement: An Overview

In light of the preceding discussion, U.S. policy toward North Korea exhibits many of the traits of a genuine engagement strategy. In particular, the Agreed Framework marked a watershed in U.S. security policy on the peninsula.[7] It represents a move away from the one-dimensional containment policy of the Cold War era, toward a more variegated vision of how best to attain security vis-à-vis the North. It seeks to contend with a problem state not through isolation and exclusion, but through dialogue and "thick" interaction. This is manifest, for example, in the mechanics of the agreement. The staged nature of the implementation process seeks to build linkages and trust between highly distrustful adversaries and attain a mutually beneficial outcome. While the immediate purpose of the Agreed Framework is to curb the North's nuclear proliferation, its broader intention is to use economic and political incentives to draw out the North on a variety of other issues, encourage economic reform, and in the process, change the North's status from a rogue state to an abiding, responsible member of the international community.[8]

On the other hand, South Korean engagement policies appear more problematic. At its inception in 1993, the Kim Young Sam government did not espouse an explicit "engagement" strategy vis-à-vis the North; instead, it offered a vision for unification based on three principles. The first—national consensus—stated that under a new civilian and democratically elected government, ROK policies toward North Korea would reflect the true will of the people. Second, the principle of peaceful coexistence and prosperity stated that unification would be preceded by a period of mutual recognition of two separate systems under one nation, where nonintervention and mutual prosperity would be promoted. And the third principle—national well-being—placed the priority of integrating the two Koreas into "one nation, one system" on the people's welfare, rather than on a particular ideology or system.[9] Despite various rhetorical embellishments, these principles were essentially reworked versions of similar principles first set out in the 1972 North-South Communiqué, and then expounded upon in the 1991 Basic Agreement on Reconciliation.[10] They did not deviate greatly from the standard boilerplate versions held by previous governments.

More explicit statements of an engagement policy began to emerge from Seoul in 1994,[11] with the most comprehensive of these in the Peace and Cooperation Initiative of August 1996. The Initiative stated that the ROK sought to reduce tensions with the North and seek a peaceful path to unification. Moreover, it laid out three negative assurances, or objectives that Seoul would *not* seek in interaction with the North. The first of these was that Seoul sought stability in its northern counterpart, and had neither the interest nor desire to capitalize on the North's internal difficulties. Second, the ROK did not seek to isolate North Korea, rather to help in making it a sound member of the international community of nations. Finally, the ROK did not seek unification through absorption, but by integration. In addition, the Peace and Cooperation Initiative laid specific means by which Seoul sought inter-Korean cooperation: it would provide technology and machinery to help solve the North's chronic food production problems, expand inter-Korean trade, expand public and private sector investment, and promote tourism.[12]

The Rhetoric and the Reality of Engagement

To its credit, the Peace and Cooperation Initiative represents a step forward in ROK policy. The negative assurances against instability, isolation, and absorption are novel as they attempt to address directly any trepidations the North may have regarding relations with its superior southern rival. The Initiative speaks of the establishment of economic linkages similar to the liberal/interdependent tradition. Through promoting people-to-people exchanges, it acknowledges the transformational effect engagement can have on the interests and preferences of North Korea, in turning it into a normal state. Tangibly, South Koreans might point to the scheduled summit between Kim Young Sam and Kim Il Sung in 1994, and more recently, to Seoul's advocacy of the Four-Power Peace Proposal as evidence of engagement's fruits.

However, upon closer analysis, the gap between lip service to liberal/transnational engagement models and practice is all too apparent. For example, while emphasizing confidence-building and negative assurances, ROK officials also accuse the North of sustaining high tensions on the peninsula, and demand that all Western powers close off contacts with Pyongyang until it makes direct conciliatory gestures to Seoul. South Korean presidential statements constantly ring with phrases such as: "The possibility is rising that the cornered North Korea will resort to reckless provocation . . . we do not know when or how North Korean leaders may try to find an escape hatch to avoid the collapse of their regime."[13] Similarly, while declaring the need to assist the North in its current food difficulties, Seoul has chosen to see rice and grain aid not in strictly humanitarian terms, but as linked with North Korean concessions on other political-military issues. It has also discouraged private sector efforts in the South to organize food aid for the North.[14] Moreover, positive assurances are always couched in statements resonating with containment logic. While Premier Lee Hong-Koo reaffirmed the Peace and Cooperation Initiative, he also added, "A war will be only prevented through the South's superior strength and strong countermeasures. . . . We must make North Korea realize that any attempts to disrupt peace on the Korean peninsula will carry a heavy price. . . ."[15] In 1994, a true engagement mentality might have seen the potential benefits from a token transmission of condolences for Kim Il Sung's death as outweighing the costs, but this was not the case. Similarly, while the December 1996 submarine incursion was a provocative act by the North, Seoul made a conscious political decision to play up the incident as a military provocation, warned the country of an all-out war, called for increases in military spending, and froze its participation in the Agreed Framework, as well as all other aid, communication, and economic activity with the North.[16]

What accounts for this gap between the rhetoric and reality of ROK engagement? At the surface, one can point to specific inter-Korean disputes that had the effect of short-circuiting any well-intentioned engagement initiatives. North Korean intransigence with regard to the Nuclear Non-Proliferation Treaty (NPT) in 1993 and 1994, the rice aid fiasco in spring 1995, and the submarine incursion in 1996 are obvious candidates. From a strategic interaction perspective, these disputes compelled Seoul to convey credibility and resolve by abandoning engagement initiatives (i.e., these actions could not go unpunished). From a domestic politics perspective, while these events were viewed by the electorate as instances of North Korean belligerence, they were also viewed as policy failures on the part of an inexperienced Kim administration. Operating in the midst of three consecutive years of local, national, and presidential elections since 1995, the government therefore had to abandon engagement and succumb to electoral pressures.

Zero-Sum Mentalities and Absorption Complexes

In spite of these factors, the gap between the rhetoric and reality of engagement is a function of two deeper and more fundamental problems. The first is an inability (on the part of both Koreas) to transcend the zero-sum mentalities of the Cold War. In Seoul's case, this understandably stems from the residual northern threat, despite the advent of the post–Cold War era. However, developments such as the effective dealignment of the North by its two primary Cold War patrons, its dire economic situation, and its isolated status as a pariah state have not fostered any perceptible change in assessments of the caliber of this threat. Instead, Seoul continues to frame its relationship with the North in terms of the acute competition of the 1960s-70s. Today, the victor in this competition is uncertain, yet Seoul still identifies any minute North Korean gains (e.g., in relations with the United States or Japan) as its own loss. Seoul's entreaties that offers of food aid, improvements in U.S.–DPRK relations, and commencing of Japan–DPRK normalization talks be contingent on North-South dialogue, effectively demand the North to admit defeat in the inter-Korea competition as a precondition to receiving help.[17]

In a similar vein, the 1991 Basic Agreement and *Nordpolitik*, while appearing to be evidence of a transformation in the ROK's Cold War thinking, still reflect a continued adherence to zero-sum mentalities. The 1991 Basic Agreement was undoubtedly a watershed development in North-South relations; however, aside from the histrionics of the moment, no tangible reduction in tensions came as a result of it. The agreement, instead, became a propaganda tool of both Seoul and Pyongyang to point out to domestic and international audience the other's lack of good faith.[18] While the ROK's successful *Nordpolitik* with communist powers appeared as a new turn in ROK security policy, emphasizing engagement and dialogue with adversaries; it, too, was motivated by classic Cold War–era motives. Normalization with the Soviet Union in 1990 and China in 1992 was of course welcomed in the language of economic interdependence, tension reduction, and engagement, yet the true benefit, as seen by planners in Seoul, was the diplomatic coup over the North. *Nordpolitik* effectively won over Pyongyang's two primary Cold War patrons, and closed the circle in terms of isolating the North. In Seoul's eyes, this was the ultimate victory in the diplomatic competition between the two Koreas. Because one side's gain is necessarily equated with another's loss, the logical policy that emerges is not one of engagement but of hard-line containment.

Underlying this zero-sum mentality is a fundamentally narrow notion of security. South Koreans can only conceive of security and how it is attained in classic power-politics terms. Security cannot be achieved through accommodation, but only through relative military advantage. States feel safe only when adversaries are intimidated and overwhelmed by superior military capabilities.[19] Such realist conceptions of security are manifest in Korean views on unification. As Patrick Morgan observes, the future, according to the Korean view, is a highly competitive and suspicious one:

> . . . states surrounding Korea are potential threats, inherently uneasy about the emergence of a stronger Korea, bound to compete for influence on the peninsula as in the past. Thus Korea has to prepare to use its elbows in the regional jockeying for power and influence that will take place.[20]

In other words, Korean visions of a post-unification Northeast Asia tend to place less faith in more liberal-type scenarios of a united Korea embedded in a web of interdependent market-democracies or transnational networks; rather, they place much more credence in scenarios of a reunified, nationalist Korea that must provide for itself in a region of aggressively intended powers. The latter is an externalization of Korea's own strategic mindset that, again, reflects well the fixation with security in narrow power-politics terms. For this reason, prescriptions about a united Korea's future also remain firmly entrenched in balance-of-power thinking and in deterrence, rather than engagement models.

Thus, ROK rhetoric toward the North, while it bespeaks of liberal engagement, still reflects strategic mindsets rooted in zero-sum thinking and power-fixated perceptions. One might surmise that the third alternative engagement model—classical or concert-type—might be a feasible path for inter-Korean relations. That is, if interaction between the two Koreas is refracted through largely realist prisms, then a collusive-type arrangement might be feasible in which the ROK engages the North by establishing a new status-quo that accommodates a modicum of North Korean interests (i.e., no rules imposed on the North but include it as part of the rule-making body). This alternative, however, is hindered by the second fundamental obstacle to engagement—absorption complexes. In other words, concert-type engagement is difficult because the two sides can only conceive of unification as dominance of one state over the other.

This absorption complex is evident in the two regimes' national visions for unification. The Democratic Confederal Republic of Koryo (DCRK), the embodiment of the North Korean vision, calls for unification under a formula of "one nation, two systems." Two subnational governments would maintain autonomy over daily affairs within their region, but would be guided by an overarching national body (the Supreme National Confederal Assembly). Composed of representatives from the two regions, the Supreme Assembly would coordinate the foreign policies of the two regions, promote uniform economic and cultural development between the regions, and generally ensure that each government's internal policies are consistent with the unity of the nation.[21]

The South Korean plan, the Korean National Community (KNC) formula or Commonwealth formula envisions a period of reconciliation in which the two governments would acknowledge the current status quo and engage in cultural and economic interchange as a means of fostering a common national community and identity (*minjok kongdongch'e*). This would be followed by the establishment of a Korean commonwealth (*Nambuk Yônhap*)—a loose federation of two systems ruling autonomously within their regions but linked through a set of overarching institutions (one people, one government, two systems).[22] This commonwealth government would then draw up a constitution for the final stage of full integration of "one people, one government, one system."[23]

While the DCRK and KNC plans differ in their specifics, they both focus on the preservation of two separate political systems as the only acceptable format for unification. This is reflected in the North Korean plan that equates the goal of full integration with two regionally autonomous systems. It is more subtly, but no less clearly, reflected in the KNC plan as well. While this advocates eventual unification under one political system, the plan's focus is on the interim commonwealth stage of two autonomous political systems.[24] Moreover, while both plans outwardly offer a vision of the two systems operating equally under an overarching confederal or commonwealth governing body, each plan implicitly assumes that its system will dominate. This hegemonic conceptualization of unification is manifest in the preconditions of the North's DCRK plan that stipulate the legalization of communist parties and the establishment of a "progressive government" in the South before a confederal system can be implemented. The South reflects this in the advocation of a proportional representation voting system for any binational bodies, which, given the ROK's 2:1 population advantage over the North, would ensure an ROK-dominated commonwealth. Thus, beneath the rhetoric of Seoul and Pyongyang's plans and proclamations lies the conviction that unification is possible only through dominance. Such zero-sum mindsets and visions of absorption make genuine embracing of engagement initiatives difficult.

Therefore, given a conceptual understanding of engagement, the ROK's professed new Peace and Cooperation Initiative toward the North does not really qualify as a bona fide engagement strategy. While critics may argue that this stems from North Korean intransigence and the imperatives of ROK domestic politics, I have argued that even if these factors were not salient, zero-sum mentalities and absorption complexes still pose fundamental obstacles to the ROK's implementation of engagement.

The Engagement Dilemma and Policy Challenges

In spite of all of these impediments to true engagement, the "default" policy for North Korea today is engagement. Whether one sees the problem of dealing with the Northern threat from either a "hawkish" or a "dovish" perspective, the optimal policy for Seoul is one of engagement. The latter perspective is intuitively more obvious and therefore is dealt with in this chapter only briefly. While engagement initiatives may entail certain initial costs in terms of unrequited cooperation by Pyongyang, these are far less than the potential costs incurred by a containment strategy that backfired and led to desperate North Korean acts of hostility. While the United States and ROK would likely prevail in renewed fighting on the peninsula, the industrial and civilian damage wrought on the South would make this a dreaded war-winning exercise. Furthermore, while coercion might be successful in eliciting North Korean cooperation, the scope and domain of this cooperation would likely be minimal. Coercion might change behavior in discrete instances, but this would not be the equivalent of a more systematic and permanent transformation of preferences and interests, which may be accomplished through an enmeshing and socializing of the North in the institutions and regimes of the international arena.

Arguing for engagement from the hawkish perspective is more counterintuitive and, consequently, requires elaboration. Four points summarize this perspective on North Korea:

1. The North is a dissatisfied, revisionist power.
2. For the foreseeable future, it is dominated by a nonreformist and militant leadership.

3. It has the incongruous combination of a strong military and crumbling economy.
4. At worst, it seeks to subvert the South; at best, it seeks to ignore Seoul and drive a wedge between the ROK and its allies.

Even under these assumptions, engagement may be the optimal policy for a number of reasons. The first reason relates to alliance relations. Throughout the nuclear negotiations in 1994 and food relief appeals in 1996, the North exhibited a clear penchant for bypassing the South and seeking improved relations with the West. This was part of an evolving North Korean strategy of survival in the post–Cold War era in which it sought to cultivate a division of interests between the ROK and its allies, and negotiate agreements that excluded Seoul. The most ambitious of these goals was a peace treaty with the United States. In Pyongyang's view, this could lead to a shift in the U.S. security presence on the peninsula from that of a Cold War patron of the ROK to one of a broker of stability on the peninsula, and in turn, a de facto guarantor against North Korea's absorption by the South.[25]

The United States and Japan have taken great care to deflect Pyongyang's wedge strategy by making improvements in bilateral relations with the DPRK, contingent on North-South dialogue. For example, in the October 1994 Agreed Framework negotiations, the United States stood firm on including a clause that commits the North to establish dialogue with the South, despite Pyongyang's eleventh-hour threats to forfeit the entire agreement over this issue. In ensuing negotiations in Kuala Lumpur in 1995 on the light-water reactor contract and the 1996 submarine incursion incident, the United States also supported the ROK agenda.[26] Similarly, Japan has held food aid and normalization treaty talks with Pyongyang, contingent on improvements in Northern attitudes toward Seoul.[27] Nevertheless, alliance tensions have surfaced as security interests on the peninsula between the ROK and its partners are not wholly congruent in the post–Cold War era. These allies are increasingly frustrated at being stymied in progress with Pyongyang by what they perceive as Seoul's zero-sum mentality, and at times unnecessarily belligerent attitudes.[28] There is growing skepticism about the good faith nature of Seoul's engagement efforts and arguments that U.S. policy to North Korea can no longer be subjected to Seoul's complaints. If Washington and Tokyo no longer allow themselves to be fettered, these dynamics could have the unintended effect of alienating the

South Koreans, rather than the North who is regarded as the primary obstacle to peace and dialogue on the peninsula. Engagement preempts such triangular dynamics (i.e., U.S.–DPRK–ROK, Japan–DPRK–ROK) that could potentially isolate Seoul.[29] Given the conditions that have evolved, entreaties by Seoul for allies to hold their bilateral dialogue with the DPRK, conditional on improvements in North-South dialogue, are more likely to succeed only if allies perceive genuine ROK efforts at engaging the North. Put another way, the likelihood of eliciting a hard-line stance of standing firm with the ROK may be greater if Seoul undertakes a series of unrequited but good faith acts at engagement, rather than continue an uncompromising, belligerent posture of bullying the North. Therefore, paradoxically, drawing out the hawk in allied governments may require a more dovish posture by Seoul. While admittedly a less-than-perfect alternative for Seoul, as interests grow more divergent, it may be the only choice.

Second, even if the South Korean hawk seeks to destroy and absorb the North, engagement may be the optimal way of achieving this goal. Several subarguments substantiate this claim. The first has to do with the transparency of policies. Containment is an inherently clearer policy to an adversary than engagement. It assumes a relationship of antagonism; it conveys the view that interests are in conflict and non-negotiable; and it draws a clear line in the sand to the opponent about what constitutes punishable behavior. By virtue of this clarity, however, containment is also easily susceptible to rally-around-the-flag effects in the target country. It gives groups in the North (most likely hardliners) an unambiguous symbol around which to cultivate enemy images and muster full support for the regime and for hostility against the South.

Engagement, on the other hand, is more ambiguous. It confuses the target state's leadership elite. It exploits cognitive inconsistencies and raises debates within Pyongyang as to whether Seoul's intentions are genuine or duplicitous. Coupled with fissures in the leadership monolith in Pyongyang stemming from the power transition after Kim Il Sung, or a divide of Old Guard versus young technocrats, these divisions over how to respond to ROK engagement could contribute to a crumbling of the North from above.

Similarly, rather than prolong the North's existence (as commonly argued by the hawk), engagement can actually hasten its demise. The reason for this is that North Korea currently faces the same reform dilemma of other nonliberal regimes in the post–Cold War era. As Ahn

Byung-joon argued, the North needs to open up to survive, yet in the process of opening up, it unwittingly unleashes, or cannot control, the forces that may ultimately lead to its demise.[30] In this sense, through mechanisms like the Agreed Framework, inter-Korean trade, tourism, and investment in special economic zones, engagement exposes the North to institutional and nongovernmental influences that push the government down the slippery slope of reform. Anathema to the hawk's preferences, this may result in a moderate improvement in the North's economic situation, but still in line with these preferences, it could spawn the conditions for upheaval from below. As history has shown, revolutions and regime instability in downtrodden states are most likely not when conditions are at their worst, but when they begin to get better.

One of the implications of the above discussion regarding the hawk's assumptions about North Korea is that the hawk generally does not seek to accommodate or integrate with the North, but to destroy it. Even if this is the case, engagement better prepares the South for such an event. The common belief is that an exclusionary and isolationist posture against North Korea, reminiscent of the Cold War, is the best way to achieve the hawk's goal. However, policies that continue to adhere to this status quo are inherently dangerous. This is because Cold War deterrence is fixated on discouraging and, if necessary, repelling a northern invasion, but it never really considers what to do *after* the North is defeated. Engagement, on the other hand, forces the ROK to think more proactively about unification.

Containment does little to reduce the opaqueness of the DPRK regime. It treats the opponent as a black box, and assumes that if one raises the costs of an undesirable action high enough, any rational-acting leadership will behave accordingly. Under these strategies, there is no need to understand the opponent or create linkages. Engagement strategies, on the other hand, promote dialogue and information exchanges, all of which provide very important benefits in terms of increased transparency. Although there have been numerous quantitative estimates on the cost of unification, some of the more underestimated and not easily quantifiable costs are those associated with a reconciliation and reacquaintance of the Northern and Southern societies after decades of nondialogue. In this regard, the process of engagement can help to reduce the start-up costs when unification arrives. The institutional ties and economic development that grow out of engagement can also help ease the costs of the absorption process and better prepare the hawk for his objective.

Furthermore, while the hawk might see a direct link between a vision of absorbing the North and a policy of nondialogue and hostility, the latter overlooks perhaps the most important factor in the success of an absorption exercise—the North Korean population. One flaw prevalent in Southern thinking about unification is attribution error—the belief that others see you the way you see yourself. In other words, after the "evil" regime in the North is destroyed, Southerners see themselves as saviors of their Northern brethren, and assume that these brethren will view things the same way. However, a policy of containment that drives the Pyongyang leadership into the ground would also alienate the Northern populace. It would reinforce decades of DPRK's demonizing of the ROK state, and effectively undercut the Southern regime's credibility as the benevolent deliverer of its Northern brethren. Engagement may be the only way to avert this as it would convey a more compassionate image of the South. It would start the process of unraveling half a century of negative indoctrination in the North, and in this manner, would lay the foundation for the Southern polity and people to emerge as a credible receptacle of popular Northern loyalty after the DPRK state collapses. In sum, containment may be more attractive to the hawk's dream of northern capitulation, but engagement better equips the hawk for his desired objective.

Conclusion

What determines the success of a state's security strategy? The commonly accepted answer is the capability of that strategy to elicit the desired behavior from the target state. In the case of Korea, the common wisdom sees the ROK's strategy of engagement with the North as ineffective because the North does not want to be engaged. While this may be true, this chapter has argued that failure could also stem from the fact that this strategy does not in fact constitute engagement. And that even if the North were less predisposed to confrontation, there are fundamental cognitive obstacles to true engagement thinking on the peninsula. Surmounting these obstacles is critical because the optimal policy for the two Koreas, whether one views strategic interaction on the peninsula through belligerent Cold War or more benign post–Cold War lenses, is engagement.

Finally, there are two additional obstacles to a successful engagement strategy even if the logic of the above argument finds acceptance among South Koreans. The first is patience—admittedly, something many

Koreans do not see as a virtue. Engagement is inherently a long-term policy. Significant efforts must be made to overcome cognitive rigidities, cultivate reciprocity, and elicit cooperation. In the interim, the engager must bear costs of unrequited cooperation, and many Koreans may not be patient enough to wait for the benefits.

Second, the history of engagement is its worst enemy. As a result of the events leading up to World War II, Koreans generally associate engagement with appeasement and weakness. This is inaccurate. Koreans should realize that engagement is a strategy not of the weak but of the strong. Engagement without capabilities may look like capitulation,but, engagement with superior military capabilities conveys credibility. The latter more aptly characterizes the South's situation vis-à-vis the North. In this sense, ROK engagement would not be a replacement for Cold War containment but would be undergirded by it.

Notes

The author thanks Wonmo Dong, Jim Landers, Kwang Woong Kim, David Steinberg, and Mira Sucharov for comments on earlier drafts of this paper.

1. In spite of the popularity of the term "engagement" in the post–Cold War era, there is a surprising absence of scholarship on it. This was in part a function of the Cold War when deterrence and spiral models were the focus of attention (for the seminal work, see Robert Jervis, *Perception and Misperception* [Princeton: Princeton University Press, 1976]). The most relevant work on engagement has been on the use of positive and negative sanctions (David Baldwin, *Economic Statecraft* [Princeton: Princeton University Press, 1985]). A new project at the Fairbank Center, Harvard University, from which the conceptual models of engagement in this paper are drawn, looks more closely at engagement strategies with regard to China (Alastair Iain Johnston and Robert Ross, "Engaging China: Managing a Rising Power," Project Proposal to Halpern Associates, n.d., 11 pp.).

2. See Johnston and Ross, "Engaging China," 4–7.

3. In game-theoretical terms, interdependent ties also lengthen the shadow of the future among states and alter the costs and benefits associating with cooperation. For example, in the liberal-interdependent view, refusing to have trade ties with the problem state is counterproductive because it effectively lowers the value of future interaction with the target state. The typical historical example often referred to in this context is European integration.

4. Commonly referred to issue-areas in which transnational coalitions have been successful in affecting state behavior are human rights, the environment, humanitarian aid, and some arms control. For the argument that the significance of transnational coalitions extends beyond, and is not exclusive to, their effects on the policy agenda of governments, see Paul Wapner, "Politics Beyond the State: Environmental Activism and World Civic Politics," *World Politics* 47.3 (April 1995), 311–340.

5. The assumptions here are that the dissatisfied power's ambitions are in fact limited (otherwise, engagement turns into appeasement and exploitation as in the case of Munich 1938), and that interests between the two parties are not in insurmountable conflict (in which case, we are talking about capitulation). Historical examples of classical engagement might be the Concert of Europe's policies toward post–Napoleonic France in 1815; Kissinger's détente policies with China and the Soviet Union in the 1970s; or what some advocate with regard to China today (see Robert Ross, "Beijing as a Conservative Power," *Foreign Affairs* 76.2 (March/April 1997), 33–44, esp. 42–44). For additional assumptions underlying these models, see Johnston and Ross, "Engaging China," 4–9.

6. Minutes, "Engaging China" Workshop, Fairbank Center for East Asian Research, Harvard University, December 7, 1996. It should be noted that these purposes, although presented as discrete end points, can also be part of a broader "socialization" process in which the behavior of the target state evolves along the various end points as it becomes more engaged. For example, as George Shambaugh argues, membership of "risky" states in international organizations may first change the target's behavior through an altering of short-run interest calculations of noncooperation; however, it may later change the target's behavior through a socialization process where it identifies with the international organization (George Shambaugh, "Threatening Friends and Enticing Enemies in an Uncertain World," in Gerald Schneider and Patricia Weitsman, eds., *Enforcing Cooperation: "Risky" States and the Intergovernmental Management of Conflict* [New York: Macmillan Press, 1996], 234–261).

7. Consummated in October 1994 after over two years of negotiation and brinkmanship, the Agreed Framework basically set out the exchange of light-water nuclear reactors and interim energy supplies for a freeze on the North's nuclear program, compliance with IAEA monitoring, and future dismantlement of facilities. For analyses and overviews of the events prior to the agreement, see United States Senate, Committee on Foreign Relations, *Implications of the US–North Korea Nuclear Agreement: Hearings Before the Subcommittee on East Asian and Pacific Affairs*, December 1, 1994, 103rd Cong., 2nd session (Washington: GPO, 1995); Victor Cha, *The Geneva Framework Agreement and Korea's Future*, EAI Reports, East Asian Institute, Columbia University, June 1995; and Michael Mazarr, "Going Just a Little Nuclear: Nonproliferation Lessons from North Korea," *International Security* 20.2 (Fall 1995), 92–122.

8. For concurring characterizations of the Agreed Framework, see Chae-jin Lee, "U.S. Policy Toward North Korea: The Dilemma of Containment and Engagement," *Korea and World Affairs* 20.3 (Fall 1996), 359–360; and Robert Scalapino, "North Korea at a Crossroads," *Essays in Public Policy No. 73* (Stanford: Hoover Institution, 1997), 10.

9. "Together on the Road to a New Korea," Inaugural Address, February 25, 1993; "Rebuilding the Nation into a New Korea," One-Hundred Day press conference, June 3, 1993; and "Toward a Great Era of National Unity," Liberation Day speech, August 15, 1994, in *Korea's Quest for Reform and Globalization: Selected Speeches of President Kim Young Sam* (Presidential Secretariat, Seoul, 1995), 5–10, 48–54, 208–214. Also see Han Wan-Sang, "The Kim Young Sam Government's Unification Policy: Basic Structure and Its Three Pillars," *Korea and World Affairs* 17.2 (Summer 1993), 213–226; Kil Jeong-woo, "The Kim Young Sam Government's

Unification Policy: Phase Two," *Korea and World Affairs* 18.3 (Fall 1994), 473–485; and Kang In Duk, "Unification Policy of the Kim Young Sam Government," *East Asian Review* 6.4 (Winter 1994), 38–50.

10. The 1972 principles called for unification through the independent will of the people and without outside intervention; unification by peaceful means; and the promotion of a grand national unity that transcended ideological differences. See "7.4 Nam-puk kongdong sŏngmyŏngsŏ (July 4 South-North Joint Communiqué)" in *Taehan Min'guk woegyo yŏnp'yo: 1972 bu juyo munhŏn* (Diplomatic Documents Annual of the Republic of Korea) (Seoul: Ministry of Foreign Affairs), 203–206. For the text of the Basic Agreement, see *Korea Update* 2.24 (December 16, 1991). Also see Kim Hak-Joon, *The Unification Policy of South and North Korea* (Seoul: Seoul National University Press, 1977); and B.C. Koh, "The Inter-Korean Agreements of 1972 and 1992: A Comparative Assessment," *Korea and World Affairs* 16.3 (Fall 1992), 463–482.

11. The change took place after the death of Kim Il Sung in July 1994. For examples, see "Toward a Great Era of National Unity," Liberation Day speech, August 14, 1994, reprinted in *Korea's Quest for Reform*; and Kim's August 1995 Liberation Day speech reprinted in "Source Materials," *Korea and World Affairs* 19.3 (Fall 1995), 531–534.

12. See August 15, 1996, Liberation Day speech reprinted in *Korea Observer* 27.3 (Autumn 1996), 485–491; also see Han Sung-Joo, *Korea in a Changing World: Speeches and Commentaries by the Former Foreign Minister* (ORUEM Publishing: Seoul, 1995), 68–76; and Chung-In Moon, "Peace and Arms Control on the Korean Peninsula: A Search for Alternatives," *Korea Focus* 4.5 (September–October 1996), 6.

13. "S. Korea President Warns Invasion by North More Likely," *AP-Dow Jones News Service*, March 12, 1997.

14. "NSP Demands Cancellation of Department Store's Campaign to Help North Korea," *Joongang Ilbo*, April 16, 1997.

15. See Lee's October 1996 speech to the National Assembly as cited in *Joongang Ilbo*, October 23, 1996.

16. Kevin Sullivan, "North Korea Apologizes for Submarine Incident," *Washington Post*, December 30, 1996, A1.

17. For comments to a similar effect by U.S. Ambassador James Laney in May 1996, see Lee, "U.S. Policy Toward North Korea," 376–1377.

18. Its fate has been largely the same as the 1972 Joint communiqué—an expedient reaction to larger regional changes (i.e., détente, and the post–Cold War)—that produced no-confidence–building on the peninsula.

19. On the notion of diverging conceptions of security and their effect on alliance relations, see Victor Cha, "Realism, Liberalism, and the Durability of the U.S.–South Korean Alliance," *Asian Survey* (July 1997).

20. Patrick Morgan, "The U.S.–ROK Strategic Relationship: A Liberalist Analysis," in Donald Clark, et al. *U.S.–Korean Relations* (Keck Center, 1995), 98.

21. Rhee Kang-Suk, "Korea's Unification: The Applicability of the German Experience," *Asian Survey* 33.4 (April 1993), 367–368; and National Unification Board, *Comparison of Unification Policies* (Seoul: National Unification Board, 1990), 99–108.

22. Executive authority, for example, would rest in a Joint Council of Presi-

dents and Council of Ministers; legislative duties would be carried out by a Council of Representatives; and administrative responsibilities would be handled by a joint secretariat in the DMZ "peace zone" and by resident liaison missions.

23. For the text of the KNC proposal, see *South-North Dialogue in Korea* Vol. 48, December 1989 (Seoul: International Cultural Society of Korea, 1989), 20–31. For analyses, see Lee Manwoo, "Domestic Politics and Unification: Seoul's Perspective," in Kihl Young-Whan, *Korea and the World* (Boulder: Westview, 1994), 174; NUB, *Comparison of Unification Policies*, 122–131; and Rhee, "Korea's Unification: The Applicability of the German Experience," 368.

24. For a concurring view on the difficulty of distinguishing whether the KNC plan is a means to an end (i.e., full integration) or an end in itself, see Kihl Young-Whan, "The Problem of Forming a Korean Commonwealth," *Korea Observer* 24.3 (Autumn 1993), 429–449, esp. 443–444.

25. For additional insights on some of the calculations behind North Korean policies, see Selig Harrison, "Promoting A Soft Landing in Korea," *Foreign Policy* 106 (Spring 1997), 57–76.

26. In the former, the United States backed KEDO's proposal that the reactors provided to the North be of South Korean origin. In the latter, the United States stood with Seoul in demanding a North Korean apology for the incident.

27. An additional precondition for Tokyo is the North's transparency regarding alleged abductions of Japanese nationals to North Korea for use as Japanese language instructors.

28. For example, while the United States sees North-South dialogue, the Agreed Framework, and a peace treaty on the peninsula as a joint U.S.–ROK interest, it increasingly sees other issues strictly in a U.S.–DPRK bilateral context (e.g., POW/MIA, missile proliferation, liaison offices), and less subject to linkage with ROK needs and desires.

29. For a concurring argument, see Kihl, "The Kim Young Sam Government's Unification Policy," 482.

30. Byung-Joon Ahn, "The Man Who Would Be Kim," *Foreign Affairs* 73.6 (November/December 1994).

6

The Dichotomy of Pride and Vulnerability: South Korean Tensions in the U.S. Relationship

David I. Steinberg

In spite of official announcements to the contrary, it is widely understood throughout Korea,[1] as well as among those concerned in Washington, that unofficial Korean-American relations have been at a very
low ebb for the past several years. Although this tide shifts somewhat
depending on the moment and incident, overall relations have generally
deteriorated. Some highly placed Korean officials have indicated that
the level of disharmony approaches, even if it does not quite equal, the
nadir of relations in the modern period that occurred during the Carter
presidency (1976–80) when U.S. troop withdrawal campaign pledges,
the "Koreagate" scandal, and Korean human rights violations under the
authoritarian Yushin Constitution were primary problems. Whatever the
present level, Korea's trust in the United States has severely eroded.

Others would dispute this statement, pointing out that there exists
extensive residual goodwill toward the United States among the population as a whole. A poll that illustrates this notes that in June 1996, 73
percent of the population had a favorable impression of the United States,
while 26 percent had an unfavorable opinion.[2] Among the more salient
issues, which this survey does not attempt to answer, are the attitudes of
the present educated elites and the bureaucracy that formulate and debate policy issues, and those of the younger generation who will inherit

these positions in the early twenty-first century. Although such a survey is not available for the current period, the impression of growing disquiet is evident, even if residual goodwill remains. It seems evident from trends in a number of surveys that those who are under forty feel quite removed from the historically close relationships between the United States and Korea that were built on the memories and experiences of wartime reliance and collaboration and foreign assistance. Historically, such problems are not new; there have been other such periods. What is new, however, are the changing factors in both states, but especially in Korea, and the external conditions that affect the intensity and consequences of such shifts.

There have been periodic critical episodes in official U.S.–Korean relations, which, although widely acknowledged among the cognoscenti, are obscured in the public rhetoric. Four low points stand out, however, as important periods of tension that affected these relationships over considerable periods thereafter. These are: the dispute over the Korean War armistice of 1953 that President Syngman Rhee refused to sign; the coup of Park Chung Hee of May 1961 against the duly elected government of Chang Myon that was supported by the United States; the Carter period of planned troop withdrawals and human rights violations; and the present circumstances.[3] All involved policy differences of major proportions. The first three were resolved or, perhaps better stated, shelved because mutual security interests prevailed over mutual discomfort. But present mutual security concerns are of a different genre than those of the past, even if North Korea remains a constant military threat in this shifting equation, for internally the North is economically no longer what it once was.

Policy tensions between the two states have grown over the past several years. They were temporarily exacerbated in 1996 by the North Korean submarine incursion incident of September and its aftermath. These were in large part resolved in the last days of that year with a statement of "regret" by North Korea over the incident and a commitment to work toward peace. South Korean President Kim Young Sam had demanded an apology from the North (and the United States had strongly supported that position) and a promise that it would never happen again. This statement was accepted, but it clearly was a tactical shift, not a strategic change in North-South relations. Following that statement, which was directed toward the external world and not toward the North Korean people, the Kim Jong Il regime returned to its vitriolic invective against Kim Young Sam and his government, and found excuses to delay participating in the proposed four-power talks, or even in the planned briefing on those talks. North Korea may have been balancing the need for better relations with the United States and for badly needed food assistance—the latter of immediate and thus higher priority—and the related need to attend the briefing and then the four-party talks, against awaiting the South Korean presidential election of December 1997 before any forward action was considered. The North Koreans may have been buying time without seriously negotiating. The defection of Secretary Hwang Jang Yop (the twenty-fourth official in the North Korean hierarchy and a critical founder of its *juche* philosophy) in mid-February 1997 in Beijing, a very serious blow to Pyongyang especially coming a few days before Kim Jong Il's birthday, could not but have a negative impact on relations. The depth of the North Korean conundrum may have been gauged by the quick change in the North Korean regime's public reaction to the defection and their willingness to let "traitors" leave.

The underlying reasons behind the tensions between the United States and South Korea was not the submarine question, the interpretations of the significance of which are still debated, nor was it Secretary of State Warren Christopher's off-hand initial remark—the all-purpose answer to any diplomatic question worldwide—that both sides should, in effect, "cool it," at which the South Koreans were naturally distressed since they had no part in causing the incident in the first place. A more basic issue was South Korean suspicions of U.S. direct negotiations with the North on Korean Peninsula Energy Development Organization (KEDO), from which South Korea was excluded, even though it will pay most of the bills for the light-water reactors (LWRs), and the suspicion that the United States was "abandoning" South Korea in favor of relations with the North. However preposterous this may sound to Americans, it was a widely, if privately, expressed sentiment in Seoul and one the American ambassador has gone to great and continuous pains to deny, as has the Acting Assistant Secretary of State for East Asia and Pacific Affairs and many other officials.[4] Yet, as one American writer noted: "But, what I am saying of present importance is that in effect the United States in 1997 has, however unspoken, a developing two Korea policy."[5] This causes intense disquiet in Seoul.

This distrust was also reflected in the spy case in which an employee of Korean extraction of the U.S. government was accused of spying for the South Koreans by stealing military secrets. Although the unofficial Korean excuse was that both sides do this in any case may have been accurate, and in spite of official denials of involvement, and virtual disappearance of the news from the Korean media, it does indicate at this juncture the extreme disquiet, indeed distrust, felt toward the United States in certain circles in Korea. There were some in Seoul who justified the incident because Korea believed that the United States was neither sharing all information on North Korea with them, nor being transparent in expressing U.S. intentions toward either state.

The issues that excite controversy and that are reported disapprovingly in the South Korean press are multiple. They feed especially on the insecurity so apparent in the South about the North Korean–U.S. tentative relationship. Most pronounced is the question of separate negotiations between the United States and North Korea and the obvious intention of the North to establish direct links with the United States while ignoring, to the extent possible, South Korea, and thus driving a wedge between the Republic of Korea (ROK) and the United States. As Ambassador Robert Gallucci has repeatedly said, the United States has gone to great pains to keep such a wedge from developing. Certainly, this was not the U.S. intent. There have been extensive and repeated suspicions, vigorously and continuously denied by the United States, that it was planning to sign a separate peace treaty with the North.

There are other issues as well, and although prominent at various junctures, they pale beside the more basic issue of U.S.–North Korean relations. Trade disputes continuously reappear. The Koreans maintain that their $23.7 billion current account deficit in 1996 was almost half with the United States, and thus they do not understand the vigor with which the United States attempts to open Korean markets, as Japan, Taiwan, and China are the nations that have large surpluses with the United States.[6] The Status of Forces Agreement (SOFA), and the disputes with the U.S. military over local civilian relations, are another category. A third category is the problem of a lack of sufficient (in Korean eyes) attention at high levels to South Korea in Washington, at least during the first Clinton administration, as opposed to nuclear proliferation issues in the North, and preoccupation with Europe and the Middle East. Madeleine Albright's visit to Korea early in her tenure as secretary of state was positive, although some observers noted that in her testimony to the Congress she characterized Asia as "almost" as important to the United States as Europe.[7]

Washington, for its part, notes conflicting and mercurial South Korean policies and pursuit of paths that are evidently motivated more by internal Korean politics and posturing than by external reality. It also notes a hard line toward the North among some in the South, one that is sometimes reflected in South Korean policy statements that, to Washington, are potentially self-defeating over the longer term. In a sense, Washington has the luxury of the absence of South Korean issues from the U.S. internal political radar screen (in contrast with the problems related to the North's nuclear program), even though some associated with the Republicans in editorial comments have accused the Clinton administration of placating the North while ignoring the South.

That the crisis has reached serious proportions is reflected in the following statement, no matter how much it may illustrate a minority position:

> Reminiscent of Syngman Rhee's stubbornness to cooperate in supporting the 1953 Armistice ending the Korean War, South Korea's President Kim Young Sam has edged toward becoming a liability in American efforts to engage the North and ensure regional stability. The legendary factionalism so characteristic of Korean domestic politics encompasses North-South relations as a whole. But unless South Korea in some way can be persuaded by the United States to back down from its unrealistic demands and preconditions, which in effect thwart much U.S. policy, Washington may eventually have no choice but to openly disagree with Seoul and part from it on how best to handle Pyongyang.[8]

If such a visible split were to occur, both distrust of the United States and anti-Americanism in South Korea would likely mushroom and the Kim Young Sam regime would also decrease in popularity.

Yet to regard these tensions as simply cyclical and of only transitory significance, evaporating in the renewed warmth of the relationship with the changing seasons, or in high level, publicly conciliatory joint statements, is to miss the point. That may have been the case in the Cold War era when rigidities were apparent, relationships highly structured, and overarching external relations paramount. Some manifestations of disagreement are, of course, indeed ephemeral. This chapter, however, contends that, more basically, the tensions between the two states are not simply seasonal, circular, or cyclical. Rather, they spiral upward in intensity with new and more critical implications because of changing internal conditions within each country, the evolving external power balances in the region, and the new nature of relationships between the two states.

Thus, in considering the Korean-American alliance, the question is not of renewing or rebuilding a relationship, but rather reconstructing anew a different one. The traditional paradigms of the alliance no longer apply. A catalogue of contemporary U.S.–Korean issues, on which there is much to comment from both sides, does not delineate the more basic forces that drive the disputes, which must be understood and faced if the longer term mutual interests of both states are to be considered.

The basic East Asian policy structure of the United States has been consistent, if generally unarticulated, for about a century and a half, from the open door policy toward China in the nineteenth century: to prevent the rise of any hegemonic power in the region. This has been the underlying, often inchoate, motivation, and wars were fought to achieve this end, even if couched in more moral terms, and treaties signed to deter this from happening. Foreign aid to Asian states was justified to Congress on these grounds. But the end of the Soviet Union and the rise of China and the continuing economic and growing military power of Japan have meant that the potential for hegemony has shifted. For the United States, then, its long-term interests lie in ensuring a close relationship with Korea, separate or preferably united, as a balance in the region—a hedge against hegemony.[9] For Korea, such a relationship is needed to protect its vital interests in the face of powerful neighboring states. Although a close relationship thus seems mutually desirable, the internal and external situation requires a paradigm shift toward a newly conceptualized association.

These new needs are influenced by a duality of Korean reactions to the changing circumstances that require understanding if the foundations for a new and vigorous partnership are possible. These are a growing, natural sense of Korean pride, and, ironically at the same time, a growing sense of Korean insecurity and vulnerability. The pride is born of a dignity associated with the economic, and to a lesser degree, the institutional accomplishments of the nation, and with it the parallel rise in Korean nationalism. The latter is a product of a greater, but unaccustomed, Korean role on the world scene, together with a loosening of international relationships, the massive internal changes that have been and are continuing, and to many Koreans an impression that the internal social and political climate leaves much to be desired. This cognitive dissonance exists simultaneously, and may be neither resolved nor amalgamated, but requires understanding if policy formulation by both governments is to be realistic, and if negotiations are to be fruitful.

The reconfiguration of the world order following the end of the Cold War and American preoccupation with its own internal budget and social problems have reintensified concern in the South about the U.S. commitment to the republic and the overall U.S. presence in the region. This has contributed to a sense of vulnerability, because for half a century South Korea has been dependent on the United States, and breaking that unidimensional reliance, which is required if dignity is to prevail, is a complex and arduous process. That reliance has forced Korea to surrender elements of its sovereignty in the face of U.S. pressures and mutual security needs. Korea is now caught between the need to regain its sovereignty, and the dignity so associated, for both internal political reasons and for international prestige (including its relations relative to North Korea) while still placating the United States, for security and economic reasons, and because the United States still has some—if substantially diminished—popular influence in Korea, which is important in a democratizing society.

The U.S. presence in Korea and the region is thus both decried and desired, sometimes at the same time and in the same circles. In spite of official American pronouncements to the contrary, there is evidence of growing disquiet in Seoul at the potentially ephemeral nature of the U.S. involvement as a stabilizing force in the region, no matter how many times military reaffirmations are given at the highest levels. This has been and is reflected in the past and planned expansion of internal Korean defense and defense production capacities, which started as a result of the Guam (or Nixon) Doctrine in 1969 that included a planned nuclear capacity in the early 1970s that the United States prevented, and has continued in varying degrees since that time. According to the Korean Ministry of National Defense White Paper of 1995–96, defense policy is "guided by the principle that we make all vital weapons systems with our own hands"[10] That paper also called for the build-up of three-dimensional naval defense forces: "Naval combat capability will be enhanced to adjust to three-dimensional warfare, following the global trend and the changing strategic environment around the Korean peninsula."[11] It is evident that the preoccupation with three-dimensional naval capacity has little to do with North Korea.

Korea's concentration on security is extensive, and extends beyond arms and matériel. The Korean government has argued that it should not be dependent on any foreign country for its staple food—rice—and thus should not open its agricultural market because the internal rice supply is a matter of national security. The United States has vigorously disputed this, perhaps both on the grounds of its commitment to the ideological principle of free trade, Korea's mature position as a member of the World Trade Organization, and, more recently, the Organization for Economic Cooperation and Development (OECD), and also because of its desire to increase agricultural exports. This past Korean position should not be interpreted as solely a political move to defend the administration's popularity, because its largely urban population still has rural roots, although that is evidently a consideration. It is a real factor in the concern and preoccupation with security self reliance. The need for self-sufficiency in rice, the national staple, was reiterated by the Ministry of Agriculture as a security measure.[12] The American argument that it is uneconomic for Korea to produce rice (at about five times the world market price) is inconsequential in Seoul. As Korean arms manufacture suffered from excess capacity and inefficient cost structures, so Korea has been, and continues to be, willing to subsidize the agricultural sector for similar security, as well as political, reasons.

The American role in the region and on the peninsula, should it materially change, could create new dynamics in this area of singular importance. A new Northeast Asian equation may be in the process of evolution in which a burgeoning South Korean relationship with China, spawned by fears or perceptions that a potential American pullback was inevitable, and accompanied and spurred by massive increases in Chinese trade and investment, could push South Korea toward a closer China relationship. Japan remains in Korean eyes the major potential security threat to the South, and the build-up of defense capabilities as reflected (but obviously not articulated) in public planning documents seems directed toward a Japan whose future roles in the region may seem far less clear should American forces be withdrawn from that country. The bilateral American commitments to both Korea and Japan contain these fears, but should either or both of these commitments lose credibility, major shifts in power relationships in the region would become evident, and the potential for a Northeast Asian arms race would become real, even without North Korea in the equation.

These problems do not mean that in the short term the security links between Korea and the United States will break. They do mean, however, that the erosion of such relationships has begun and could increase in momentum and intensity unless efforts are made to stop this attrition. It is evident that Korea has been considering contingency planning for such shifts, and it is the purpose of this paper to delineate some of the issues. If this special relationship between Korea and the United States is to shift or be retained, then it should happen as a result of conscious decisions involving both parties and assessments of the national interests of each. It should not be a product of inattention, inertia, misunderstanding, complacency, or ignorance.

The Rise of Korean Nationalism

The growth of Korean nationalism is not a new phenomenon, although the intensity with which it has expanded, and the freedoms under which public expression of such views are now allowed, give its development much greater attention, and thus a self-perpetuating momentum. This heightened nationalism directly affects the receptivity of Koreans toward American influence.

Korea is unique.[13] It is the only nation in which people, ethnicity, language, culture, society, family, and "blood" and "race" (to use Korean phrases) are melded into a single group. The absence of minorities, and problems of being surrounded by more powerful and often belligerent neighbors, have created a sense of unity that prevails over the turbulent factionalism that has been characteristic of Korea's political scene. This has probably been the explanation for Korea's durability as a separate cultural group. Under such circumstances, nationalism is equated with cultural survival. It should neither be underestimated nor dismissed. Nationalism has been expressed, quite naturally given Korea's unfortunate colonial experience, in suspicions concerning Japanese future relations with Korea. What is palpably different over the past generation has been the relationship between the rise of nationalism and anti-Americanism.

The growth of anti-American sentiment, even though limited in comparative international terms, has increased in intensity and is a significant factor in Korea today. "Anti-American nationalism is surprisingly virulent in the South, where military dependence on the United States has generated strong undercurrents of xenophobia that are sweeping aside the gratitude felt by the older generation for the American role in the Korean War."[14] Many trace its explosion to the charges of U.S. complicity in the suppression of the Kwangju uprising of 1980, and to which the United States immediately objected, but belatedly denied, in a white paper only some nine years following the event, but its presence is essentially inherent in the continuously unbalanced relationship between

South Korea and the United States since the former's liberation in 1945. The overwhelming importance of the United States is one that smarts and grates on the Korean sense of pride, and understandably so. Having liberated Korea, fought a war to ensure its survival, fed and aided the country, continuously provided a security umbrella, and occasionally supplied a political imprimatur (or withdrawn one) to a regime, the role of the United States could hardly have been treated with indifference. When this is combined with the obvious mistakes in U.S. policy for almost a century (dating back to the Taft-Katsura secret agreement of 1905, as the Koreans will remind Americans since it has been on the college entrance examinations in Korea; and the charge that the United States was responsible for the division of the peninsula and thus the Korean people), together with support to dictatorial governments to ensure the security umbrella, a powerful case can be, and in some circles is, made for freeing Korea from the American embrace.

This embrace is not only related to security—it is cultural as well. The destruction, begun on Independence Day in 1995, of the Japanese colonial headquarters in downtown Seoul at a cost of over $100 million was a nationalistic (and political) statement of importance by the Kim Young Sam government. The constant reminders throughout the country of the destruction of temples and cultural sites during the Japanese invasion of 1592 under Hideyoshi are fresh and constant reminders of the need for patriotism.

This concern is directed toward the American presence and influence as well. Distrust is reflected in contemporary Korean literature, which, since liberalization in 1987, is far more free to express these views. Those most popular works have been quite explicit:

> However, it is true most Koreans no longer love and trust the United States implicitly as they used to a quarter century back, and have come to regard the United States with suspicion and distrust. To put it simply, most Koreans no longer feel that Korea owes an everlasting debt of gratitude for what the United States did for them; they now feel that the United States owes them apologies and compensation for the harm they did to Korea in the course of pursuing their imperialistic objectives. Some have claimed that the Americans were worse than the Japanese.[15]

Nationalism has produced the *minjung* (mass or people's) movement, which is essentially a search back to discover and extol the indigenous roots of Korean culture and society.[16] Its positive elements include a reappreciation of much in Korean society that once was regarded as outmoded or inappropriate in the modern world; its negative aspects include denigration of much that is foreign, and thus much that is American. The *minjung* movement has assumed a left-leaning stance, because of its strongly antiforeign orientation, but this should not disguise in some respects its very deeply felt hold on much of a public that is politically, conservative. This dichotomy is accompanied by a second, between the internal forces of the *minjung* movement and its associated sentiments, and that of the government's policy of globalization that reflects Korea's continuous reliance on the external world for both markets and security. The society as a whole, and individuals within it, are caught in this contradiction—self reliance and nativism. As one Russian émigré author (Vassily Aksyonov in *The Island of Crimea*) wrote, "Every peninsula fancies itself as an island. Conversely, there is no island that does not envy a peninsula."[17]

The argument that continuing American influence is assured because Korean elites are in large part American trained and that the highest prestige accrues to the products of the American post-graduate educational system,[18] and even because of the expanding Korean minority in the United States (now close to two million), is spurious. The institutional configuration and the bureaucratic culture derive not from the American experience, but more from the unfortunate Japanese colonial bureaucratic heritage, the hierarchical Korean social system, and traditional Confucian concepts of power and authority. Koreans in the United States have exhibited a most modest degree of political influence, given their overall economic and educational achievements.

More important than explicit anti-Americanism is its corollary—the increasing feeling that the United States cannot be trusted. This mistrust is widespread. Americans may, and do, state that this trust was early based on a misapprehension and a naive Korean assumption of American altruism as the guiding principle of American policy on the peninsula (although it may have been by a significant percentage of the American people), when in fact it has been based on perceived American interests related to preventing Soviet hegemonic control. Altruism has been important as an element in some activities and of some organizations, but it has not been the motivating force of U.S. policy. Yet this emphasis on American altruism has been propagated by both governments during the early period of controlled information, and it could be argued that the expression within Korea at that time of alternative and more realistic assessments of the alliance would have been treated as virtually subversive under South Korea's stringent regulations.

American preoccupation with nuclear proliferation, at the expense, in Korean terms, of South Korean interests reflects a division in priorities that is important that Americans understand, even if it does not change their policies. Koreans are less worried about nuclear issues than conventional warfare, and some raise the issue of the apparent American double standards of nonproliferation that are so apparent in U.S. policies over the last generation (e.g., Israel versus Pakistan or India). As many ardently anticommunist Chinese were proud of the People's Republic of China's ability to develop nuclear weapons, so many Koreans might have exhibited such nationalistic pride, coupled with fear, if any Korean regime had been similarly successful.

The insecurity that is so apparent in the press, and in personal conversations in Korea, stems from a variety of dissatisfactions related to internal issues as well as an increasingly amorphous international environment. The series of physical disasters during the Kim administration (collapsing bridge and buildings, explosions, etc.) coupled with the pervading atmosphere of corruption, a weak government and vacillating policies, all contribute to this uncertainty. The flagrant expenditures of the nouveau riche and increasingly observable income disparities also augment these uneasy emotions and unstable balance. As more Koreans travel abroad and as more expensive goods are imported, nationalistic and, increasingly, class issues are accentuated. These nationalistic reactions are in direct conflict with the government's policy of *segyewha*, or globalization. The press is a party to this emotion, and public opinion and the press feed on one another and affect governmental attitudes as well. The result is that international discontent enhances internal unease, and the reverse is apparent as well. The breakdown of what are perceived as traditional Korean values (sometimes portrayed in mythic proportions) causes much concern in spite of their continued relevance in the political culture.

Korean Political Influences on the Alliance

The opening of democratic procedures in 1987 as the Cold War waned prompted further stresses on the alliance. Democratization has been a continuous American objective in Korea, but obviously on a lower level of priority than the other two objectives—security and market openings. Democratization ironically increased the public debate on the other issues, thus broadening further avenues for anti-Americanism. Although subtle pressures for conformity exist both in the media and in all walks of life—some imposed from the top, some generated from the bottom—the relative freedom with which the alliance is debated is, on the one hand, highly laudable, but on the other, ferments both aspects of the split personality of defiance and vulnerability.

Politics has had a less salutary history than economics in modern Korea. Koreans seem dissatisfied with the "imperial" presidency (the present), but scorn a weak, "watery" one (the last). There is continuing concern about corruption and a loss of traditional values. Pride in accomplishments—on hosting the Olympics and the Asian Games before it, on winning the 2002 World Cup site with Japan, on APEC and ASEAN relations, and on joining the OECD (whatever the problems)—are commingled with fear of market openings; reluctance to reform the financial sector; dissatisfaction with the results of the political process, if not with the democratic system; and concern with the physical collapses of structures and environmental degradation as indicative of more deeply rooted vulnerabilities. The corruption that is so widespread and endemic is an embarrassment to the Korean people. Regimes are under pressure not only to stand up to the United States, but also to seek its approval; they pursue an acceptable accommodation with the North, but must appear stalwart and vigilant. The right wing that expects the North to collapse must be considered as well as those who, in a sense of ethnic solidarity, want to provide humanitarian assistance to the North in its difficulties, as well as others who want a weakened continuation of the North until such time as quiet, uneventful absorption can take place. These differences fuel debate over Korean government policies and the U.S. position.

Korean internal political events have affected the alliance as well, although to the outside observer this may be less apparent. The Kim Young Sam government, starting with a popularity in 1993 that was the highest recorded (over 80 percent) since polling began in Korea, had fallen by early 1997 to some of the lowest figures in polling history (approximately 10 percent—some claim that it has reached a single digit). There have been real contributions of the regime to the democratic process, most importantly the retirement of the military as a potential threat to the democratization movement except under the most dire contingencies. But the early reformist efforts to restrain corruption through the "real name" bank account system of 1993, the dismissal of officials who could not account for their wealth, stress in the Blue House on unostentatious living, and the early Kim Young Sam attempts to control the influence of the *chaebol*, have all been marginalized by the further reliance on these organizations, on which the health of the economy now in fact depends, especially in a period of slowed growth. The continuous revelations of corruption not only among previous leaders, with whom the present president was closely associated since 1990, but also in the present administration, have been an embarrassment. The Hanbo steel mill scandal of early 1997, and the collapse of that group with almost $6 billion in unmanageable debt, exacerbates and graphically illustrates the problems.[19] There is also a feeling among the public that the full range of the corruption has not been exposed. Corruption charges and convictions have affected the Blue House, the Cabinet, the National Assembly, and the military leadership. All these problems have been accentuated by the popular belief that the presidency has become almost "imperial."

It may be argued that the depth of the internal political problems compounds the sensitivity of the U.S. relationship. Senior private Koreans have suggested that the United States quietly declare a moratorium on trade and on other criticisms until the political issues are resolved. Some in the United States argue that as Korea wishes to be, and be considered as, a major economic power, it must abide by the economic rules of that game; past rhetorical excesses of market openings and calls on Korean vulnerability have diminished Korean credibility, continued trade and market frictions are therefore likely.

The President was caught in a series of problems that include intensive labor disputes as a result of his apparent promises to the OECD to reform the restrictive labor practices. He did this in legislation passed surreptitiously by the National Assembly (at the end of 1966 and subsequently amended in March 1997 after a nationwide furor) in a manner that antagonized much of the nation, even if some of the reforms were badly needed for increased international competitiveness. In dispute were both issues connected with the political activities of labor unions, government recognition, and provisions of the laying-off of workers. Foreign intervention into the labor dispute on the side of the workers was the subject of severe criticism of the state. At the same time as he arranged passage of the labor legislation at a 6:00 A.M. end of session of the National Assembly, revision of the law strengthening the internal operations of the Agency for National Security Planning (which President Kim had weakened in 1993) was passed, and this caused concern among intellectuals that the regime was preparing further to restrict free expression of ideas.[20] In late February 1997, the National Assembly began debate on their reconsideration.

Under these circumstances, a series of internal political ploys appear to be useful. One is to blame the economic slowdown and the current account deficit on excessive foreign imports, especially luxury goods from the United States that are economically marginal (as the major item of U.S. imports is agricultural products), and on OECD regulations on both labor and market openings.[21] But it was the administration that was pushing for OECD status as one means to enhance political appeal and ensure the administration's place in Korean history, and globalization was the government's policy of choice. This antiforeign reaction feeds on the nationalism so prevalent in the society, and, of course, prompts the United States and other states to counter these arguments.

The second ploy is to demonstrate the strength of the leadership in foreign affairs, in contrast to its internal weaknesses, and this means standing up to Japan (always a popular position) on issues that remain highly sensitive and explosive, whether they involve a disputed island or the remembrances of colonial things past. More importantly, it involves challenging the United States, especially when the latter is engaged in attempting to prevent the collapse of North Korea and its return to the nuclear option it was pursuing. Disputes over food aid to the North, and the issue of direct talks with the Northern leadership are thorny questions. Although the United States and Korea may not differ over longer-range strategy, since the official policies of both do not want to see the early and uncontrolled collapse of the North, there are evident strains in the tactics. These strains not only result from perceived shorter-term national interest differences, but also in the need to appear strong when in fact the government is at its weakest ebb since President Kim Young Sam's inauguration in February 1993.[22] It is evident that not only is the Kim Young Sam administration a "lame duck," it is virtually disintegrating because of its internal problems. The results of the December 1997 election are thus in great doubt.

The president needed a compliant National Assembly for both the rest of his administration and for the future. He also needed a successor who would treat him and the administration in his post-power period with the respect and dignity that have been lacking with regard to previous administrations after their tenure. To do so he would be dictated by popular and press responses, or his perception of those responses, to act so that his successor would come from the New Korea Party he founded. The picture is further clouded because factions of President Kim's own party opposed him, and they used these crises to diminish his and his supporters' influence within the party.[23] The President seemed no longer in a position to control his successor candidate because of the scandals linked to him. Nationalism is normally a safe umbrella under which to operate in such circumstances.

In such a situation, negotiations with the United States become difficult. Democracy, as Churchill remarked, is a messy system, and nowhere is it more evident than in contemporary Korea. Any newly constructed alliance must take into account the process by which Korean decision-making is reached.

This year, 1997, and the following year are likely to be a difficult period. Labor problems will continue throughout the spring, as will debate over corruption issues, and productivity normally drops in the summer, while in the fall the presidential campaigns will pervade the society. The new president will likely inherit a difficult economic situation. All of this means that politics will continue to pervade international relations and affect the American alliance.

The Realignment of Power

The end of the Cold War has quite obviously changed the power relationships in East Asia. Even before this happened, however, South Korea's policy of Nordpolitik—to develop diplomatic and trade relations with China and the Eastern Bloc nations—was eminently successful and was spurred by the Seoul Olympics of 1988. The result was the effective isolation of North Korea, and its continuing diminution of economic strength.[24]

The rationale for the U.S. security relationship diminished with Russia no longer considered to be a major military ally of the North, although North Korean military power remained formidable. More importantly, the new power structure created ambiguities in the region— it was no longer simple to delineate friends from foes, trade and investment no longer related solely to diplomacy, and Korea pursued a foreign policy more independent from U.S. influence than theretofore.[25] Korea's involvement in multilateral organizations from the Asia-Pacific Economic Cooperation (APEC) to the ASEAN Regional Forum and beyond are related to this search for reassurance in international affairs, and not simply to economics.[26]

The economic growth of Korea and the end of the Cold War, together with increasing internal American pressures to balance the budget and cut defense spending, have resulted in growing sentiments to diminish the American military presence both in Korea and in Japan. Diverse groups, such as the very conservative Cato Institute, and leading academicians, such as Chalmers Johnson, have regarded the alliances in East Asia as anachronistic remnants of an earlier era that ought to be discarded. These sentiments do not go unnoticed in Korea or elsewhere, and coupled with the evident history of a limited American attention span in foreign affairs, contingency planning for a post–U.S. period in the region continues, and anxieties are further intensified, in spite of U.S. announcements to the contrary.

American troops in Korea are symbolic to both sides. To Koreans, however, the presence of U.S. troops in Korea and Japan is not necessarily based on the same rationale accepted in the United States. American troops in Japan are considered to be important not in the defense of Japan against now nonexistent enemies, but rather as a deterrent to Japanese rearmament, which would set off an explosive arms race in Korea based on both historic memories and nationalistic sentiments, and perhaps elsewhere as well. American troops in Korea are often considered by some thoughtful Koreans, including a ranking North Korean official who made a quasi-public statement several years ago, as protection against a resurgent Japan.

American public sentiment seems reluctant to accept the complexities of these arguments. Many in the Congress have called for Japan to spend more on defense to save U.S. resources, without understanding the sensitivities in the region of an even more powerful Japanese military, although Korea feels this issue more acutely than other states.

The Alliance Reconsidered

For all of these reasons, the Korean-American alliance needs to be reconsidered.[27] It must be taken out of the intense, zero-sum game that is presently Korean internal politics, and, similarly, placed at a bipartisan level in the United States. A quiet, profound rethinking of the overall needs for the alliance, not simply the presence of certain levels or composition of U.S. forces on the peninsula, is required. The premises on which the alliance was first built need to be reexamined to test their present validity. The vested interests of all those concerned must be noted, but not allowed to prevail over sound analysis and concern over the longer-term national interests of the two states.

This is not easily undertaken. But to allow the drift in the relationship is to cause even more problems later. To this writer, the intertwined long-term national interests of both states in the region are evidence that a close relationship is desirable, but what kind of a relationship needs discussion.

In a sense both Korea and the United States have given up a certain amount of sovereignty in their relationship. Korea has handed over command of its troops in periods of crisis, while the United States has not been able to negotiate earlier with the North because the South did not approve.[28] These anachronistic patterns need to be resolved in a period of peer relationships if the historical impedimenta to better relations are to be removed.

This writer proposes that the premises for a long-range relationship be in part built along the need for regional force and influence balance, with Korea, separately in the South or preferably united, acting with the United States to ensure stability in the region, while Korea's national interest involves a close relationship with a major power outside the region to balance its comparatively modest influence compared to Japan or China.[29]

These national interests need analysis out of the glare of the footlights by respected parties from both states and all political parties. Venues for such activities should be encouraged. There is now no forum for this type of discussion that is free from public scrutiny or expression of particularized interests.

In a democracy, or a society such as Korea, that is in the process of democratization, such discussion must eventually evolve into public education and dialogue with the educated elite. If foreign policy is too far removed from those who vote, and if the media are excluded from the process, then it becomes subject to revision through the ballot over immediate issues that may undercut the longer-term needs of the state. Both governments, but especially the Korean, which has little history of explaining policies to the people, need to deal more openly with its population, and demonstrate that whatever position is proposed, whether a close relationship, a distant one, or even the termination of the alliance, people's needs remain served. An imperial approach to such policy issues will only result in future and more dire problems. An American government that ignores the issue, and neglects to explain it to its own populace, because no immediate threat is apparent, is creating problems that will become more intractable in the future. The U.S. political system should downplay what the media has begun to call a political triumph of U.S. foreign policy on the peninsula by its engagement with North Korea. Although this engagement is highly desirable, and there is evident progress, the complexities, both internal and external to the peninsula, should prompt those in the United States who look to quick solutions to postulate progress with less hubris.

Notes

The views expressed in this essay are those of the author alone, and do not necessarily represent those of any institution.

1. All references to Korea are to South Korea. When North Korea is meant, it is specifically stated.

2. U.S. Information Agency. *Opinion Analysis*, July 16, 1996. This nationwide poll indicates that the lowest approval level was reached in June 1995 (45 percent), and that the June 1996 reading was the highest since September 1983 (84 percent). This poll does not differentiate responses by age, education, regional, or other characteristics. A *Choongang Ilbo* poll of August 1995 found that the United States was regarded as friendly by one-third of younger Koreans, but by 72.2 percent of Koreans in their fifties and sixties. The United States was distrusted by 16.7 percent of the younger, but by only 4.2 percent of the older. Another poll (*National Strategy*, August 1995, translated in *Korea Focus*, July–August 1995) indicated that 21.5 percent of the younger population and only 9.2 percent of the older population felt that the United States was hostile to Korea (see David I. Steinberg, "Continuing Democratic Reform in the Republic of Korea: The Unfinished Symphony," in Larry Diamond, ed., *Deepening Democracy in Korea,* forthcoming). Stephen Noerper in his *The Tiger's Leap. The South Korean Drive for National Prestige and Emergence in the International Arena* (Sofia: St. Kliment Ohridski University Press, 1996, pp. 141–143) notes polls showing favorable attitudes toward the United States precipitously dropping from 1985 to 1990: from 70 to 24 percent. Another poll indicated that two-thirds of Koreans in 1990 believed that U.S.–Korean relations were in trouble. The abrupt swing in sentiment over one year in the USIA poll without any intervening critical event throws into question the usefulness of this data for forecasting.

3. One could argue that there were two other events that shaped Korean-American relations that were more subtle. These were the Nixon (Guam) Doctrine of 1969, in which the United States declared that it would no longer fight ground wars in Asia, and that resulted in Park Chung Hee distrusting the security umbrella of the United States, specifically regarding it as ephemeral, and attempting to build up internal defense production capacities, including nuclear capabilities; and the Kwangju massacre of 1980, which had an important and lasting effect on anti-Americanism in Korea.

4. Charles Kartman in his testimony before the House International Relations

Subcommittee on Asia and the Pacific on February 26, 1997, stated: "In this longer-term perspective, our security alliance with South Korea remains at the heart of our policy on the peninsula. . . ." Kurt Cambell, deputy assistant secretary, ISA, Department of Defense, that same day testified, "I would begin any statement with recognition of a fundamental point—the forty-three-year-old U.S. alliance with the Republic of Korea has been a profound success and continues to serve as the foundation for a broad, solid bilateral relationship."

5. Mark P. Barry, "U.S.–DPRK Relations: 1997 and Beyond." A paper given February 8, 1997, and distributed by Nautilus via Internet, February 14, 1997. Dr. Barry is director of the Summit Council for World Peace, which operates the Summit Council Humanitarian Relief Fund Project, authorized by the U.S. Treasury to transfer funds to the UN World Food Program for DPRK relief.

6. Calculations differ significantly between the United States and Korea on these figures.

7. Tom Plate, in the *Los Angeles Times*.

8. Barry, "U.S.–DPRK Relations: 1997 and Beyond." "Some U.S. officials say South Korea's hostility toward the North has begun to pose as much or more of an obstacle to a reduction of tensions on the peninsula than any recent provocation by Pyongyang." R. Jeffrey Smith, Washington Post Service, *International Herald Tribune*, February 18, 1997.

9. Some Koreans have argued that the U.S. policy of preventing any hegemonic power in the region has evolved in the present era into a new policy of ensuring its own hegemonic role. For a statement of policy, see Department of Defense, Office of International Security Affairs, *United States Security for the East Asia-Pacific Region*, February 1995, "United States interests in Asia have been remarkably consistent over the past two centuries: peace and security; commercial access to the region; freedom of navigation; and the prevention of the rise of any hegemonic power or coalition." p. 5.

10. Ministry of National Defense, *The Republic of Korea*, *Defense White Paper 1995–96*, Seoul, 1996, p. 22. On the issue of a potential South Korean nuclear capacity, "A third threat [to U.S.–Korean relations, the other two being an aggressive North Korea or its collapse] could materialize from South Korea moving to become a nuclear power itself. Seoul's leaders need to be clear that they are not going down this road. Such a course would set off reactions from China and, especially, Japan. It would also serve to undermine, frontally, U.S. ties and commitment to South Korea. It is very important that there be no ambiguity about this." Leslie H. Gelb, "South Korea and the Global Order," in Han Sung-joo, ed., *The New International System. Regional and Global Dimensions*. Seoul: Ilmin International Relations Institute, 1996, p. 319.

In a poignant scene from a 1996 Korean television docudrama, the Park Chung Hee regime is forced to dismantle its nuclear program, and the military officer who informs the young Korean nuclear physicist that he no longer has a job was pictured as Chun Doo Hwan, thus emphasizing the ties between the United States and the dictatorial regime. Don Oberdorfer (personal communication) has indicated that the Park government did not completely dismantle the program, although Park vastly reduced it, but the subsequent Chun government did so.

11. Ibid., p. 96. If Japan is the focus, Korea's military spending in 1995 was $20 billion, while Japan's was $26 billion. Based on estimates in 1995, if Japan keeps

military expenditures at 1 percent of GDP, Korean military expenditures will exceed Japan's by the year 2000. Rand, "Long-Term Economic and Military Trends 1994–2015, The United States and Asia," Charles Wolf, Jr., et al., ed. 1995. However, Korea plans to increase its defense spending by about 17 percent in 1997 alone.

12. *Korea Herald*, supplement, January 29, 1997.

13. This refers to the Korean peninsula as a whole.

14. Selig S. Harrison, "The United States and the Future of Korea." Conference paper for the symposium "The Two Koreas and the United States." Dallas, March 1997.

15. Ji-Moon Suh, "America and Americans as Depicted in Korean Fiction." *Journal of American Studies* (Seoul), vol. 28, number 2, Winter 1996, p. 388. See also Harrison, p. 216.

16. For example, see Kenneth M. Wells, ed., *South Korea's Minjung Movement. The Culture of Politics and Dissidence*. Honolulu: University of Hawaii Press, 1995.

17. This is reflected both in the appeal (some perhaps government inspired, some autonomous) for a "buy Korean" policy. *Juche* (self reliance or autonomy), as the official ideology of North Korea, is nationalism transformed into a state religion.

18. Many Koreans returning from graduate work in the United States feel they must be more nationalistic than others to gain peer social or academic acceptance.

19. The Hanbo scandal dramatically illustrates the need for reform of the financial sector and its institutions. But freeing these institutions from government formal and informal control will likely increase *chaebol* influence, which is already extensive, thereby heightening concentration of wealth and power, and creating economic, social, and political problems.

20. For a discussion of the issue, see David I. Steinberg, "Human Rights and Civil Society in South Korea: The Influence of Orthodoxy and Ideology" (in Korean), *Sasang*, Winter 1996.

21. Both the British and German ambassadors have also protested the efforts to boycott the imports from those countries. Consumer goods are about 11 percent of imports. See "Buy Korean," *Far Eastern Economic Review*, March 6, 1997.

22. See the *International Herald Tribune*, February 18, 1997.

23. Under these troubled circumstances, some are speculating on the administration's potential willingness to change from a strong presidential system to a parliamentary one. Rumors have abounded for years that Kim Young Sam, on joining the government party in January 1990, made such a commitment, but later reneged on it. Kim Jong Il has continuously advocated such a system. The fears of a parliamentary system, which might be more immediately responsive to public needs, might also serve to perpetuate dominant party power, for the single five-year presidential term would no longer be the locus of power. That would rest with a prime minister who could continue in office as long as his party had a majority in the legislature.

24. Some Koreans have argued that the very success of this policy resulted in spurring on the North Koreans with their nuclear adventure, and thus the policy, although accomplishing its shorter term goals for the South, may have created longer-term problems with the North.

25. It should be remembered that Korea has broken from U.S. influence in the Middle East. For example, it had extensive construction contracts in Libya, and close relations with Iraq, and closed the Israeli Embassy in Seoul for a period.

26. See, for example, David I. Steinberg, "South Korea in Southeast Asia: Enhancing Returns and Reassurances," *Southeast Asian Affairs 1995*. Singapore: Institute of Southeast Asian Studies, 1995.

27. For an analysis of this, see Richard Halloran, "Distrust," the *Korea Times*, January 17, 1997, in which he calls for a "wise men's" group consideration of the continuing validity of the relationship in its present form.

28. This has been analogous to Israel effectively prohibiting the United States from negotiating with the Palestine Liberation Organization for many years. Whether the U.S. Congress would have approved of such actions is a separate issue.

29. After all, this was in fact the basis for Korea's first independent treaty—with the United States in 1882.

Part III
The Two Koreas and Their
Asian Neighbors

7

The North Korean Crisis and Japan's Choice

Masao Okonogi

Introduction

Concerning the future of North Korea, many talk as if its fate has already been set. When President Kim Il Sung died, there were those who predicted its implosion within three to six months. However, as former CIA Director John Deutch stated in the U.S. Senate Intelligence committee on December 11, 1996, it is still uncertain whether North Korea would: (1) collapse internally or implode because of incredible economic problems; (2) invade the South over one issue or another; or (3) lead to some peaceful resolution and reunification with the South. His evaluation, "how that proceeds between those three directions will be resolved in the next two or three years," is correct.

However, we should not forget about the importance of timeframe when we discuss and compare various scenarios. In other words, although there are many scenarios, they would not all come about simultaneously. Even in the case of the three scenarios above, what we have to be most vigilant about now is North Korea's possible invasion of South Korea and its sudden collapse. Once these scenarios are successfully avoided, there would again be more scenarios until peaceful reunification. For example, in the second scenario, violent, sudden collapse is expected within two or three years, but if North Korea opens up and makes reforms toward progress, the result would be a more moderate form of internal collapse. It would take at least ten to twenty years until peaceful unification is ultimately achieved. If this is so, we must examine carefully, at each stage, the nature of the North Korean crisis, set concrete goals accordingly, and formulate the most adequate policy.

The Future of North Korea: Three Scenarios

Deepening diplomatic isolation, worsening economic difficulties, solidifying North-South gap, the death of President Kim Il Sung . . . North Korea faces what may be called the most extreme difficulties in almost all spheres of international relations, economic systems, and political regimes since its establishment as a nation. Facing a food crisis due to floods for two consecutive years, the formal successor to the president of Democratic People's Republic of Korea (North Korea or DPRK) and general secretary of Korean Workers' Party (KWP) Kim Jong Il's problems are so immense that they seem impossible to overcome. However, looking at the prospects of North Korea's future more concretely, two big hurdles lie ahead. Depending on whether North Korea is able to overcome these hurdles, three scenarios of differing timeframes come to mind.

The first hurdle is an issue already confronting Kim Jong Il. That is, taking advantage of the October 1994 U.S.-DPRK Agreed Framework to improve foreign relations and to introduce foreign capital and technology, thereby putting the failed North Korean economy on the road to reconstruction as soon as possible. The three-year period from 1994 to 1996 had been set as a buffer phase to Kim Il Sung's last injunction for an economic reconstruction policy of "agriculture, light industry, and trade first." To achieve this, however, requires economic cooperation between North and South Korea and normalization of relations with Japan. Furthermore, North Korea must now solve its immediate food crisis, which will necessitate the prolongation of the buffer phase. With the end of the "three years' mourning" next July, what Secretary Kim Jong Il faces now is an economic crisis, not a political crisis.

In the first scenario, the October 1994 Agreed Framework does no more than lay the groundwork for a breakthrough. If North Korea fails to make progress in relations with the United States, South Korea, and Japan while implementing the first phases of the Agreed Framework, its international isolation and economic difficulties will be further exacerbated and it will face insurmountable difficulties. In other words, not only will its food problems remain unsolved, but a dangerous situation will emerge in which North Korea will not be able to devise a new economic plan even after Kim Jong Il's formal succession to supreme leadership. If this is so, domestic distrust toward Kim Jong Il's leadership will increase. International isolation and collapse of the economic system will facilitate North Korea's political crisis. The possibility that this scenario will be accompanied by aggressive action beyond North Korea's borders cannot be discounted, because, for North Korea, the situation above equals that of an economic sanction.

In the second scenario, the North Korean economy begins down the path of reconstruction, although there remains serious doubt about this possibility, but that alone will not immediately guarantee the long-term stability of the Kim Jong Il regime. An opening up of the North Korean economy, accompanied by improved relations with Japan and South Korea, would give rise to another type of contradiction in North Korea—between the old political structure to which Kim Jong Il is attempting to succeed and the open economic policies that would be newly implemented. The issue is whether or not North Korea can implement opening and reform in stages after the Chinese model.

The appeal to traditional culture seen in the process of constructing a succession system—for example, an emphasis on skill in the literary and military arts, loyalty and filial piety, politics of benevolence and virtue, and other Confucian values—attests to a regressive phenomenon in North Korea's political system. Uncovering and mobilizing the old values still surviving in North Korean society will make the work of succession to political authority easier, but this will mean holding off addressing the difficult issue of reform. As a result, as the economy continues to open up and people's livelihood improves, the leadership and the populace of North Korea will see a gap between politics and economics that needs to be closed.

In essence, North Korea is facing the same dilemma that the Soviet Union and China faced. Clinging to the old political system and placing restrictions on people, goods, money, and information makes economic reconstruction impossible. Freedom in these areas, however, will bring to the surface the contradictions of the old system and produce political instability. Contact with the outside world that comes with economic opening and improvements in people's livelihood will, in the end, necessitate a reform of the economic system (through the introduction of a market economy), and reform of the economic system will in turn lead to a reform in ideology and the political system. About this time contention between conservatives and reformers within the North Korean leadership should grow more fierce.

As a result of such contention, policy disputes could easily turn into power struggles and, regardless of whether the conservatives or the reformers win, contradictions, once they have surfaced, will only grow more serious. In the end, they will bring on a collapse of the trinity consisting of the supreme leader, the political system, and the state. Whether one likes it or not, South Korea will absorb North Korea and the Korean peninsula will be unified.

In the third scenario, the North Korean leadership demonstrates unexpected authoritative skill (managerial skill) and succeeds in implementing opening and reform as in China—such results would not be undesired. In fact, wary of the cost of unification attendant on an early collapse of North Korea, South Korea might even welcome a long-term coexistence with an open and reforming socialist North Korea. If North Korea succeeds in its experiment of "survival," both North and South Korea will be able to achieve a peaceful coexistence lasting perhaps a decade or more, as happened in East and West Germany.

Such North-South coexistence cannot last forever. Opening and reform, and, above all, greater North-South exchange, will lead to changes in the belief system (values) of the North Korean people. Like East Germany, North Korea will find itself unable to resist a systemic transition. The third scenario thus ultimately reaches the same end as the second. Over the long term, both the systemic collapse of North Korea and the unification of the Korean peninsula are inevitable.

Food Crisis and War: the Worst Case Scenario

As mentioned in the beginning, the scenario that we must be most vigilant of is the internal and external use of violence. Central Intelligence Agency Director Deutch differentiates between the internal collapse scenario and a war-contingency scenario. Further, an implosion in the next two or three years would happen when North Korea's food and energy situation reaches the bottom level with no aid from neighboring countries. But if maintaining its political regime becomes impossible, would North Korean leaders accept their fate accordingly? Three years ago, when economic sanctions against North Korea were about to be adopted in the United Nations, the North Korean government made a declaration of war. Along these lines, an internal collapse in the next few years would actually turn the food crisis into a war scenario, or at least something that could easily entail war.

This is not unthinkable. For example, despite the resolutions of the submarine incident and the recent Hwang Jang Yop exile, another unexpected incident with no external food aid will greatly worsen North Korea's situation. Secretary Kim Jong Il will have to proceed with his formal succession to supreme leader during the food crisis and the North Korean leadership will have to adopt a kind of brinkmanship policy. Enforcing that policy may force the surrounding countries to choose between war or aid. If the October 1994 U.S.–North Korea Geneva Agreement or the Korea Energy Development Organization (KEDO) framework, which is based on the agreement, is abandoned, we would have to judge that war is near. Also, if Kim Jong Il delays his formal succession to the supreme leadership post, he would not be able to resolve the political mistrust that would emerge internally.

To make matters more interesting, Secretary Hwang Jang Yop, who applied for asylum at the South Korean (Republic of Korea, or ROK) Embassy in Beijing on February 12, explained North Korea's crisis from food and economic difficulties and denied the possibility of the internal collapse scenario but expressed strong fears about the possibility of a war scenario. For example, he said, "even in a feudal society, if the situation becomes as bad (as North Korea's) a farmers' uprising would occur, but since the dictatorship is so strict and the suppression so merciless, we cannot expect the people to come out of their suffering by themselves." He also stated that, "although (North Korea) faces some economic difficulty, there is no danger of North Korean collapse since it is politically united." In addition, he stressed the need for food aid and stated, "even if food aid is given, North Korea will not become rich and its military strong. It would just be weathering hunger. However, if it receives aid, no matter how secret it is kept, the North Korean people would come to understand. This is the only way to prevent war."

Of course, there is debate about whether the political unity within North Korea is as strong as Hwang stated. [If a farmers' uprising does not occur, and the food crisis worsens and reaches a dangerous stage because the political unity is maintained within the leadership, the claim that the war scenario is likely—rather than the internal collapse scenario—in the form of uprisings and coups d'état, is logical and consistent.] As long as the North Korean leadership is united and centered around Kim Jong Il, and ideological indoctrination toward the people maintained, and the further the militarization of the Kim Jong Il regime progresses, the possibility of war, rather than internal collapse, increases. Thus, a debate about the possibility of a soft-landing of North Korea would not be too late even in the immediate future.

Even so, there is no need to think in only pessimistic terms. In fact, since Kim Jong Il's fifty-fifth birthday on February 16th, North Korea's attitude has rapidly changed in a positive way. On February 17 the North Korean Foreign Ministry spokesman stated, "It is our position that if he sought asylum, it means that he is a renegade and he is dismissed." On February 21, shortly after the announcement of the death of North Korean Defense Minister Choe Kang and the list of the funeral committee, the spokesman made a statement that a joint briefing regarding the four-party talks would be held in New York on March 5. North Korea chose to resolve the Hwang Jang Yop incident quickly, and to respond to the joint briefing it had been delaying. This was also a measure in response to U.S. and South Korean food aid through the United Nations World Food Program. Furthermore, on March 7, U.S.–North Korean governmental consultations were held at the deputy assistant secretary level.

Of course, this kind of trend does have its limits. But the fact that the North Korean leadership restrained itself from an emotional response, and did not lose its diplomatic flexibility and mobility, should be noted. If Kim Jong Il could not constrain the hardliners who support a retaliation toward the Hwang exile, the dispatch of KEDO engineers and the realization of a joint briefing on the four-party talks would be impossible. A severe "war of attrition" would have made Kim Jong Il's formal succession to the supreme leadership difficult. As mentioned before, this difficulty would have been a prelude to a "war" scenario. Therefore, the most important points in predicting the future would be to see whether North Korea succeeds in acquiring food aid within the next few months, and whether Kim Jong Il can actually become president of the country and/or general secretary of the KWP. If the process is carefully observed, we would be able to know the degree of unity and stability of the Kim Jong Il regime.

Even if the formal succession is realized, the possibility of a "war of attrition" during that process would cause North Korea to exhaust its power in the game with South Korea. An increase in fleeing civilians spilling over into military defections would be terminal. In this sense, we should not underestimate the gravity of the Kim Jong Il military regime and force it into a corner. However, after Kim Jong Il formally becomes the supreme leader, there is a reasonable possibility that North-South talks will resume between Kim Jong Il and South Korea's president. That is because once President Kim Young Sam's term is completed, there would be more leeway to gain justification for resuming talks. As a result, there remains the possibility of a major breakthrough in North Korea's relations with the United States, Japan, and South Korea, and of the opening of a new road for survival. Therefore, the three scenarios given regarding North Korea's future are still relevant.

Moderation and Cooperation: The Preferred Policy of Japan

The question of which of these three scenarios will actually occur depends to a great extent on the actions taken by North Korea itself, and this should not be taken for granted. The leadership in North Korea, well-versed in diplomacy, will likely apply their skills to overcoming the first hurdle; even so, there is no guarantee that cooperation between North and South Korea and normalization of Japan–North Korea relations will be achieved in the short term. Consequently, should North Korea choose once again to employ the nuclear card, circumstances will immediately revert to the stage prior to Kim Il Sung's meeting with former president Jimmy Carter— that is, a crisis situation will once more arise.

Such being the case, the engagement policy based on moderation and cooperation must be the fundamental guideline. Moderation means recognizing the three scenarios as three stages of differing natures and proposing the most appropriate policy for each stage, and cooperation means putting these policies into practice through close cooperation with Japan, the United States, and South Korea. Our objective is to promote gradual change in North Korea and to portion out the costs of unification of the Korean peninsula while avoiding violent confrontation. Japan's policies, too, should be designed with this viewpoint in mind.

Our policy of engagement at the first stage is to adhere to the U.S.– North Korea Agreed Framework and improve relations with North Korea within this framework. Of utmost importance are the normalization of Japan–North Korea relations and cooperation between the North and the South. Reconstruction of the North Korean economy is impossible without considerable financing and technological transfer from Japan and without economic cooperation from South Korea. With reconstruction the economy will become more open to the outside. If these goals can be achieved, North Korea can end its international isolation. Thus, we should not summarily reject the policies of North Korea but continue to tolerate them in part and include North Korea in a new international system within the context of a post–Cold War era.

The greatest difficulty for North Korea will probably be in achieving the "staged opening and reform." As already seen, I am not necessarily optimistic about the possibility of this being achieved successfully. While I hope that such pessimism is unwarranted, we may face an extremely thorny problem in the intermediate term (5–10 years): an internal collapse of North Korea, despite having avoided a confrontational scenario at the first stage. Furthermore, there are limits to the external assistance that can be provided should systemic collapse occur within North Korea, for overdependence on the outside, in and of itself, will only hasten systemic collapse.

In addition, the trinity of the supreme leader, the political system, and the state might not permit a "collapse by stages" in North Korea. The country's present political system has been personified in *suryon* (the supreme leader), and this concept is inextricably bound with the state known as the Democratic People's Republic of Korea. For that reason, the fate of the nation lies in Kim Jong Il's assuming power as Kim Il Sung's successor. If it is indeed impossible to separate the supreme leader from the political system, then the fate of all three elements in the trinity are bound together. The collapse of the leadership would be followed by the collapse of the political system and then by the collapse of the state.

Therefore, we must develop two completely contrary policies. We must be simultaneously prepared (1) to continue promoting opening and reform in North Korea through economic exchange, and (2) to deal with a sudden internal collapse of North Korea. From such a perspective, the role Japan can play is in no way a small one. The large-scale transfer of capital and technology to North Korea from Japan, foreseen once Japan–North Korea relations are normalized, will, even if only temporarily, activate the North Korean economy and promote the attainment of coexistence between North and South Korea. Once the infrastructure has been improved to a certain degree and the facilities of key industries renovated, the cheap but good quality labor resources of North Korea can be utilized to develop labor-intensive export industries in North Korea.

One should note in this regard that the economic cooperation provided to North Korea by South Korea and Japan complement each other. Any capital and technology transferred to North Korea from Japan after a normalization of relations would be of a "reparations" nature in connection with its history of colonial rule. In other words, these would be public funds outside the realm of commercial considerations, and most of these funds would probably be used to improve North Korea's infrastructure. Given the likelihood of arrears in trade payments, private Japanese corporations will not be willing to invest their own money in a country as risky as North Korea. If infrastructure is improved, however, North Korea could be an attractive source of labor for South Korean corporations troubled by skyrocketing labor costs. South Korean corporations can also be expected to develop export markets for the light industrial products produced in North Korea.

On the other hand, a sudden internal collapse of North Korea followed by absorption into and unification with South Korea will have serious consequences not only for the Korean peninsula but for Northeast Asia as a whole. The causes of greatest concern in such a case would be the enormous cost of unification and the outflow of refugees from North Korea. South Korea alone cannot bear the cost of unification, estimated to be more than US$200 billion. Therefore, the formation of an international consortium is inevitable and, regardless of whether one likes it or not, Japan will be expected to play a central role in this. Another point the Japanese must bear in mind is that while the majority of North Korean refugees will likely head for China or South Korea, the nearly 100,000 North Koreans and their wives residing in Japan who returned to North Korea from Japan in the 1960s still have family and relatives in Japan.

Finally, if North Korea's experiment in "survival" succeeds and unification of the Korean peninsula is achieved after a lengthy North-South coexistence through a revolutionary process resembling that in Eastern Europe, what kind of circumstances will we then face? Indeed, in this case as well, one system will collapse and there will still be the problems of unification costs and an outflow of refugees. At the same time, one could certainly not expect a decade or more of opening and reform to go for naught. During that time, North Korea would, to a certain degree, improve its infrastructure, and its citizens would, to a certain degree, gain experience in market economics while acquiring immunity to the chaos of unification. This itself is nothing less than a form of portioning out the tangible and intangible costs of unification.

Unified Korea and Japan: A Japanese Viewpoint

According to my personal observations, many South Koreans seem to believe that the Japanese do not desire unification of Korea. In the most extreme case, it is believed that the Japanese will oppose and obstruct unification. The reason, it is said, is that the emergence of a unified state with a population of seventy million will most definitely present a threat to the Japanese. However, the reality is that most Japanese do not have a concrete image formed about a unified Korea and Japan's relations with it. What most Japanese are vaguely concerned about is not unification itself, but the immense confusion that may occur in the process toward unification. For example, in the case of sudden North Korean collapse, the possibilities of a second Korean War, the necessities for vast amounts of financial aid, and the outflow of refugees can be conceived, and each possibility will have grave consequences for Japan.

Some Koreans point out that, like the Korean War during 1950–53, a second Korean War will bring about a large wartime demand and stimulate exports from Japan, which in turn will favorably influence the Japanese economy. Also, it is feared that, with that opportunity, Japan's military role will be expanded. However, the majority of Japanese do not fear the positive effects of export expansion, but they do not look forward to being demanded by the international community to contribute more than the financial support given during the Gulf War. In fact, if the Korean peninsula is unified by war, Japan will have to share not only part of the war costs, but also part of the unification costs. That may become a big burden for Japan's financial reconstruction efforts. Also, many Japanese fear Japan, as the rear area base for U.S. forces, becoming the target of North Korea's missile attacks and subversive activities, rather than desire becoming a military power. Furthermore, some Japanese worry that the deficiencies of Japan's system of military support for U.S. forces will become apparent by a second Korean War, and thus jeopardize a U.S.–Japan alliance.

As to the possibility of a strong unified state emerging and becoming a threat to Japan, many Japanese, at present, are not considering it a serious problem. Although it cannot be doubted that a unified Korea may become the next economic power, by looking at the example of unified Germany, it may take ten to twenty years. Considering the population and gaps in the gross national products of South and North Korea, South Korea will face bigger economic difficulties than unified Germany did. Also, the political and psychological distrust between the North and the South is larger than Germany's. North Korea does not know market economy or political freedom. Therefore, in a period of economic difficulty and political instability after unification, only the ROK government will be equipped to pursue cordial and cooperative relations with surrounding countries. That is the necessary condition for achieving Korean unification successfully. Such a rational policy will also be promoted by Japan's cooperative attitude.

However, despite all this, it cannot be denied that many Japanese vaguely worry about a rise of extreme nationalism in a unified Korea and of that nationalism's being directed toward Japan. For example, if an emotional conflict occurs between Japan and Korea, the possibility of a unified Korea turning to China to counter Japan, and making efforts toward its own military build-up, cannot be denied. In fact, at the November 1995 summit, when Presidents Kim Young Sam and Jiang Zemin took a unified stance in criticizing Japan, possibilities for PRC–ROK collaboration were reported in the Japanese and Korean media. Also, there have been instances such as the 1991–92 ROK *Defense White Paper* in which Japan was treated as a hypothetical enemy. Furthermore, in February, when the Takeshima (Dokto) issue came to fore, South Korea undertook military exercises in the seas near Takeshima. These examples are enough to increase Japanese suspicions with regard to a unified Korea's attitudes toward Japan.

Such mutual distrust and perception gaps are negative factors that will destabilize relations between a unified Korea and Japan. As with many other cases, the communication gap is the biggest problem between Japan and Korea. However, in spite of this, it is not necessary to think about the relationship in only a pessimistic way. With the unification of Korea, one of the most destabilizing factors in Northeast Asia will be removed. A new economic unit of seventy million people in the neighborhood will emerge. As long as Korea maintains a system of democracy and an open market economy, and chooses to live as a commercial state, the unification of Korea will be a positive factor for Japan, in the long term. Also, in order to alleviate unification costs, a unified Korea will make more efforts than the present toward liberalization of its economy. Koreans know that unification of Germany was achieved within the integration of West Europe.

Also, Japan's active cooperation toward the unification of Korea will be a good opportunity to change the Koreans' image of Japan. In fact, as long as the Korean mistrust of Japan is derived from the unfortunate past of colonial rule, a new experience equal to the magnanimity of the past would be necessary to change the present image. It is earnestly desired that North Korea's opening and reform be encouraged, and that the Korean peninsula be peacefully unified through the thoroughly coordinated and joint efforts of both Japan and Korea. That would indeed guarantee cooperation between a unified Korea and Japan.

8
China and the Two Koreas

Quansheng Zhao

It took thirty-five days for Beijing to handle the defection of Hwang Jang Yop, a top North Korean Communist Party ideologue. On February 12, 1997, Hwang walked into the South Korean Embassy in Beijing,[1] and stayed there for five weeks. On March 18, 1997, Hwang was transferred to the Philippines, previously arranged as a transit place for him on the way to South Korea. This case of defection not only presented a drama in the dynamics of North-South relations in the Korean peninsula, but also highlighted the diplomatic dilemma China has faced. This dilemma began in the late 1980s when Beijing started the process of normalizing relations with South Korea, while attempting to keep working relations with the North. To work out a solution for the case of Hwang Jang Yop, there were extensive negotiations in Beijing among and between diplomats from China, North Korea, and South Korea.

Beijing attempted to avoid choosing sides in a dispute between an old communist ally and a new commercial partner. Chinese Foreign Ministry spokesman Guo Chongli indicated several days after the defection that the negotiations may "take a very long time," citing examples of the standoff in Lima, Peru, where Tupac Amaru guerrillas had been holding diplomats and other officials hostage in the Japanese ambassador's residence for two months.[2] A month later, Chinese Premier Li Peng reiterated the issue, "China will exercise caution, and we will handle the issue by proceeding from the maintenance of peace on the Korean peninsula." What China needs to solve this dilemma, as former South Korean Foreign Minister Han Sung-Joo pointed out, "is right timing and right method."[3] Beijing's extreme cautious actions toward this incident demonstrated a high degree of sensitivity in China's policy toward the two Koreas.

In order to fully understand Beijing's considerations behind its Korea policy, it is necessary to first discuss the changing priorities in Chinese foreign policy from the era of Mao Zedong to the era of Deng Xiaoping and the post-Deng era.

Changing Priorities in Chinese Foreign Policy

The death of Mao Zedong in 1976 brought the ten-year Cultural Revolution to an end. After a one-year transitional period under the leadership of Mao's hand-picked successor Hua Guofeng, Deng Xiaoping overcame political disgrace and returned to power in 1977, achieving the status of China's permanent leader in 1978.[4] (He had been purged twice by Mao in 1966 and 1976 during the Cultural Revolution, but was rehabilitated in 1973.) This change of leadership marked the beginning of a new period in contemporary Chinese history.

The Mao Zedong era, which lasted from 1949 to 1976, was a radical revolutionary period highlighted by the Cultural Revolution, which caused what the Chinese Communist Party (CCP) itself has described as "the most severe setback and the heaviest losses . . . since the founding of the People's Republic."[5] The Deng Xiaoping era (1978–97), a period of pragmatism, has led to "a new situation in all fields of socialist modernization." In both the Mao and Deng periods, as Kenneth Lieberthal points out, "each of China's principal domestic strategies—from the First Five-Year Plan and the Great Leap Forward of the 1950s, through the Cultural Revolution of the 1960s and 1970s, to the Four-Modernization of the 1980s, has had clear and direct implications for its posture toward the rest of the world."[6]

The Deng era (and the post-Deng era) can be regarded as a post-revolutionary era, clearly different from the Mao era in its national priorities and behavior toward the rest of the world community. A revolutionary state conducts a continuous revolution internally and externally, whereas a post-revolutionary state sets economic development as its first priority, thereby introducing a more mass-regarding political climate.[7] A revolutionary state regards itself as an outsider trying to change the status quo within the international community, whereas a post-revolutionary state acts like an insider seeking maximum opportunities for its development from within the existing order. In addition, a revolutionary state emphasizes ideological considerations, whereas a post-revolutionary state believes that pragmatism better serves its national interests.

The transition of the Chinese leadership's interpretations and perceptions of China's internal and external environments has brought considerable changes in Beijing's foreign policy priorities. Such changes of world views frequently form the basis for determining priorities, or at least for determining how such enduring priorities as regime survival and the promotion of national interests can be best advanced. Therefore, we should pay close attention to the transformation of the Chinese leadership's interpretation of the internal conditions and external environment, and the effects of this transformation on the priorities of Chinese foreign policy.

China experienced a fundamental change from the era of revolution to the era of modernization. Under Mao, the regime emphasized revolutionary objectives: dramatic and sweeping social reform in the domestic arena and survival as a communist nation in the international environment. This period was characterized by an emphasis on revolutionary ideology, a lack of respect for the prevailing international norms and extreme sensitivity to outside threats. This perception of external threats to the new communist regime often led the Beijing leadership under Mao to meet perceived threats to security with military means.

In the post-revolutionary era, or the era of modernization, China has moved beyond a single-minded preoccupation with world revolution. As the world becomes increasingly interdependent, particularly in terms of economic integration, the Beijing leadership has gradually recognized that the concept of regime survival has broader meanings. National security today is not only related to political and strategic issues, but also to economic development. Beijing, of course, recognized the importance of the economic aspect earlier, but felt that economic security and development could be achieved in self-sufficient, classless, and socialist fashion. Now the leadership has realized that economic development by necessity in this age also means economic interdependence, which requires less antagonistic world behavior than Maoist ideology would prescribe. Deng Xiaoping has warned on several occasions that China may face the danger of losing its *qiuji* (global citizenship) if its economy fails to catch up with that of the rest of the world. The People's Republic of China's (PRC) leadership now has multiple goals for national development and places particular emphasis on economic development and modernization.

An examination of China's foreign relations with the countries in the Asia-Pacific region, the two Koreas included, highlights three basic trends—modernization, nationalism, and regionalism—influencing China's foreign policy.[8] Modernization refers to China's concentration on economic growth. Since 1978, two years after the death of Mao Zedong, Deng Xiaoping repeatedly emphasized the need to shift China's priority from "revolution" to "modernization." In the beginning of 1980, Deng raised three tasks for China to work on for the decade ahead (the 1980s): to "oppose hegemonism" and to "preserve world peace"; to work on "China's reunification with Taiwan," and to "step up the drive for China's four modernizations." Deng singled out the third task as the most important one by stating, "Modernization is at the core of all these major tasks, because it is the essential condition for solving both our domestic and our external problems,"[9] and "nothing short of a world war could tear us away from this line."[10]

Nationalism has emerged as a leading ideological current behind China's drive toward modernization. It has increasingly become one of the primary driving forces behind Chinese foreign policy. In the post–Cold War era, nationalistic feelings appear particularly strong among Chinese intellectuals and government officials as well as in other circles of Chinese society. China's nationalism has long been a focus of Chinese foreign policy studies.[11] A focus on regionalism allows China to remain a regional power, concentrating its political, economical, and military activities primarily in the Asia-Pacific region,[12] in spite of its global aspirations.

The new orientation of Chinese foreign policy in the era of Deng was further confirmed by what was called "the 28–character strategy" raised by Deng Xiaoping in the wake of the Tiananmen incident of 1989, when China was facing economic sanctions from the West, disintegration of the Soviet Union, and the collapse of communism in East Europe. These strategies included the following seven phrases:

lengjing guan cha—watch and analyze [the developments] calmly;
wenzhu zhenjiao—secure [our own] positions;
chen zhe yingfu—deal with [the changes] with confidence;
tao guangyang hui—conceal [our] capacities;
shanyu shou zhou—be good at keeping low profile;

jue bu dang tou—never become the leader;
you suo zuo wei—make some contributions.

In other words, in order to concentrate on economic development (or modernization), China should keep a low profile in international affairs. Deng's idea is that "by the middle of the next century," China should "have basically realized modernization," and then it can be said that China "has succeeded."[13]

China's Balancing Policy Between North and South

The changing priorities in Chinese foreign policy in the Deng and post-Deng era have inevitably produced a profound impact on Beijing's policy toward the two Koreas. Historically, China and Korea shared complex and intimate relations, which were symbolized by a hierarchical tributary system. As Chae-Jin Lee points out, "Korea's tributary relations with China began as early as the fifth century, they were regularized during the Koryo dynasty (918–1392), and became fully institutionalized during the Yi dynasty (1392–1910)."[14] These tributary relations came to an end when China was defeated in the Sino-Japanese war of 1894–95, and was forced to sign the treaty of Shimonoseki with Japan. Consequently, Korea became a colony of Japan, which lasted until 1945 when Japan was defeated in World War II.

China did not get involved in Korean affairs until October 1950, when the new Chinese communist leadership made the momentous decision to cross the Yalu River and enter the Korean War, thereby placing itself in direct military confrontation with the United States. This conflict was to end in a military stalemate three years later. The casualties for both sides, the estimations for which vary, were tremendous. According to Chinese statistics, U.S. casualties reached 390,000, whereas Chinese casualties were 366,000, with 115,000 dead and 221,000 wounded.[15] One other account[16] claimed that the number of dead on the Chinese side alone reached 400,000. China's decision to enter the Korean War[17] had other lasting consequences for the Asia-Pacific region. It prompted President Harry Truman to order the U.S. Seventh Fleet into the Taiwan Strait to guarantee Taiwanese security, thereby internationalizing the issue of Taiwan and making it a focus of future conflict between Beijing and Washington. The war also left the Korean peninsula with the long-term legacy of North-South division.

There are major changes in China's policy toward the two Koreas between the era of Mao and the era of Deng. Modernization and regionalism have played leading roles in China's policy shift toward the Korean peninsula. In the 1950s, the PRC, inspired by its perceived threat of the invasion of Western imperialism, provided substantial military support to North Korea in its war with the South. It is no doubt that strategic and political calculations dominated the PRC's Korea policy. Beijing has also learned lessons from the war in terms of casualties and political implications for China's foreign policy and the evolution of East Asian international relations—the war proved very costly for China.

With changing international and domestic environments, Beijing made substantial adjustment in its Korea policy. Despite its openly stated alignment with Pyongyang, China long ago ceased to support North Korean military attack on the South since the complete withdrawal of its military forces from the North in 1958. Since the opening of the Deng era, Beijing has consistently expressed interest in avoiding another major military conflict and, therefore, has a particular interest in the creation and maintenance of a peaceful and stable situation in the Korean peninsula, leading toward the peaceful unification of North and South Korea.[18] Beijing hailed the talks that took place in September 1990 between North Korean Prime Minister Yon Hyoung Muk and South Korean Premier Kang Yong Hun as "a good beginning" that "will help alleviate tensions and promote the process of Korean reunification."[19] Beijing has also encouraged both Pyongyang and Seoul to create a nuclear-free Korean peninsula,[20] considering the move to be in line with China's national interests.

There were sporadic quarrels between Beijing and Pyongyang during the past several decades. Its nadir was in 1969 (at the peak of the chaotic period of China's Cultural Revolution), when Chinese and North Korean forces clashed along their border. With Beijing further strengthening its ties with Seoul, there were signs in the mid-1990s that the Beijing-Pyongyang relationship appeared to become cool. In July 1995, for example, a North Korean official told an American delegation of the New York-based Council on Foreign Relations who were visiting Pyongyang, "If you need to balance China's growing power, you should establish relations with us."[21] This comment could remind people of the balancing game played by North Korea with China and the Soviet Union during the 1970s and 1980s. Bilateral economic exchanges between China and North Korea were also reduced. According to an unpublished study by the American Enterprise Institute's Nicholas Eberstadt and three other scholars, China's food exports to North Korea dropped from $149 million in 1993 to $55 million in 1994, and its coal and oil exports fell from $264 million to $194 million.[22] It would be interesting for East Asian specialists to watch the changing dynamics of this triangular relationship among Beijing, Seoul, and Pyongyang when approaching the twenty-first century.

The PRC nevertheless managed to maintain a workable relationship with North Korea. High-level bilateral visits took place virtually every year since the beginning of the Deng era. Political developments in China and Eastern Europe since the late 1980s brought Beijing and Pyongyang closer together. Kim Il Sung was one of the few world leaders who openly supported Deng Xiaoping's military suppression of student demonstrations in 1989.

From the 1960s to the mid-1980s, Pyongyang was able to play the Beijing card against the Moscow card, effectively preventing China from moving closer to Seoul. As the international situation changed, especially after the Soviet Union and Eastern European countries established diplomatic relations with South Korea, the PRC gained more freedom and confidence in expanding its relations with South Korea. In fact, in the post–Cold War era beginning with the late 1980s Beijing has had strong incentives to develop relations with Seoul, because a closer relationship might increase China's leverage in dealing with the Korean problem and with East Asia as a whole. As one U.S. official in Washington suggests, "Having good relations with both [Koreas] puts China in the best possible situation" in world politics as well as regional affairs.[23]

Several events that took place in 1990 were described in a *Beijing Review* article as indicative of South Korea shedding "the cloak of the Cold War." These events were the establishment of diplomatic relations between South Korea and the Soviet Union; three meetings of the prime ministers of North and South Korea, and the decision reached by China and South Korea to set up nongovernmental trade offices in each other's capitals. These developments are seen as part of the "realignment of relations among Asian nations."[24]

The changes in institutional macrostructure and power-regime macrostructure have also played a major role in the evolution of China's policy toward Korea, a policy that was significantly altered in September 1992, when China finally agreed to establish official diplomatic relations with South Korea. It had taken more than two years for Beijing to follow

Moscow's lead in establishing relations with Seoul.

A major difficulty in establishing relations with South Korea was China's need for North Korea's support for survival of Beijing's communist regime after the Tiananmen incident in 1989. Beijing and Pyongyang were isolated at that time, both from other remaining socialist countries and from the international community at large, and relied on each other for moral support. The collapse of Soviet communism and the development of political democratization and pluralization in the former Soviet Union and Eastern Europe caused alarm in Beijing. In some countries, local communist parties formally relinquished their monopoly of political power; in others, their power simply collapsed. Beijing's leaders were pleased to announce to the Chinese people that Kim Il Sung firmly supported the 1989 military crackdown that was ordered by Deng Xiaoping against the student demonstrations. When Kim Il Sung paid his twenty-ninth visit to China in October 1991,[25] this political and moral support was highlighted.

Furthermore, these mutual institutional supports between the two countries translated into personal relations at the micro level. The Chinese attachment to North Korea throughout the 1980s was underpinned by personal ties and sympathies. Leaders such as Deng Xiaoping, Chen Yun, Yang Shangkun, Li Xiannian, Peng Zhen, Wang Zhen, and Bo Yibo held leading positions during the 1950s, and were personally involved, to varying degrees, in the Korean War. Their contemporaries in North Korea, headed by Kim Il Sung, also retained power. This decades-long friendship was sustained and enhanced through frequent, mutual public or private visits.

In the aftermath of the Tiananmen incident, the struggle for succession to political authority from the aging leadership became the predominant concern of the Chinese Communist Party. This struggle had a profoundly deadening effect on all aspects of Chinese domestic and foreign policy, rendering the formulation of new initiatives and imaginative policy virtually impossible. It was much more difficult for the Beijing leadership at that time to break or downplay its ties with North Korea than it was for Gorbachev, who shared with Kim Il Sung neither age nor personal ties. This could explain why Beijing was relatively slow in developing official relations with Seoul.

On the other hand, however, China had long shifted its priorities from political campaigning to economic modernization. Economic development was one of Beijing's primary incentives for normalizing relations

Table 8.I

China's Trade with South Korea and North Korea, 1980-84
(US$ millions)

Year	South Korea	North Korea
1980	188	677.5
1981	280	531.0
1982	139	585.4
1983	120	527.7
1984	434	498.2
1985	1,161	488.3
1986	1,289	509.8
1987	1,679	513.3
1988	3,087	579.0
1989	3,143	562.7
1990	3,821	482.7
1991	5,812	610.4
1992	8,218	696.5
1993	9,078	890.0
1994	11,660	623.7

Source: Compiled from Chae-Jin Lee, China and Korea, pp. 140, 146.

with South Korea. China's modernization programs cannot be realized without extensive external support and exchanges from industrialized countries that can provide advanced technology, capital, markets, and managerial skills. South Korea was apparently a nearby supplier of these resources, in addition to Japan and Western powers, making China's suppliers more diversified.

Table 8.1 shows that South Korea has become increasingly important as a trading partner for China. In 1994, for example, Sino-South Korean trade reached US$11,660 million, far exceeding trade with North Korea of US$623.7 million.

In his November 1995 state visit to South Korea, President Jiang Zemin reemphasized the importance of China's ties with South Korea and projected that the 1995 bilateral trade would reach the level of US$15 billion.[26] As a newly industrialized country and a close neighbor, South Korea can also provide China with valuable experience and lessons in terms of economic development strategy, especially in "export-led" industrialization. South Korean businessmen began to conduct direct investment and joint ventures in China. The actual investment in China

Table 8.2

South Korean Investment in China, 1988-93

Item/Year	Number of cases (in millions of dollars)	Amounts approved (in millions of dollars)	Actual investment (in millions of dollars)
1988-89	1	13.8	12.8
1990	35	50.0	48.3
1991	107	121.9	91.0
1992	260	330.9	168.6
1993	630	570.3	153.9
Total	1,043	976.9	474.6

Source: Chungguk Pyonram (China Almanac) (1994), p. 634. Quoted from Chae-Jin Lee, *China and Korea*, p. 156

increased quickly, from $48.3 million in 1990 to 153.9 million in 1993 (see table 8.2). In April 1994, South Korean Technology Minister Kim Si Joong announced that conglomerates, including Samsung and Hanjin (the owner of Korean Air), would cooperate with China to produce mid-sized commercial airplanes.[27]

The geographic distribution of South Korean investments in China has indicated that they are primarily concentrated in the Bohai Sea area, most notably in Shandong province, and the Northeast region, accounting for 85.9 percent by the end of 1993 (see table 8.3).

The first official step to enhance bilateral relations was the agreement to set up trade offices in each capital in October 1990. South Korea quickly appointed a former assistant foreign minister as the head representative of its trade office, and both offices formally opened in the spring of 1991, leading to the following year's normalization of relationships between the two countries.

Still, China has to balance actions between the two Koreas to meet various demands from both external and internal fronts. It appeared that it is in China's interests that Beijing maintain a warm relationship with both North and South Korea. It is believed that Beijing does have a certain degree of influence on Pyongyang in terms of its policy toward Seoul. In May 1991, for example, North Korea announced a dramatic reversal of its "one Korea" policy, saying that it would seek separate U.N. membership, which had been demanded by South Korea. This policy shift was reportedly based on Kim Il Sung's "confederate system" idea of "one nation, one country, two systems, and two governments," which is supported by

Table 8.3

Geographic Distribution of South Korean Investment in China
(by the end of 1993)

	Number of cases approved	Percentage (in thousands of dollars)	Total amount	Percentage
Bohai Sea area				
Shandong	293	28.1	374,331	38.3
Tianjin	109	10.5	131,053	13.4
Beijing	69	6.6	62,362	6.4
Hebei	27	2.6	23,553	2.4
Subtotal	498	47.7	591,299	60.5
Northeast region				
Liaoning	221	21.2	125,155	12.8
Jilin	99	9.5	46,186	4.7
Heilongjiang	79	7.6	76,990	7.9
Subtotal	399	38.3	248,241	25.4
Central China				
Jiangsu	44	4.2	45,897	4.7
Shanghai	19	1.8	18,612	1.9
Zhejiang	11	1.1	6,676	0.7
Subtotal	74	7.1	71,186	7.3
South China				
Guangdong	40	3.8	42,609	4.4
Fujian	10	1.0	16,195	1.7
Hainan	2	0.2	800	—
Subtotal	52	5.0	59,604	6.1
Other regions	20	1.9	6,594	0.7
Total	1,043	100.0	976,923	100.0

Source: Chungguk Pyonram (China almanac) (1994), p. 635. Quoted from Chae-Jin Lee, *China and Korea,* p. 161.

the PRC.[28] Beijing is reportedly to have played a key role in Pyongyang's sudden shift,[29] engaging in much behind-the-scenes maneuvering. In late 1990, Beijing made it clear to Pyongyang that China would not commit itself to meeting North Korea's demand for a veto of any South Korean application to join the United Nations.[30] In April and May of the following year, frequent consultations were held between Beijing and Pyongyang on the U.N. membership issue, including a visit made by Chinese Premier

Li Peng to North Korea in early May.[31] Immediately after North Korea's announcement to seek separate U.N. membership, Li Peng commented that this move was "an interim measure before the unification," and would be "welcomed by the international community, including China."[32] The two Koreas now have separate U.N. memberships, a major step toward peaceful settlement in the Korean Peninsula.[33]

China's balancing act between its policies toward both countries is also reflected in the controversial issue of nuclear development in North Korea. In the spring of 1994, the International Atomic Energy Agency (IAEA) under the United Nations unearthed fresh evidence of North Korea's clandestine nuclear program; and IAEA director Hans Blix called the Yongbyon facility, which Pyongyang described as a radiochemical laboratory, "the most proliferation-sensitive facility" of North Korea's seven nuclear installations. Since then, Pyongyang has been under tremendous pressure from Washington and Seoul, including possible economic sanctions from the international community, to further open its nuclear installations for international inspection.[34] On the one hand, while admitting that China did not have accurate information regarding North Korea's nuclear weapons development program,[35] Beijing opposed economic sanctions on Pyongyang. In meetings with South Korean President Kim Young Sam and Foreign Minister Han Sung Joo during their March 26–30 visit to Beijing, Chinese leaders made clear that it would oppose any economic sanctions on North Korea, and would even be reluctant to support a resolution from the United Nations Security Council. Rather, Beijing would like to have more time to "work its persuasion on Pyongyang before any U.N. sanctions are imposed," demanding that the Security Council should downgrade its plea for inspections of the North's nuclear installations from a resolution to a nonbinding "statement." A vote on a resolution would require China to go on record with either a veto or an abstention; a statement requires no vote. [36]

On the other hand, Beijing, Washington, Tokyo, and Moscow have already reached a consensus on prohibiting the development of nuclear weapons in the Korean peninsula, particularly in North Korea. Such cooperation serves not only China's security interests, but also its economic interests.

The death of Kim Il Sung in July 1994 and his replacement by his son Kim Jong Il did not change China's policy toward the Korean peninsula. In his October–November 1994 visit to Seoul, Chinese Premier Li Peng assured South Korean President Kim Young Sam that China was positive toward the Geneva nuclear accord signed between North Korea and the United States in September.[37] Soon after, Chinese President Jiang Zemin also expressed "strong support" for the nuclear deal to U.S. President Bill Clinton when the two met at the APEC summit in Jakarta.[38] At the same time, Beijing indicated that it supported replacing the Panmunjom armistice with a permanent peace treaty—a position strongly supported by Pyongyang, but not Seoul. These actions further demonstrated that China was playing both sides of the Korean equation, and Beijing was in favor of resolving the North's nuclear issue but without hurting its interests in the North.[39]

Conclusion

The future of Korea—specifically, the North-South conflict and the issue of Korean unification—is closely connected to China. As Jiang Zemin emphasized when he met Kim Il Sung in October 1991: "China is concerned about the situation on the Korean peninsula, since détente and stability in this region has a direct bearing on the overall situation in Northeast Asia."[40] Chinese interest in the development of the two Koreas is also accentuated by the involvement of the United States, Japan, and Russia.

There are also historical connections. In Korea's early history, the peninsula was divided into three kingdoms: Silla, Koguryo, and Paekche. In the seventh century, Silla, the kingdom located in the south, entered into a political and military alliance with China's Tang dynasty, and in A.D. 668 unified the Korean peninsula into a single country. During the unification process, the Chinese and the Silla state also repulsed a Japanese expedition sent to aid Paekche. From that time on, Korea remained a unified country, with only occasional and relatively brief periods of political division. It was not until the conclusion of World War II in 1945, that the peninsula was once again divided, bringing to an end a history of political unity exceeded in length only by that of China itself. Although the Korea of today is substantially different from the Korea of the period of the three kingdoms, both domestically and internationally, there are at least three clear links with the past. First, the issue of Korean unification is still closely tied to significant influence from external powers including China, Japan, and the United States.

Second, there have been close connections between Korea and China. The Korea problem—North-South conflict and the issue of unification—remains an important consideration in Chinese foreign policy, and vice versa. Indeed, China has been actively involved in the conflicts related to Korea, the most notable of these, as discussed earlier, being the Korean War of 1950–53.

Last but not least, both the Chinese and the Koreans have always had a strong sense of political continuity and a keen desire for national unification; therefore, the unification issue in both countries has always occupied central positions in both countries' domestic politics and foreign policy.

Inevitably, there will also be problems between the countries; their differing political systems and levels of economic development are sure to contribute to the friction. The ground for cooperation, however, will be much greater than that for conflict. Each side, for instance, may regard the other as a counterweight to the increasing economic and military strength of Japan. This possibility was confirmed by the fact that Japan's past experience of militarism was jointly condemned by China's Jiang Zemin and South Korea's Kim Young Sam, during Jiang's state visit to Seoul in November 1995. [41]

There are about two million Korean minorities in China, most of whom live in the bordering Jilin province. The most well-known Chinese-Korean community area is the Yanbian Korean Minority Autonomous Region. In general, this large number of Korean minorities have played positive roles in facilitating Sino–South Korean relations. But as the bilateral relations developed rapidly in the past years, some problems have emerged. The most noticeable problem is that a sizable number of Chinese Koreans have been "recruited" to work in South Korea as a way of making quick money. By the end of 1996, there were more than 77,000 Chinese working in South Korea, and more than half were illegal residents. Furthermore, a few South Korean swindlers went to the Korean Chinese communities in Yanji, Changchun, and Harbin to "recruit" laborers or to "make investment" there. These "recruiters" or "investors" disappeared as soon as they collected fees and funds from the local Chinese Koreans. The total losses of the Chinese-Korean community is estimated to be as high as RMB280 million (about US$30 million). Some South Korean visitors even openly advocated that these Korean-Chinese regions were actually parts of Korean territory. These problems prompted Chinese Premier Li Peng to ask the South Korean government to exercise more "self-control," when he met South Korean Prime Minister Lee Hongkoo in Beijing in 1995.

Another major concern is that the PRC must adhere to certain principles regarding its own unification policy toward Taiwan. While actively promoting relations and contacts with Taipei, Beijing is extremely sensitive about the Independent Taiwan movement, which has increased its influence within and outside of Taiwan in recent years. One of the fundamental principles of Chinese foreign policy is to oppose firmly any form of policy that will create a situation of "two Chinas." Any move toward strengthening relations with Taipei from either Seoul or Pyongyang will jeopardize its relations with Beijing. This concern has been demonstrated by the unhappiness of Beijing toward a controversial plan between Taiwan and North Korea to ship Taiwan's nuclear waste for storage in North Korea. As some experienced Asia watchers put it, "North Korea knows all too well that its most important patron can be extremely testy when it comes to any fancy Taiwanese maneuvers."[42]

Notes

1. See Shim Jae Hoon, "Man in the Middle," *Far Eastern Economic Review* (February 27, 1997):14–15.
2. Kevin Sullivan, "N. Korean Defector Leaves Beijing for Philippines," the *Washington Post* (March 19, 1997):A24.
3. Steven Mufson, "China Steps Back From Diplomatic Row," the *Washington Post* (February 16, 1997):A35.
4. Steven Mufson, "Premier Li Smooths Over Divisive Issues with U.S. as China's Congress Winds Up," *The Washington Post* (March 15, 1997):A24.
5. National Public Radio, Washington, D.C., March 5, 1997.
6. In July 1977, Deng Xiaoping attended the Tenth CCP Central Committee's Third Plenum, and was reinstated to all his offices: Party vice chairman and member of the Politburo Standing Committee; vice premier; and PLA chief-of-staff. He emerged as the CCP's third-ranking leader, after Hua Guofeng and Ye Jianying. A year later in December 1978 at the Third Plenum of the Eleventh Central Committee, Deng consolidated his power and achieved what Doak Barnett called "political primacy," although he never took the Party's top positions as did Mao Zedong. (By 1981, Hua Guofeng formally lost all three of his positions—party chairmanship to Hu Yaobang, premiership to Zhao Ziyang, and the CAC chairmanship to Deng Xiaoping.)
7. See Central Committee of the Communist Party of China, *Resolution on CPC History (1949–81)*. Beijing: Foreign Languages Press, 1981, p. 32.
8. Kenneth Lieberthal, "Domestic Politics and Foreign Policy," in Harry Harding, ed., *China's Foreign Relations in the 1980s*. New Haven, CT: Yale University Press, 1984, pp. 43–70.
9. Brantly Womack, "The Party and the People: Revolutionary and Postrevolutionary Politics in China and Vietnam." *World Politics* 39, no. 4 (July 1987):479–507.
10. For detailed analyses of the directions of Chinese foreign policy, see

Quansheng Zhao, *Interpreting Chinese Foreign Policy*, New York: Oxford University Press, 1996.

11. See Deng Xiaoping, "The Present Situation and the Tasks Before Us," January 16, 1980, in Deng Xiaoping, *Selected Works of Deng Xiaoping (1975–1982)*. Beijing: Foreign Language Press, 1984, p. 224.

12. See Deng Xiaoping, "Building A Socialism with A Specifically Chinese Character," June 30, 1984, in Deng Xiaoping, *Selected Works of Deng Xiaoping, vol. 3 (1982–1992)*. Beijing: Foreign Language Press, 1994, p. 73.

13. Some of the excellent examples in this regard are: Jonathan Unger, ed., *Chinese Nationalism*, Armonk, NY: M.E. Sharpe, 1996; Allen Whiting, "Chinese Nationalism and Foreign Policy After Deng," *The China Quarterly* 142 (June 1995), pp. 295–316; James Townsend, "Chinese Nationalism," *The Australian Journal of Chinese Affairs* 27 (1992), pp. 97–120; and Michel Oksenberg, "China's Confident Nationalism," *Foreign Affairs 65* No. 3 (1986/87), pp. 501–523.

14. "Regionalism" used here should not be confused with central-local relations used in China's domestic politics.

15. See Deng Xiaoping, "With Stable Policies of Reform and Opening to the Outside World, China Can Have Great Hopes for the Future," September 4, 1989, in Deng Xiaoping, *Selected Works of Deng Xiaoping, vol. 3 (1982–1992)*, Beijing: Foreign Languages Press, 1994, pp. 305–311.

16. Chae-Jin Lee, *China and Korea: Dynamic Relations*, Stanford, CA: Hoover Institution, 1996, p. 1.

17. Deng Lifeng, *Jianguo houjunshi xingdong quanlu* [The complete records of China's military actions since 1949]. Taiyuan: Shaanxi renmin chubanshe, 1994, pp. 312–313.

18. Jonathan Adelman and Chih-yu Shih, *Symbolic War: The Chinese Use of Force, 1840–1980*. Taipei: Institute of International Relations, National Chengchi University, 1993, p. 189.

19. There are many studies analyzing the Korean War. One may see, for example, Allen Whiting, *China Crosses the Yalu: The Decision to Enter the Korean War*, New York: The Macmillan Company, 1960; Bruce Cumings, *The Origins of the Korean War* (two volumes), Princeton: Princeton University Press, 1981 and 1990; Sergei Goncharov, John W. Lewis, and Xue Litai, *Uncertain Partners: Stalin, Mao, and the Korean War*, Stanford: Stanford University Press, 1993; and Jian Chen, *China's Road to the Korean War*, New York: Columbia University Press, 1994.

20. Some scholars believe that from the security perspective, China would not want to see a united Korea. Chalmers Johnson, for example, argues that Beijing "prefers a structurally divided Korea that is unable to play its full role as a buffer between China, Russia, and Japan, thereby giving China a determining influence on the peninsula." See C. Johnson, "Korea and Our Asia Policy," *The National Interest*, no. 41 (Fall 1995), p. 67.

21. "Korea's First High-Level Talks," *Beijing Review* 33, no. 39 (September 24–30, 1990):15.

22. Xu Baokang, "A Good Foundation for Solving the Nuclear Problem in the Korean Peninsula," *Renmin ribao*, December 2, 1991, 6.

23. Nayan Chanda, "Lesser Evil," *Far Eastern Economic Review* (December 21, 1995):17–18.

24. Ibid.

25. Nayan Chanda, "Chinese Welcome North Korea's Kim, But Relations Are Subtly Changing," *The Asian Wall Street Journal Weekly*, October 21, 1991, 24 and 26.

26. Hu Xueze and Bing Jinhu, "World Situation Unstable Despite Detente," *Beijing Review* 34, no. 2 (January 14–20, 1991):27–31.

27. Lincoln Kaye, "Friend in Need," *Far Eastern Economic Review* (October 17, 1991):14–15.

28. *Renmin ribao*, November 16, 1995, p. 1.

29. "South Korea: Aircraft for China," *Far Eastern Economic Review* (April 21, 1994):83.

30. "China Backs DPRK Reunification Efforts," *Beijing Review* 34, no. 20 (May 20–26, 1991):8–9.

31. Damon Darlin, "North Korea Reverses Position on U.N., Seeks Admission Separately From South," *The Asian Wall Street Journal Weekly*, June 3, 1991, 18 and 23.

32. Ted Morello, "Veto Vanishes: Thaw Clears Way to (United Nations) membership for Koreas," *Far Eastern Economic Review* (December 5, 1990):15.

33. *World Journal*, April 12, 1991, 1.

34. "Li Peng on Domestic and World Issues," *Beijing Review* 34, no. 26 (July 1–7, 1991):24–29.

35. It is interesting to note that the PRC has been firm in opposing Taiwan's U.N. membership, fearing the creation of "two Chinas." See next session for detailed analysis.

36. Nayan Chanda, "Seal of Disapproval," *Far Eastern Economic Review* (March 31, 1994:14–15.

37. South Korea: Information Gap," *Far Eastern Economic Review* (April 21, 1994):13.

38. "Making Haste Slowly: Seoul, Tokyo, Play up to Beijing on North Korean Issue," *Far Eastern Economic Review* (April 7, 1994):6. For a detailed analysis of China's assessment of North Korea, see Garrett Banning and Bonnie Glaser (1995), "Looking Across the Yalu: Chinese Assessments of North Korea."

39. Shim Jae Hoon, "Sitting on the Fence," *Far Eastern Economic Review* (November 10, 1994):15.

40. "Beijing Backs North Korea Pact," *South China Morning Post* (November 15, 1994):1.

41. Shim Jae Hoon, "Sitting on the Fence," *Far Eastern Economic Review* (November 10, 1994):15.

42. "North Korea Leader Pays 39th China Visit," *Beijing Review* 34, no. 41 (October 14–20, 1991):7.

43. "Zhonghan tongsheng ling riben shise" [Both China and South Korea criticized Japan], *Yazhou zhoukan* [The international Chinese newsweekly], November 26, 1995, p. 24.

44. "Nanhan pianzi pian chaoxian tongbao" [South Korean swindlers cheat minority Koreans in China], *Yazhou zhoukan* [The international Chinese newsweekly], November 25–December 1, pp. 50–51.

45. Ibid.

46. Charles Lee and Julian Baum, "Radioactive Ruckus, Nuclear-waste Plan Comes Between Taipei and Seoul," *Far Eastern Economic Review* (February 6, 1997):16.

9
Russia's Policies Toward the Two Koreas

Evgeniy P. Bazhanov

Traditional Policies

The Korean peninsula was the focus of Russia's attention after Czar Alexander II established his rule in 1860 over the maritime province adjacent to the "Hermit Kingdom." Ever since then, Russia, for various reasons and in different ways, has participated in the struggle of major powers (Japan, the United States, China) for control in this East Asian nation. Once in a while Russia would slacken its activities on the Korean peninsula, only to return there later with renewed vigor.

At the end of World War II Stalin's strategy in Korea included three goals: assurance of the USSR's national security; expansion of the sphere of communism's influence; and satisfaction of Russia's traditional great-power ambitions. The Soviet Union, although weakened by the bloody and destructive war against fascist Germany, spared no effort to build and strengthen a loyal regime in the North.[1] Stalin did not plan to extend his control to the South of Korea until the end of 1949. He feared an attack from the Republic of Korea (or South Korea, ROK) and tried hard to suppress the aggressive moods of North Korean leaders.[2] Stalin's approach changed in 1950; in April of that year the Soviet dictator officially blessed North Korea's invasion of the South.[3] The change was prompted by the victory of the communists in China, the Soviet acquisition of the atom bomb, general aggravation of Soviet relations with the West, and a perceived weakening of Washington's will to get involved militarily in Asia.

When Stalin realized that the war in Korea could not be won, his main preoccupation became to avoid a direct, large-scale conflict of the USSR with the United States and, at the same time, to keep Americans tied up in the Korean war as long as possible. According to the Soviet leader, in the interests of "socialism," the longer Washington was involved there, the better it was for the overall international situation.[4] After Stalin's death the new Soviet leadership hurried to terminate the bloody conflict on the Korean peninsula and adopted the policy of a status-quo, nonviolent competition between the North and the South.[5] A huge material and military aid was poured into North Korea (Democratic People's Republic of Korea, or DPRK).[6] However, by the beginning of the 1960s, ideological and political contradictions developed between Moscow and Pyongyang. Nikita Khrushchev was concerned that the leftist fever that infected Beijing and Pyongyang at the time would set the Far East afire in war.[7] The next Soviet leader, Leonid Brezhnev, and his administration tried to bring the DPRK back from its "tilt" toward the PRC. North Korea was perceived by the Kremlin as a strategic ally, a Far Eastern outpost in the overall confrontation of the USSR with the United States. While it disliked Kim Il Sung's *juche* and "cult of personality," Moscow continued to help its ally and ignore the ROK.[8]

With Gorbachev's ascent to power in Moscow in 1985, Soviet–North Korean cooperation intensified, including the development of peaceful nuclear energy. From the very outset of his rule, Gorbachev denounced inequality in relations among socialist countries and sympathized with intentions of smaller states to rely on their own resources and to have freedom of choice and actions. He expressed readiness to increase economic aid to partners and to extend his military, political and moral support to them. Moscow modified its attitude toward Pyongyang accordingly.

Officials in the Kremlin stressed that the DPRK was a strategic ally that was extremely important to the national interests of the Soviet Union and security in the Far East. A consolidation of friendly ties with Pyongyang was declared one of the priorities of Soviet foreign policy. Moscow began to offer its support to North Korea more actively and openly. Soviet pronouncements, tailored after those coming from Pyongyang, were increasingly critical of U.S. attempts to form a trilateral Washington–Tokyo–Seoul military alliance and to include South Korea in closed economic groupings. Contacts between the Soviet Union and the DPRK in military, scientific, cultural, and sports fields quickly intensified.

Kim Il Sung reacted with satisfaction to the changes in the Kremlin and to new Soviet policies. Pyongyang expressed its approval of Moscow's domestic and foreign policy initiatives and was receptive to advice, opinions, and requests made by the Soviet leadership. Pyongyang upheld Gorbachev's initial foreign policy proposal in the Asian-Pacific region and agreed to the expansion of Soviet military presence in the DPRK, the Soviet–North Korean military cooperation reached such magnitude that it provoked concern on the part of China.[9] Pyongyang later withdrew its reservations regarding Soviet–North Korean military cooperation, but only because of some improvement in relations between Beijing and Moscow.[10]

At the same time, however, irritating problems began to crop up in Soviet–North Korean relations, consequences of growing differences between the Soviet Union and the DPRK in various spheres. The factors that influenced Soviet–North Korean relations the most were the following:

1. Diverging foreign policy orientations. The foreign policy positions of the Soviet Union and the DPRK began to head in separate directions on several key issues, including approaches to inter-Korean ties, the geopolitical situation in the Asian-Pacific region, conceptual views on the contemporary world, and overall international relations. Pyongyang finally decided to reject the Soviet "new thinking" as heretical and "dangerous for socialism."[11] On its part, Moscow had became critical of Pyongyang: it qualified North Korea's behavior in the international arena as "irrational and unpredictable." Experts in the Kremlin stressed that Pyongyang refused to recognize new realities and was stuck on obsolete notions of class and ideological struggle.[12]

2. Events in Eastern Europe. The North Korean leadership was shocked by the events in Eastern Europe. Kim Il Sung and his associates were afraid that these events could be repeated in North Korea. Pyongyang was inclined to blame Gorbachev, not only for welcoming East European revolutions, but also for instigating them.

3. Democratization of Soviet society. Pyongyang disapproved of the democratization of Soviet society, seeing it as a serious ideological challenge. Soviet public opinion progressively rejected the social model of the DPRK as Stalinist and totalitarian. It is plausible to suggest that, had the East European scenarios been repeated in North Korea, they would have been approved by the majority of the politically aware public within the USSR.[13]

4. The Soviet–South Korean rapprochement. North Korea's irritation with Moscow grew as Soviet–South Korean dialogue intensified. Commenting on Kim Young Sam's visit to the Soviet Union in April 1990, the North Korean press called it "a hostile, criminal act."[14] Further, Pyongyang qualified the negotiations between Gorbachev and Roh Tae Woo in San Francisco in June 1990 as "unforgivable, criminal dealings."[15]

There were also other factors that contributed to the worsening of Soviet–North Korean bilateral ties. In 1988, the Soviet Union reduced its military aid to the North and, afterward, rejected all Pyongyang's attempts to strengthen cooperation between the two ministries of defense.[16] The volume of trade and economic cooperation between the USSR and North Korea declined as well. Whereas, driven by strategic and political motives, Moscow had often in the past sacrificed its interests in order to prop up its North Korean ally, now the Soviet leadership had no desire or the ability to do so. The Kremlin stressed that no matter how hard the Soviet Union tried to help its neighbor, it would be difficult for the DPRK to solve its problems unless the North Korean economy was reformed, unless the confrontation and arms race underway on the Korean peninsula ceased, and unless the North shed its semi-isolationist policy regarding business contacts with developed countries.[17]

As a result of general foreign policy changes within the Soviet Union and in Moscow's position toward the Korean peninsula, North Korean authorities came to the conclusion that the Soviet Union was no longer an ideological, military, and political ally of the DPRK. Pyongyang could not rely on the Soviet Union as a guarantor of North Korea's security or as a source of military and economic aid necessary to maintain the balance of forces on the Korean peninsula.

Evidence of Gorbachev's first action toward South Korea after his ascendancy to power is found in a Politburo document dated May 11, 1986. The document states that it was necessary to weaken the position of the United States in Korea and to elevate the Soviet role in the settlement of the Korean issue. In this context, the document suggested changes in Moscow's approach to South Korea, "which was becoming a factor of global, military-strategic balance." The following concrete measures were envisaged:

1. To take steps, initially unofficial, preferably through third countries, which would show Seoul that Moscow welcomed a more self-reliant and independent posture of South Korea vis-à-vis Washington and Tokyo. If Seoul went along these lines, contacts between the USSR

and South Korea could become possible at a later date.

2. In external propaganda about South Korea, to encourage an anti-American mood among its population.

3. To draft a concept of different methods of penetration into South Korea, targeting first its economy.[18]

According to these guidelines, Soviet diplomats and other officials established contracts with their South Korean counterparts in Washington, Paris, San Francisco, and Tokyo. Their message was clear: A dialogue could develop between Moscow and Seoul in the event the ROK freed itself from U.S. control.

The tone of Soviet propaganda concerning South Korea changed from hostile to neutral toward the local authorities. Blame for the problems of the Korean peninsula was now placed on the United States. Trade with South Korea was permitted through third countries, soaring to $133 million in 1986 (there had already been occasional business transactions between the two sides in previous years). Trade volume grew in 1987 by 50.4 percent to $200 million. Unofficial, very cautious contacts continued. However, there was no substantial improvement in Moscow-Seoul relations.

The real breakthrough came as a result of the Seoul Olympic Games of 1988. The primary reason for this change was that Moscow's perception of South Korea underwent a complete turnaround as a result of Seoul's surprisingly adroit conduct of the Olympic games. A great number of influential Soviet citizens visited the South and acquired firsthand knowledge of the friendliness of the local populace, the great interest by South Korea in developing mutually beneficial ties with the Soviet Union, and the spectacular achievements of South Korea in the economic and social fields.

A lobby developed within Gorbachev's immediate entourage that strongly advised the secretary general not to miss such "tremendous opportunities." As a result of the lobby's insistence, Gorbachev, in his Krasnoyarsk speech of September 16, 1988, immediately following the Olympic Games, indicated the opening of possibilities for business transactions with South Korea: "It seems that within the context of a general improvement in the situation on the Korean peninsula, opportunities can open up for forging economic ties with South Korea."[19]

Seoul's reaction was enthusiastic. To capitalize on the momentum, the Central Committee of the CPSU, together with the Council of Ministers of the USSR, adopted a resolution on the development of unofficial commercial, cultural, scholarly, sports, and other ties with the ROK.[20]

In December 1988 an agreement to have an exchange of trade represen-
tations in an unofficial capacity was achieved between the USSR and
the ROK. The Korean office in Moscow was virtually mobbed by hundreds of Soviet enterprises and ministries proposing different deals even
before it was fully established.

Pressure increased on Gorbachev to promote détente with South Korea even further. It came from two different directions: the Soviet Union
and South Korea. Gorbachev, however, was not yet ready to give diplomatic recognition to the ROK. Talking to Chinese Premier Li Peng in
May 1989, Gorbachev explained, "Kim Il Sung and the North Korean
leadership are probably afraid that we can go from trade contracts to
political ties with South Korea. This, however, is out of the question. We
are not going to agree on cross-recognition. At least for today, this is not
our policy."[21] Foreign Minister Eduard Shevardnadze made similar assurances to Pyongyang on a number of occasions.[22]

It seemed for a while that rapprochement between the USSR and the
ROK would slow and bog down at the unofficial level. While Moscow
was restrained by its fear of antagonizing Kim Il Sung, South Koreans
were repeatedly cautioned by Washington against "hasty actions" in relations with the Soviet Union. A slowdown in Seoul's overtures toward
the USSR was noticed in Moscow.[23]

However, Soviet–South Korean relations continued to move forward.
Both nations benefited from the changing international environment
characterized by a deepening détente, shrinking resistance to dialogue
between Moscow and Seoul from U.S. quarters, and flourishing trade
and economic cooperation of the ROK with the PRC and Eastern Europe. Normalization of Soviet–Chinese relations in May 1989 also contributed to reduced tensions on the Korean peninsula.

Later, two additional factors came into play. First, as mentioned earlier, regressive tendencies in USSR–DPRK relations intensified because
of ideological and political differences. Moscow's readiness to appease
North Korea was rapidly declining as Pyongyang strongly criticized
Moscow's internal and foreign policies. After the fall of the East European Stalinist regimes, both the Soviet government and the public underwent a profound ideological transformation. North Korea was no
longer considered to be an ideologically close country, but the South
was becoming closer in this sense to the USSR.

A second factor was the Soviet economy. As the economic situation
severely deteriorated, the importance of South Korea to the Soviet Union

increased: Moscow urgently needed and sought South Korean capital, technology, goods, and credits.[24]

On May 23, 1990, a personal envoy of President Gorbachev, A. Dobrynin, arrived in Seoul to discuss the first USSR–ROK summit. It was agreed that Gorbachev and Roh Tae Woo would meet in San Francisco on June 3 following Gorbachev's visit to Washington. The San Francisco summit was a complete success from Moscow's point of view. Its main outcome was an agreement on establishing diplomatic ties.[25]

Relations with South Korea immediately became a priority in Russia's Asian-Pacific foreign policy.[26] In just a few months after official relations commenced, Moscow-Seoul political dialogue could only be compared in intensity with that between the Kremlin and the White House. By the end of 1990, a solid foundation had been laid for the development of Soviet–South Korean ties in both the political and economic spheres.

In the spring of 1991, just before going to Japan, Gorbachev was asked by South Korean authorities to make a brief stopover on the island of Chejudo. Gorbachev was extremely pleased with his visit. On the way home, the Soviet leader commented that not only was the reception the warmest accorded to his party on a government level, but also the warmest by the general public as well. Gorbachev was impressed with President Roh Tae Woo's support of Moscow's policies.[27]

Special emphasis was made by the Soviet leadership on forging close economic links with the ROK. During the Chejudo negotiations, Gorbachev insisted on expanding the scope of cooperation from simple trade to investments, joint ventures, and joint efforts between Soviet and South Korean scholars and managers. Upon returning from his trip, Gorbachev stressed at a meeting with close associates that South Korea was the most promising partner of the Soviet Union in the East, and that opportunities there should not be lost.[28] Another dimension to the partnership between Moscow and Seoul, from Gorbachev's point of view, was the commonly shared fact that the Soviet Union and the ROK were both leaving behind similar totalitarian practices and trying to introduce democracy to their respective societies.[29]

In reality, though, the USSR and the ROK had only just begun the road to full cooperation and friendship. Right after the normalization of relations, the Soviet leadership felt somewhat disappointed. The Kremlin had expected to receive $6 billion in cash as aid, but the South Koreans now talked of $3 billion and only $1 billion of that in actual cash.[30]

Evolution of the Policies of the Democratic Russia toward the Two Koreas

After emergence of the democratic regime in Russia in 1991–92, relations between Moscow and Seoul continued to develop. South Korea looked like a bright spot in Russia's interactions with Asian-Pacific nations. South Korean companies, interested in Russia's natural resources and its military and space technology, kept a high profile in the Russian market. Some of them continued to look at opportunities for major investment, and Moscow, in turn, solicited Korean capital and pressed for resumption of the $3 billion loan that had been frozen by Seoul after collapse of the USSR. In the end, Yeltsin succeeded in regaining the loan.

Moreover, the two sides needed each other politically. The Kremlin played "the Korean card" to put pressure on Japan, and generally displayed an interest in the political role of South Korea in East Asia and, for the future, an interest in unification of the Korean nation. South Korea looked to the Russian connection as a counterbalance to American and Japanese influence in the region and as an instrument for deterring the North. Cultural links between Russia and South Korea were reinforced as well, partly due to the 600,000–strong Korean community in the former Soviet Union. It became fashionable in South Korea to send students to study and earn degrees in Russia, and politicians and prominent business people used trips to Moscow to build up their prestige at home. For example, a leader of the opposition Peace and Democracy Party, presidential candidate Kim Dae Jung, had defended his Ph.D. thesis in the Russian Diplomatic Academy. For Russians, South Korea remained one of the most attractive destinations, and the media marveled at the achievements of the ROK economy. Russo–South Korean relations were, in a way, almost a unique case of neighboring nations praising each other's achievements. South Koreans found that Russians praised them too much; Russians smiled when they heard overly optimistic comments about Russia's future from Koreans.

Up to the present, exchanges between Russia and the ROK have remained relatively dynamic. High-level political contacts are frequent, and the two sides regularly confirm a convergence of views on most international issues, including security and confidence-building measures on the peninsula. Joint adherence to democratic values is also expressed. Official Seoul continues to support the internal polices of President Yeltsin, and economic, cultural and other ties keep developing. Russian and South Korean navy squadrons recently exchanged official visits for the first time, and there was agreement to hold joint naval exercises in 1997.

However, not everything had been rosy between Moscow and Seoul; in 1993 the atmosphere in bilateral relations deteriorated to a certain degree. South Koreans were unhappy about a number of problems and the overall attitude of Moscow toward its partners. South Korean businessmen increasingly complained about the harsh conditions of the Russian market. A very negative reaction was expressed regarding Moscow's decision to postpone payments due on the $3 billion loan. Seoul newspapers called it "an act of arrogance beyond our understanding and patience." Notwithstanding requests and explanations from the Russian government (which Seoul characterized as "awkward"), Seoul froze the remaining half of the loan, and the opposition used this opportunity to attack the ruling party for grave mistakes in foreign and economic policy. Russians, in turn, showed displeasure at fluctuations in Seoul's behavior in the economic sphere, its unreliability, and the dishonesty of some Korean businessmen. Contention grew over the Russian moratorium on fishing in the central part of the Sea of Okhotsk and Moscow's demands to get compensation for the territory of the old diplomatic mission in Seoul.

In political relations, the Russian foreign minister in 1993 denounced demands by certain South Korean officials that Moscow renounce military clauses in the Soviet–North Korean alliance treaty of 1961. South Koreans were also bitterly disappointed when a special state committee in Russia concluded that Moscow could not be held responsible for the shooting down of the KAL 007 passenger plane over Sakhalin in 1983. The South Korean media called it a Cold War position, and Seoul demanded partial material compensation for "the unforgivable destruction" of the airliner. The Russian government, badly short of cash, limited itself to expressing apologies. South Koreans also complained about the discharge of nuclear waste by Russia in the Far Eastern seas, and Seoul was distressed by the Kremlin's sudden cancellation of a high-level economic meeting in May 1994.

The overall image of Russia in the ROK is further tarnished by the political instability and miserable socioeconomic conditions in the Russian Federation. Moscow's weakening international positions and its inability to influence North Korean behavior have reduced its political value in the eyes of South Korea.

Although the Russian government at times was irritated with Seoul, its basic attitude toward the ROK remains unchanged. Moscow is interested in promoting cooperation with Seoul and does not feel that relations are declining. Such optimism is shared by the Russian public at large, despite individual complaints about the operating style of South Korean businessmen and the "aggressiveness" of politicians. High hopes for South Korea's participation in the Russian economy, however, have diminished.

In June 1994 President Kim Young Sam paid an official visit to Russia, and the two sides confirmed their mutual desire to develop bilateral relations. Kim agreed to postpone repayment of the Russian debt to the ROK in exchange for Yeltsin's commitment to apply stronger pressure to oppose Pyongyang's nuclear weapons program.

Problems between Russia and South Korea on the whole seem minor and manageable if one compares them with the stormy Moscow-Pyongyang "alliance" in recent years.

The advent of the new anti-Communist regime in Moscow further complicated matters, as leaders of the democratic movement felt nothing but contempt for communists both inside and outside of Russia, and the DPRK, with its pure, Stalinist-type dictatorship, seemed the worst possible case. Such views were shared by most of the Russian media, which mercilessly attacked Kim Il Sung and his "kingdom." A strong belief existed in the Russian capital that the DPRK was doomed and would soon go down the drain, following the examples of the USSR and Eastern Europe. The argument was advanced in the government that Russia should distance itself from a decaying international pariah so as not to be compromised in the eyes of the world and the future democratic leaders of Korea.

Even less desire existed in the Kremlin to bolster the DPRK economically. Not only did Moscow not want to prolong the Kim Il Sung system, but economic cooperation with North Korea was simply not profitable, and crisis-stricken Russia curtailed all the aid that had been provided in the past for ideological and political reasons. Politically, the Kremlin now clearly disapproved of Pyongyang's intransigence in inter-Korean relations and its confrontational foreign policy. Russian democrats did not want to supply the DPRK with weapons and they did not want to be linked to North Korea's security by guarantees or by anything else.

Pyongyang reacted to changes in the former Soviet Union with disgust and fear. The new Russian ideological and political order was not merely alien to North Korean communists but was seen as a source of subversive influence on their own people. They felt that this influence could not be simply spontaneous, that Russian anti-Communists would join Seoul, Washington, and Tokyo in plotting to destroy socialism in the northern half of the Korean peninsula. Negative feelings toward Moscow were reinforced by a disastrous economic situation in the DPRK, caused in part by the cessation of Russian assistance. The drastic decline in supplies from Russia frustrated the DPRK military programs and deepened an alarmist mood in Pyongyang.

Thus, Russo–North Korean relations got off to a bad start in 1992. While continuing to develop ties with the ROK, Moscow ignored political contacts with the DPRK. The Russian foreign minister declared that Moscow would stop all military cooperation with the North and pressured it to drop its nuclear plans. Yeltsin described the 1961 Soviet–North Korean security treaty as existing only on paper, and Information Minister Poltoranin, while in Tokyo, advised the Japanese not to pay war reparations to the DPRK to prevent prolongation of this repressive, obsolete regime.[31]

Pyongyang initially responded in kind, but with time it decided to ease tensions. It was necessary to keep channels open with a big neighboring state upon which North Korea still depended in many ways (half of the DPRK's trade volume remained connected to Russia). Besides, the Russian Federation continued to experience internal upheavals, and hopes were rekindled in Pyongyang that the former friend could still come back to its senses. Moscow agreed to reciprocate by restoring a working relationship, encouraged by the argument that expansion of links with Pyongyang was advantageous to everyone, including South Korea. The ability of the Kremlin to influence Kim Il Sung in the right direction would be welcomed in all quarters.[32]

At the end of summer 1992, the Russian Foreign Ministry advanced a thesis that Moscow should seek balanced relations with both South and North Korea, and that it was important for Russians and Americans to maintain their security arrangements on the peninsula in order to ensure stability. But these attempts to patch up differences with Pyongyang and overcome the government's South Korean "tilt" did not succeed. By 1993 Russo–North Korean relations had reassumed an almost hostile character. The sharpest controversy grew up around the question of Pyongyang's compliance with the nuclear Non-Proliferation Treaty (NPT). In 1993 Russia stopped the delivery of three nuclear plants. Foreign Minister Kozyrev stressed that there was the danger that other "atomic candidates" would follow the North Korean example, creating a nuclear zone along the southern borders of the Commonwealth of Independent States.[33] Moscow's pressures and threats to support international sanctions provoked counterthreats and reprisals by North Korea, which declared a fifty-mile military zone in the Japan Sea that hurt Russia's interests and was considered by the Kremlin to be illegal and liable to military incidents between the two "allies." Pyongyang also warned that it would block projects involving Russia and the two Koreas, and loudly denounced—as did the ROK—Russia's discharges of nuclear waste in the Japan Sea.

There were several real incidents. Russia ordered home its scientists who had secretly agreed to help Korean military programs. Sharp criticism was directed against Korean workers' brigades logging in Russia's Far East, labeling them as concentration camps and as centers of smuggling. Moscow granted North Korean refugees political asylum and gave them permission to emigrate to the ROK. It also agreed to allow repatriation of Sakhalin Koreans to the South. These acts increased Pyongyang's irritation with the Kremlin. Economic cooperation continued to dwindle as Moscow sternly demanded repayment of the old $3.5 billion debt, refused to buy inferior North Korean goods, and fell from the DPRK's first to third largest trading partner. In mid-1994 Yeltsin further infuriated Kim Il Sung by threatening to support international sanctions against North Korea if it persisted in its attempts to acquire nuclear weapons capability. Moscow suggested that an international conference be held on the issue and, if it failed to achieve its objective, to proceed with sanctions. Some initial differences between the Kremlin and the White House on the issue were rather quickly overcome as a result of Moscow's statements.[34]

Pyongyang was disgusted with Russia's decision to give Seoul secret archives on the Korean War, with an official admission in Russia (in speeches, textbooks, public documents, etc.) of the fact that the North attacked the South in 1950. Unrelenting attacks of the Russian media on Kim Il Sung and his son and on the internal situation and foreign policy of the DPRK added to Pyongyang's trauma.

Mutual dissatisfaction was intensified because of the 1961 Treaty. In January 1993 Moscow gave a new interpretation of the first article of that document. It was stressed that military assistance would not be provided by Russia to the DPRK automatically, but only in case of an "unprovoked aggression" and exclusively on the basis of Moscow's own appraisal, as well as in accordance with the Russian Constitution. This position was reiterated on a number of occasions by top officials (though sometimes statements from the Kremlin sounded contradictory). Finally, on August 7, 1995, the Russian foreign ministry presented the DPRK with a draft of a new treaty. North Koreans were told that the existing treaty no longer corresponded to the realities of life and had to be replaced. Pyongyang agreed to examine the draft.

The problems created in Russo–North Korean relations in the late 1980s to early 1990s still exist. However, a number of important factors have been moving the Kremlin lately to a more positive posture vis-à-vis the DPRK.

There is growing awareness in the Kremlin of a potential danger of renewed hostilities on the Korean peninsula, and Moscow wants to resume a more active role in mediating differences between Seoul and Pyongyang, especially since it has realized that the North Korean regime will not necessarily collapse in the immediate future and that its collapse may actually create even greater security risks. Such an approach requires an improvement of relations with the DPRK and a more balanced policy on the peninsula.

Great power ambitions also push Moscow toward North Korea. Restoration of links with North Korea is justified on the grounds that Moscow created Kim Il Sung's regime and spent much time and money nourishing it, and while leaders come and go, people's memories and friendships endure. A powerful pro-North lobby, consisting of military men, diplomats, scholars, and former technical advisers to Pyongyang, advances such a thesis. These feelings are reinforced by envy toward American activities in the DPRK. It seems to the Russians that the United States is winning Moscow's ally over to the American side. This is evident in the North's attempts to sign a peace treaty exclusively with the United States, in the Seoul-Washington proposal on four-power peace talks, and in the forthcoming cooperation between the DPRK and the United States in the nuclear field.

Russian ambassador to the DPRK, Valerii Denisov, argues that the United States is undertaking a broad offensive, irrespective of Russian interests, aiming at expanding U.S. influence over the northern part of the Korean peninsula in order to become the sole master of Korea's destiny.[35] Ambassador Denisov stresses that an active Moscow does not coincide with American national interests.[36]

At the same time, as observers in the Kremlin notice, Washington

still keeps basically unchanged security links with the ROK and continues to dominate in the South. Russia also feels that its prestige and
influence in the ROK have diminished lately, precisely because of
Moscow's weakening position in the North. Experts remind that back in
the 1980s South Korea decided to develop the Soviet connection because Moscow seemed able to influence positively the North Korean
leadership. However, as soon as the Kremlin and the Blue House for-
malized mutual relations, Seoul began to pressure Russia against continuing military and other aid to the DPRK. When Russia did downgrade
its cooperation with the North, the South, instead of being satisfied, lost
respect for the Kremlin since it now lacked leverage vis-à-vis the North.
So Moscow, taking such reactions of the ROK into consideration, feels
that improvement of relations with the DPRK, among other things, will
help to restore Russian credibility and prestige in the South.[37]

Anatolii Torkunov, rector of Moscow State University of International
Relations, notes that only by exerting influence over both Korean states
can Moscow "stay in the game" and secure its position vis-à-vis a future
reunified Korea. A deterioration of relations with the DPRK has "limited Russia's possibilities to positively influence developments in the
immediate neighborhood of its border."[38] In its turn, China is cited nowa-
days in Russia as a perfect example of how to manage relations with the
DPRK. It is pointed out that the PRC has been able to develop excellent
rapport and close economic cooperation with the South without undermining its position with the North.[39]

Economic considerations are a third driving motive for Russia's activities in the DPRK. Moscow has recognized that the only way to get back
North Korean debts is to smooth tensions with the DPRK. It is deemed
profitable to continue employing North Korean wood cutters and other
workers in the Russian Far East and to buy the DPRK's valuable raw
materials in exchange for finished goods. Russia may also someday participate in the modernization of the numerous Soviet-built enterprises in
the DPRK (by providing spare parts for them). Deliveries of nuclear reactors to the North and involvement in the development of the free economic zones in the border areas are mentioned among economic aims of
Russia vis-à-vis North Korea.[40] Another argument is that only through a
joint effort with the DPRK would it be possible to realize some of the
large-scale Russian-South Korean projects, such as a gas pipeline from
Yakutia to the ROK via the Northern part of the Korean peninsula.[41]

The ideological factor, that is, spreading the democratic gospel, no longer figures prominently in Russia's policies toward the DPRK. North Korea is no longer abhorred by the ruling elite of Russia as it was two years earlier. As for various groups of the opposition, the DPRK has become their new "darling." The Russian communist party established permanent contacts with the North Korean ruling circles, regularly sending to the North high-level delegations. In joint statements and other documents the two sides swear to unite "in the struggle for socialism and against reaction." Russian communists use every opportunity to praise *juche* ideology—"great achievements" of the DPRK in the socialist construction and in pursuing an "independent, proud" foreign policy.[42]

Russia's strongest nationalist party, the Liberal-Democratic party, headed by V. Zhirinovsky, is even more eloquent in praising Pyongyang. During his visit to the DPRK in October 1994 Zhirinovsky said: "The world is now in the grip of unrest and disorder, but Korea is advancing in close unity based on self-reliance and its own political philosophy, thus becoming a country envied even by Russia, which was once the strongest power, and an oasis for the world."[43] On June 4, 1996, during Russia's State Duma hearings on the Korean problem, the chairman of the Duma's Committee on Geopolitics, Mitrofanov (Zhirinovsky's "shadow" foreign minister) roundly denounced the Kremlin's policies in Korea. Mitrofanov claimed that Moscow had betrayed the DPRK, joined the international anti-Korean chorus, and, as a result, North Koreans who had "loved" Russia and Russians "had no choice but to consider us as at least an unfriendly country."[44]

Mitrofanov insisted that North Korea was a "strategic ally, who was betrayed for the sake of futile and senseless economic contacts with the ROK."[45] The Liberal-Democratic party harshly criticized South Korea's policies toward Russia as "insulting." From its point of view Russia "had to warn and threaten South Korea with strong actions in order to make it more respectful."[46] The Liberal Democrats demanded resumption of military cooperation with the DPRK and, in fact, supported North Korean nuclear programs. A nuclear-armed North Korea is viewed by them as a contributing factor of Russia's defense against Washington and its allies.[47]

Since 1994 Moscow has been persistently trying to put its relations with Pyongyang back on the normal track. Of special importance was a visit by Russian Deputy Foreign Minister A. Panov to the DPRK in September 1994, following Kim Il Sung's death. Panov conveyed Yeltsin's message to Kim Jong Il and reached an agreement with North Korean counterparts to activate bilateral ties on the basis of the following principles: respect for mutual sovereignty, noninterference in each other's internal affairs, and freedom to choose the social model.

Lately the political and economic dialogue between the Russian Federation (RF) and the DPRK has become more vigorous. In 1996 a Russian governmental delegation, headed by Vice Premier V. Ignatenko, visited North Korea and held the first session of the Joint RF–DPRK commission on trade, economic, scientific, and technical cooperation. Then, a State Duma delegation, headed by its speaker V. Seleznev, also toured the North, and finally, there was a round of consultations at the level of deputy foreign ministers.

Both sides have agreed to renew the treaty of 1961 while keeping the original intact.[48] In January 1997 Deputy Foreign Minister G. Karazin visited the DPRK and fruitfully discussed provisions of the new treaty. The discussion continued in the second part of 1997. A dialogue between Moscow and Pyongyang has been resumed on the Korean settlement.[49] All in all, it can be said that the political climate in Russo–North Korean relations has been slightly improved. Russia is a more active player in this process, since North Korea aims now at getting closer to the United States. The "Russian card" is useful for teasing Americans, but Pyongyang is cautious not to overplay that card.

There are also signs of a movement in bilateral economic relations. Between 1988–91 trade between the two countries fell by about 60 percent; between 1992–94 it further decreased from US$600 million to US$140 million. Russia's share of North Korean imports fell from over 60 percent in 1988 to less than 10 percent.[50] The fall of oil deliveries was especially painful to the DPRK's economy. In 1996 a number of agreements and understandings were reached that could reactivate the bilateral cooperation. They concern the following issues:

- revitalization of cooperative ties between Russian organizations and North Korean enterprises built in the past with Soviet assistance (examples: the Kim Chaek metallurgy plant, plants of car batteries and microelectrical engines);
- joint development in the DPRK of magnesite deposits;
- joint development in Yakutia of coal deposits;
- normalization of the process of wood-cutting in the Russian Far East;
- resumption of cargo shipment lines between Russia and North Korea;

- construction of a gas pipeline, Yakutia–South Korea, through North Korean territory;
- repayment of the DPRK's debts to the RF;
- reinstitution of clearing and barter methods to bilateral trade;
- establishment of joint ventures (there are now about forty of them);
- utilization of North Korean workers in agriculture, construction, and mining in Russia;
- modernization of Soviet-built enterprises in South Korea.

Military cooperation between Russia and North Korea is also being gradually restored. There is an exchange of defense ministry delegations on the basis of the agreement signed back in 1992.[51] Russia is ready to resume military supplies to the DPRK, underlining the fact that North Korea is a member of the United Nations enjoying equal rights and not subject to any sanctions, so there exists no legal obstacle to commercial deliveries of arms and weapons.[52]

At the same time officials point out that Russia can only supply weapons to meet defensive requirements of Pyongyang (not offensive), as well as on the basis of commercial profitability and taking into consideration the overall security situation in the Far East. Zhirinovsky's Liberal-Democratic party favors subsidies for the supplying of weapons to "a friendly North Korean state."[53]

On the whole, Russia's objectives on the Korean peninsula can be summarized as follows:

1. maintaining stability in Korea;
2. establishing balanced relations with two Koreas;
3. helping with inter-Korean dialogue;
4. cooperating with other big powers in Korea; and
5. opposing domination of the Korean peninsula from external forces.

Notes

1. For details see Natalia Bazhanova. "Between Dead Dogmas and Practical Requirements." Seoul: *The Korea Economic Daily*, 1992, pp. 19–169 (Korean language).

2. Natalia Bazhanova. "Samaya Zagadochnya voina XX stoletia." ("The most mysterious war of the XX century"). Moscow: *New Times*, 1996, no. 6, p. 30.

3. See Evgueni Bajanov. "Assessing the Politics of the Korean War, 1949–1951." *Cold War International History Project Bulletin*. Washington, D.C.: Woodrow Wilson International Center for Scholars, Winter 1995–1996, issues 6–7, pp. 54, 87.

4. See Natalia Bajanova "Assessing the Conclusion and Outcome of the Korean War." Paper at the conference "The Korean War," Washington D.C., July 24–25, 1995, p. 7.

5. Ibid, pp. 8–10.

6. See Natalia Bajanova. Vneshneeconomicheskie svyazi KNDR (DPRK's Foreign Economic Relations). Moscow: *Vostochnya Literatura*, 1993, pp. 8–99.

7. Nikita Khrushchev. *Memuary* (Memories). Moscow: Mezdunarodnye otnoshenia, 1991, pp. 342–345.

8. Eugene Bazhanov. "Soviet Policy towards South Korea under Gorbachev." In Il Yung Chung (ed.), *Korea and Russia. Towards the 21st Century.* Seoul: Sejong Institute, 1992, p. 82–83.

9. Ibid, p. 85.

10. N. Bazhanova. Vneshneekonomicheskie svyazi KNDR. Moscow: *Vostochnya Literatura*, 1993, p. 134.

11. See Eugene Bazhanov, "Soviet Policy Towards South Korea under Gorbachev." In Il Yung Chung (ed.), *Korea and Russia. Towards the 21st Century.* Seoul: Sejong Institute, 1992, pp. 84–85.

12. The All-Russian Center for Preservation of Contemporary Documents (VTsKhSD) (Moscow), File 8, list 6, units of storage (4 of S.) 205, pp. 130–131.

13. Such predictions could be found in at least 50 to 60 articles published in major Soviet newspapers throughout 1990. E. Bazhanov and N. Bazhanova, "Soviet Views on North Korea," in *Asian Survey*, vol. 31, no. 12, December 1991, pp. 1124, 1135–1138.

14. *Nodong shinmun*, April 10, 1990, p. 2.

15. *Nodong shinmun*, June 12, 1990, p. 2.

16. VTsKhSD, File 8, list 6, collection 153, pp. 60–62.

17. N. Bazhanova. "No Elder and Younger Brothers." *Pravda*, 6 August, 1990.

18. ARCPCD, File 8, List 6, u. of s. 205, p. 162.

19. *Pravda*, 18 September 1988.

20. ARCPCD, File 8, List 6, u. of s. 205, pp. 190–192.

21. Negotiations between M. Gorbachev and Li Peng, 16 May 1989.

22. "On the Visit to the DPRK of the Foreign Minister of the USSR Eduard Shevardnadze." *Pravda*, 24 December 1983.

23. ARCPCD, File 8, List 6, u. of s. 192, p. 114.

24. *Pravda*, 18 August 1989.

25. ARCPCD, File 8, List 6, u. of s. 109, p. 17–18.

26. *Pravda*, 1 October 1990.

27. "A Summit Between the Presidents of the USSR and the Republic of Korea." *Izvestiya*, 20 April 1991.

28. "Developing Ties with Far Eastern Neighbors." *Komsomolskaya Pravda*, 28 April 1991.

29. *Trud*, 20 April 1991.

30. ARCPCD, File 8, List 6, u. of s. 92, pp. 80–81.

31. See Eugene Bazhanov and Natacha Bazhanova, "The Evolution of Russian-Korean Relations," in *Asian Survey*, vol. 34, no. 9, September 1994, pp. 792–793.

32. Ibid.

33. A. Kozyrev's interview, *Izvestiya*, 18 June, 1994, p. 1.

34. Stephen Foye, "Joint Russian-US statement on North Korea," in RFF/RI, *News Briefs*, vol. 3, no. 26 (1994), p. 4.

35. Valerii Denisov, "Rossiya na Koreiskom poluostrove," in *Segodnya*, November 4, 1994, p. 4.

36. Valerii Denisov, "Otluchenie ot integracii," in *Nezavisimya gazeta*, 26 August, 1994, p. 4.

37. See E. Bajanov and N. Bajanova, *DPRK Report*, July–August 1996, Moscow, ICIP, p. 5.

38. Anatolii Torkunov, *Problemi bezopasnosti na Koreiskom poluostrove.* Moscow: MGIMO, 1990, p. 14.

39. *Obschaya gazeta*, 20 July, 1996, p. 3.

40. See Natalia Bajanova, "The economy of the DPRK," *Macro-issues*, Moscow, ICIS, 1995, pp. 35–41.

41. Proceedings of a seminar on Russo–North Korean relations, Moscow, ICIP, July 11, 1996, p. 28.

42. N. Stepanov, "KNDR na vernom puti (The DPRK is on the right track)," in *Pravda*, September 6, 1996.

43. KNCA, Pyongyang, October 4, 1994, quoted from SWB FE/2118 D/4, October 5, 1994.

44. *The DPRK Report*, May–June 1996, Moscow, ICIP, pp. 3.

45. Ibid.

46. Ibid.

47. R. Ivanov, "Koreiisky factor (The Korean Factor)," in *Patriot*, August 10, 1996, p. 3.

48. *The DPRK Report*, May–June 1996, p. 2.

49. *The DPRK Report*, May–June 1996, p. 3.

50. Russia's Ministry of External Economic Relations. A report, Moscow, 1996, pp. 15, 20–21.

51. A. Torkunov, E. Ufimtsev, *Koreiskya problema: novy vsglyad* (The Korean Problem: a New View). Moscow 1995, p. 181.

52. Diplomaticheskii Vestnik, MID Rossiiskoi Federatsii, 1996, March, p. 30.

53. *The DPRK Report*, May–June 1996, p. 4.

Part IV
The United States and the Two Koreas

10

The Two Koreas and Northeast Asia in the Post–Cold War Era

Donald P. Gregg

I will try to weave together some thoughts in a framework of how countries and civilizations can relate to each other effectively in the post–Cold War era. There is a very distinguished American scholar who thinks we can't: Sam Huntington. Professor Kim referred to his book, *The Clash of Civilizations*, and I've just written an article trying to refute Huntington's thesis because I think it is a recipe for a disaster.

Let me read a couple of things that Huntington has to say. He says the essential aim of the United States and all the western leaders should be "to preserve and renew the unique qualities of western civilization." As for the United States, Huntington says it should adopt "an Atlanticist policy of close cooperation with its European partners, one that will protect and promote the interests, values, and cultures of the precious and unique civilization they share." He then turns to Latin America, which he feels may be able to get its act together so that it can join Europe and North America as what he calls "the West." Then, referring to Asia, he says no such conversion is possible with Asian society. Instead, Asia is likely to pose continuing economic and political challenges to the United States specifically and the West, more generally.

Huntington's prediction is that the world is going to divide into a tripolar world, with the West, Asia, and the Islamic world contending

This is a revised version of Ambassador Gregg's oral presentation.

along cultural issues that he believes will be even more difficult to deal with than the balance of power or military-economic issues, which have been the traditional concerns of this century. Some of the recent developments in Northeast Asia tend to bear out the threat that is implicit in the thesis that Huntington lays out. Just a year ago, for example, China resorted to firing missiles in the Taiwan Strait and the United States responded by sending two carrier battle groups into the straits. When two countries of that size are reduced to that sort of ugly muscle-flexing, it would indicate that the dialogue that had led up to such an event had been either totally wrong or nonexistent. In November 1996, I met with Ambassador James Laney, and as recently as last November he said to me that Jim Deutch, the then director of the CIA, had been unable to get from the South Koreans any assurance that they would not retaliate against North Korea on the submarine incident without telling us in advance. And he said that he had been totally unable to convince the South Koreans that the United States was not going to suddenly fall into the arms of North Korea and abandon the South.

Bob Gallucci spoke at the March 1997 SMU conference of the cabinet meeting that was providentially interrupted by a call from Jimmy Carter from Pyongyang saying, "I've got good news for you." It might be interesting for me to relate a follow-up meeting in the White House three or four days later where President Clinton and his team were trying to digest the very counter-intuitive message that Jimmy Carter had sent, which was that North Korea wanted a new relationship with the United States. And so, the White House reached out to a very disparate group of people including Jim Lilley, myself, Selig Harrison, along with several other people. We were invited into the White House to discuss what President Carter's message meant and whether it could be taken seriously. The underlying thread of this meeting was, "Can we take this message from Jimmy Carter seriously or not?" It was interesting the way it came out. One of the pivotal factors was the fact that Jimmy Carter had taken with him a man fully fluent in Korean, a foreign service officer named Dick Christensen who is now our Charge in Seoul. Dick had been able to hear the full flow of conversation both ways and verified what had been said. Kim Il Sung had been saying, "I want a new relationship with the United States." He'd been saying that to people like Billy Graham and Bill Taylor. But the message hadn't really come through because it was so counterintuitive. I think the reason he said that was that the success of the South Korean *Nordpolitik* had isolated North Korea. They (the North) had no concessional aid from anyone else, and they were facing a very different political landscape. There was a continuing threat from Japan and so Kim, who was a very smart, ruthless man, made the essential decision: let's reach out to the United States.

So we decided to take that seriously and that led to the negotiation of the framework agreement. But it also led to what I think was the cause of an estrangement with the South Koreans, which still sputters on. Kim Il Sung unfortunately didn't live long enough to hold his scheduled meeting with Kim Young Sam, and the statement that came out of Washington very quickly after his death was hard for me to fathom. I don't know who wrote it and I don't know where it came from, but from my visit at the White House, I can imagine people saying, "Kim Il Sung seemed like such a nice guy, isn't it too bad that he died." That was the underlying tone that angered the South Koreans because they have a long memory of what Kim Il Sung has done to them starting in 1950, and I think that is what created the gap between us, in which the North Koreans have maneuvered quite successfully ever since.

Things have gotten better. I think Madeleine Albright is going to be an excellent secretary of state and her February 1997 visit to Seoul was successful. I think she has started an engagement with Korea but I agree with Dave Steinberg that these are like blips on a fever chart. They are not reflective of any real change in the tension that exists. Now why does this tension exist? I saw parts of it when I was Ambassador. In three-and-a-half years in Seoul, I never was able to make a publicized appearance on any college campus anywhere in Korea. Once a Korea University professor invited me to come over to speak to his class. He said "I will not announce it and if you've got the guts to do it, I've got the guts to hold a class." And so, I went over and did it and there were five hundred riot police outside the gate.

I got an honorary degree from Sogang University when I left and it was given to me at night during Christmas vacation to avoid starting a riot. One of my favorite projects is to try to get Koreans, Japanese, and Americans to talk to each other because I feel that the hope of stability in Northeast Asia lies in that triangular relationship. While I was still in Korea, I sponsored a conference at the University of Pusan. We all thought Pusan had a long history of Japanese involvement and so I went down there, and lo and behold, they wouldn't let me on the campus to preside over my own conference.

So, something was bugging the students. Part of it was the Taft-Katsura Pact, part of it was the perception of arrogance on our part, and I think part of it was their lack of surety that we really want to stay involved in Asia on a long-term basis. They don't want to be abandoned.

The Koreans have an extraordinary sense of history and I like that. I think they have the feeling that the evils of history need rectification and they go about it with a vengeance, quite differently from the Japanese. But, I think that our failure to engage China has sent a signal of doubt about our long-range staying power in Asia to everybody. I think that our failure to begin to talk to *ourselves* about what we intend to do with our troops in Northeast Asia after the North Korean threat is gone, is also real evidence to Asians that we really haven't made up our mind about what we're going to do. Now there are certainly people in Washington who can't wait for the North Korean threat to be over so they can say, "OK, bring the boys home, let's save all that money." There will be people in Okinawa who will say, "Yankee, go home," and there will be a certain number of students in Korea who will say, "Yankee, go home," and if we have not built a policy that ensures against that, that may well happen. I think that would be a tragic policy failure on our part. But there certainly was nothing in the first Clinton years that really seriously addressed what we intend to do long-range.

I think that kind of thing plays into the Huntington thesis because it can be taken as evidence by Asians that Asia is a second-class policy priority for America. They believe we will make up our mind about what we're going to do on our time, and will play it by ear, not really thinking things out in advance. So I think we stand a little bit guilty as charged there.

The Huntington thesis is also terribly dangerous in terms of what it says about military security because if we turned inward culturally, as he suggests we should, our ability to maintain troops in Japan and Korea, which I think are really the foundation for stability in that area, will not be sustainable. If we began to turn inward culturally, I think the Asians would begin to regard our troops in Korea and Japan as the Sioux tribe used to regard the forts that we built out in their territory during the Indian Wars, as hostile outposts of an uncaring larger force. In the 1990s we can't maintain that sort of a presence, and so we would have to withdraw. And every television camera in the area would be on us as we withdrew. A signal of American irresolution would have been sent all over the area. We must not let that happen.

I think one of the most hopeful things that has happened in Northeast Asia recently was the negotiation by the United States of a Statement of Regret from the North Koreans about their submarine incident of September 1996. I go a long way back in Asia. I was in Japan in 1968 when the North Koreans seized the Pueblo. I was part of a very concerted effort to find a way, overt or covert, where we could hit back at the North Koreans for what they had done to us. I was part and parcel of that, and we were furious. We could not find anything effective to do that would not either have gotten the entire crew killed or risked the starting of a second Korean War. That same pattern held through a whole series of ghastly incidents perpetrated by the North. You could start with the Blue House Raid in 1968. You could go on to the digging of tunnels under the Demilitarized Zone (DMZ) discovered in 1972, the horrendous attempt to kill President Chun Doo Hwan in Rangoon in 1983, the ax murders in the DMZ of two American officers in 1976, or the blowing up of a Korean airliner in 1987. For none of these incidents were the North Koreans ever punished or ever caused to utter one word of regret. (I think after the ax murders there was some carefully couched statement because that had involved the killing of two Americans and it was in front of the eyes of the West.) So for the North Koreans to be forced to make their statement and to not only say they were sorry but that they would take steps to see that it didn't happen again, is a very significant thing. I think it was only possible to negotiate that because we still are credible to the North Koreans in a military sense through the maintenance of our troops in Korea and, there, through repeated Team Spirit exercises.

I used to teach a graduate-level course at Georgetown University called "Force and Diplomacy." A lot of my students took the course to try to disprove the title. Most of them I think I convinced that force and diplomacy work hand-in-hand. If you don't believe that, think of how ineffective we were in Bosnia until we hit the Bosnian-Serbs with a little NATO air power. So for us to stay engaged in Asia, we need a military base. For us to maintain that base we have to engage with our Asian friends in a more thinking, sensitive way than perhaps we have done in the past. We need to sit down and discuss these things out of the limelight in a way where the Asians can know that we are truly serious about working with them as friends and on how we can continue to make good on the gains that we achieved during the Cold War.

I feel that the fruits of the Cold War lie in our ability to trade, with our former enemies as well as our old friends. It is an opportunity to tie the world together in new forms of economic interdependence that may make the making of war more difficult than it has been in this century. But I don't see this outreach, which is spearheaded by the business community, supported politically. I see economic expansion but political contraction or stasis. And for the economic expansion to be sustained over time, it needs to be supported by political thought, which also is reaching out. We are not doing that as well as we should. Somebody mentioned at the SMU conference in 1997 that we were going to keep the pressure on the Koreans to continue to open up their markets even when they have asked for a moratorium. We became the largest exporter of foreign goods to Korea last year. We exported $26.6 billion worth of goods to Korea in 1996. We have a $4 billion trade surplus with Korea but we don't seem to be willing to cut them any slack. I think that's a mistake. We have a huge deficit with Taiwan, with China and Japan. So there needs to be more connections made between what we're doing economically and what we're doing politically.

As I was looking around, trying to refute Huntington, it was very difficult to find anybody who set out a framework that I thought might work for the rest of this century and the first decades of the next. And I finally came up with a quote from George Kennon made in 1966, thirty years ago this month. I used to hand this out to my students at Georgetown because I thought it was a marvelous way for a large power to outline a philosophical approach to foreign relations. Kennon calls it "the quest for concept." He defines concept as a blending of purpose and principle. And his definition of concept is this, "What we need to strive for is concept based on a modest, unsparing view of ourselves, on a careful examination of our national interest devoid of all utopian and universalistic pretensions and upon a sober discriminating view of the world beyond our borders. A view that takes account of the element of relativity in all antagonisms and friendships but sees in others neither angels nor devils, neither heroes nor blackguards. A concept finally, which accepts it as our purpose, not to abolish all violence and injustice from the workings of international society but to confine those inevitable concomitants of the human predicament to levels of intensity that do not threaten the very existence of civilization."

I think the strength of that is that it could be said by a Confucian, it could be said by a Muslim, and it was said by George Kennon who is still very much at the forefront of policy thinking.

So I am going to close with that. I think when there is weak foreign policy being conducted by governments, there is a greater need than ever for NGOs and universities to step to the fore.

11

The U.S.–North Korea Agreed Framework and the Korea Policy of the United States

Robert L. Gallucci

I would like to present an orientation to U.S. policy toward Korea beginning with the negotiation of the Agreed Framework and moving to the current situation. The theme I would like to weave through the presentation is the connection between U.S. interests and U.S. policy.

So, let me begin then with an interpretation of the Agreed Framework and how it relates to our interests. If I can please take you back to the spring of 1993. Obviously, you can start this discussion at any point in the flow of events, but there is something special about the spring of 1993: it was the beginning of the first Clinton administration and it was the period in which the North Korean nuclear situation, as we came to know it, began to ripen to crisis. I would identify U.S. policy in the new administration, in the Clinton administration, as a continuation of the Bush administration policy. We defined U.S. interests as first to defend South Korean sovereignty, and second to prevent the proliferation of weapons of mass destruction globally, but particularly in Northeast Asia. The objective, of course, was to do both of those, if possible, without military conflict. The Clinton administration also emphasized another traditional U.S. interest: to promote democracy and free market, the free enterprise system. This was the general approach taken by the administration in terms of how we defined our interests.

So as we looked at the North Korean case in 1993, policy objectives flowed from those interests. The political objective, in the first instance, followed from what North Korea had done. They had refused to accept so-called special inspections from the International Atomic Energy Agency (IAEA) in Vienna. The North said that it would not accept inspectors at sites that had been identified by the Agency, and when the Agency reported the matter to the Security Council, the North Koreans not only rejected safeguards, but said they were going to withdraw from the Nuclear Non-Proliferation Treaty (NPT). This would have been the first time any state had ever done that under what you might call "not very good circumstances." So, the first political objective of the administration was to get North Korea to change its mind, to accept the IAEA safeguards and to withdraw its announced intent to withdraw from the NPT. This political objective was not only relevant to the North Korean case and intrinsically important to our objectives in Northeast Asia, but it was a "regime objective." We were concerned about the global regime of the IAEA safeguards, we were concerned about the global NPT regime, and these were major political concerns.

There obviously was a security objective here as well, and that went to the North Korean nuclear capability. In retrospect, a lot less was said about North Korean nuclear capability than probably ought to have been said. First, many of us who had spent portions of our lives focused on nuclear proliferation were mesmerized to some degree by what was a rather large nuclear weapons program underway in North Korea. There was an operating research reactor—relatively small as research reactors go—that probably had 30 kilograms of plutonium in its core, or roughly around five nuclear weapons. We were impressed with that. And that of course a year later, not June of 1993 when we first began negotiations with North Koreans, but June of 1994, that material would be pulled out of the reactor, put in a storage pond, and thus moved one step closer to a reprocessing facility that could extract the plutonium from the spent fuel and make it available for the manufacture of nuclear weapons. So this focused our attention.

Second, the North Koreans had a reprocessing facility, in other words, they had the technical capability to do what I just said was the next step in manufacturing nuclear weapons. Third, and to some degree even more disturbing, they had two relatively large production reactors under construction, one rated at 50 megawatts, the other rated at 200 megawatts. The relevant thing about these two reactors is that they would have produced, once operating, about 150 kilograms of plutonium each year. That translates to roughly thirty nuclear weapons every year of operation. So in addition to the political objectives, we had a fairly substantial security objective in terms of the nuclear program itself. That nuclear program we judged would have a significant impact not only on South Korean security, but also on Japanese security. As we looked about, in terms of the North Korean relationship to the rest of the world, we were concerned that this might also have an impact on global security, because the North Koreans were known to have export relations with some other countries of concern. The North Koreans were exporting missile components to Iran. One of the concerns, then, was that this nuclear weapons program would result in the export of nuclear material, if not nuclear weapons, to the Middle East. So our security objective was fairly broadly drawn.

In addition, the North Koreans had then, and indeed still have, a very well-developed ballistic missile program. Not only have they built extended-range SCUD missiles that have ranges in the hundreds of kilometers, but they are building two other classes of ballistic missiles, one with the range of 1,000–2,000 kilometers, and the other in the range of 4,000–6,000 kilometers. It is clear that these missiles are designed for some other purpose than a conflict with South Korea. We must be concerned with the impact this would have on Japanese security. Moreover, if these missiles were to be exported, the missile arches, if drawn from Iran, would have a serious impact on our interest in gulf security and in protecting the security of our friends in the Middle East. So, there was a ballistic missile concern as well. In assessing the overall situation, we also looked at the military situation on the ground. The conventional military disposition of forces was pretty unhappy. Combined forces in Korea were confronting a million-man army in the North, usually assessed at about 60 percent forward deployed, substantial artillery dug in deeply along the Demilitarized Zone (DMZ), and capable of targeting Seoul, a city of 13 million people.

There was also quite clearly a political or ideological objective in our interest to promote the free market over a command economy, democracy over totalitarianism—translated in the Korean context to mean that we were interested in promoting a transition in the regime in North Korea. In other words, we were interested in promoting the reunification of the Korean peninsula. Those were our objectives and interests.

Let us switch now to the negotiations. In October 1994, some fifteen months after the negotiations began, we concluded the Agreed Framework with North Korea. Now, we can assess that Framework in terms of U.S. interests. Politically, we did pretty well, but not perfectly. Under the terms of the Agreed Framework, the North Koreans accept IAEA safeguards, and they even accept those "special inspections" that really crystallized the situation in the early days of 1993—but they did not accept them right away. They ultimately agreed to accept the special inspections when significant nuclear equipment for the construction of light-water reactors (LWR) would begin to be introduced. So the safeguards issue is addressed, but not immediately. The concern that the North would pull out of the NPT is resolved because North Korea agrees to put aside its intent to withdraw from the treaty. However, the North will not be in full compliance with the treaty until it accepts special inspections and is in compliance with its safeguards agreement.

In security terms, the nuclear issue was the key objective to us as negotiators. That objective was substantially achieved because the agreement froze, at that moment, the North Korean nuclear program. The spent fuel containing the plutonium would not be taken out of the pond, but recanned for ultimate removal from North Korea. The research reactor would not be restarted. The two large production reactors would not be completed. The nuclear program goes into a kind of cryogenic arrest. It is frozen right in place. Ultimately, as the North Koreans get their benefits of two large LWRs, these nuclear facilities designed for nuclear weapons development are all dismantled. So, on the nuclear issue, in terms of security, we did pretty well.

In the other areas with other objectives that go to our other interests, I would say we opened the door. We created an atmosphere that would contribute to our success. It is a sort of permissive outcome, not one that really leads directly to the conclusion that we wish to realize. The ballistic missile problem is still there; it is not included under the terms of the Agreed Framework, but it is under the "umbrella" of the Agreed Framework in the sense that there have already been two discussions with the North Koreans about their ballistic missile program. We are beginning to address it.

The larger problem is political. Our hope was to promote a transition in North Korea, to promote unification through a process of North-South dialogue, that is, direct discussion between Pyongyang and Seoul. That has not happened. Again, we think the atmosphere was improved by putting the nuclear issue aside, but we have not had the political success we had hoped for.

Now, let me digress for a moment and say that there is another interpretation of what the Agreed Framework has accomplished, and it is much more critical than the presentation I just offered. It goes something like this: under the terms of the Agreed Framework, North Korea immediately gets a lot of what is called heavy fuel oil, and over the long term it gets two rather large power reactors, 1,000 megawatts each, valued at something on the order of $4 or $5 billion; and, as the critique goes, by giving North Korea these benefits, it in fact sustains the regime, and prolongs the transition that we wanted to have occur; and, therefore, the Agreed Framework cuts against the fundamental interests of the United States. A second critique is that the course of negotiating this Agreed Framework over those many months was so agonizing an enterprise for the alliance between the Republic of Korea (South Korea, or ROK) and the United States, it so stressed the alliance; it in fact resulted in that well-known wedge being driven between the South Koreans and the Americans. The result was a loss of South Korean confidence in its ally, the United States, and the undercutting of the willingness of Seoul to engage the North Koreans. Now, if you believe those two critiques, you do not see the Agreed Framework as contributing to some of the objectives and serving some of the American interests I initially noted.

On the nuclear point, I would argue that we are in fairly good shape. It is very hard to say that the Agreed Framework does not address that concern, but you may not see it as such a plus in political terms. The question now is what policy should the United States adopt, in light of its interests. I am assuming here that some circumstances are different now, in the spring of 1997, than they were in the spring of 1993, but U.S. interests probably have not changed. That is my working assumption. With respect to what has changed, I am going to identify two very large ones. The first is that North Korea is a great deal weaker now than it was four years ago. A very important question is just how much weaker. I unfortunately do not have the answer to that question but I know that there is sort of a continuum here. The continuum goes from a North Korea that is experiencing a certain amount of malnutrition, to the other end of the continuum, a North Korea that is about to experience a famine. The North is, in fact, somewhere along that line, I just am not sure exactly where they are, but I tend to believe it is more rather than less serious. The second point is that there is an inference that most people draw from the economic condition of the North Koreans to the political stability of the regime, such that the more severe the economic situation, the more likely it is that this regime will not survive. That is important because as we go back to the question of what U.S. policy should be in light of its interest with a changed condition, it seems to me that there are risks and opportunities now. I know I will shock you when I say that I think we ought to seize the opportunity, and avoid the risks. The opportunities can be seen when the North Koreans behave as something approximating a normal country: we see the North Koreans apologize for sending their submarines South. That was interesting, and I think most observers thought this was connected to the economic condition in the North, and the concern in the regime that the economic condition not worsen any further and lead to political instability. So, we have the North Korean apology, we have the North Korean grudging acceptance of the defection of a rather senior person from their regime, and we have the grudging acceptance of North Koreans of the briefing given by the South Koreans and the Americans over the possible conduct of the four-power talks. So we have some indicators here that North Koreans are being propelled in the direction of a more cooperative posture with respect to South Korea and the United States. There is opportunity here. The risk from an American perspective, it seems to me, is that with the North Koreans located somewhere on the starvation continuum, we are in a very difficult situation. If we are not careful and simply try to take advantage of that weakness, kick them while they are down, so to speak, we might get an outcome we do not wish to get. Now, some do not believe this is very plausible, but I want to suggest to you here that if the only option that we give to the North Koreans is one in which they confront starvation and political collapse, then a military adventure, with all the ambiguities surrounding this adventure, may look better than certain starvation, political collapse, and absorption by the South, fully and totally on terms that the South may dictate. What I am suggesting to you here is that is a risk, it seems to me, and we ought to be thinking about providing another option for the North other than such a catastrophic one. At the same time, I think there is a risk here that the North may look ripe for the picking at any moment to the South, and if the South were to judge that to be true, and if the domestic context in South Korea would appear to be supportive of such a conclusion, once again, one could have military conflict with rather catastrophic results. This is not, I think, in the interest of South Korea and certainly not in the interest of America; it is a risk to be avoided. What does that mean in terms of U.S. policy? It seems to me that, looking at the opportunities and the risks, we, the United States, should be looking for ways of promoting that well-known soft landing. In other words, promoting the objective of transition in the

North without suffering the consequences of a military conflict.

That leads us to the second changed circumstance, which is painful to describe, and that is, a rather sharp increase in South Korean suspicion, South Korean resentment, and South Korean unease with its ally, the United States. Now, initially, I experienced this in negotiating with the North Koreans, in the conduct of the negotiations and then afterward, even after we had the Agreed Framework and we went through the pain of agreeing that the language was indeed acceptable to Seoul as well as to Washington and Tokyo, and then found that many South Koreans were depressed. Indeed, some in the government in Seoul were saying that the fundamental element of the deal that made it work—the delivery of $5 billion in LWRs—was going to result in the South Korean people paying for somebody else's LWRs to be built in North Korea. And I remember telling the South Koreans over and over and over again, the only reactors that would be built in North Korea would be South Korean reactors. I assure you that I never told the North Koreans anything else. But there were months, actually about ten months, of suspicion that the Germans would build these reactors, that the French would build these reactors, the Russians would build these reactors, Westinghouse would build these reactors. I kept telling the South Koreans that there are lots of people that would build these reactors, but I could only find one group that would pay for the reactors, South Koreans. I said, "Don't worry, this is the only deal that works," and indeed, in August, the deal was made, and the North Koreans agreed to accept whatever reactors the Korean Peninsula Energy Development Organization chose to construct. The Korean Peninsula Energy Development Organization, affectionately known as KEDO, has a board of directors that is composed of an American, a South Korean, and a Japanese. I was chairman of that board and we, not surprisingly, chose South Korean reactors. That is the story.

This did not put the matter to rest in terms of suspicion. The Agreed Framework provides for liaison offices to be open. North Korea opens one in Washington, Washington opens one in Pyongyang. These offices, from October 1994 to March of 1997, still have not been opened, but the South Koreans are concerned about a rush to normalize, negotiating a separate peace arrangement. This goes to the fear of a separate political arrangement between the United States and North Korea. There is nothing of the sort, but the suspicion is there. The Agreed Framework is regarded by many in South Korea as sustaining North Korea. Why give them heavy fuel oil, they ask? And by the way, many South Koreans cannot recall why they are being asked to pay for these LWRs. It seems they have forgotten. Well, there is a very good reason: that is the way the deal was structured and they agreed to a very significant role in financing and construction, but right now, now that we all have the benefits of a defused nuclear weapons threat, it does not seem like it makes a lot of sense.

To some in the South, there is the U.S. reaction to the submarine incident. I do not know if you recall, but the initial American reaction to the submarine incident was not everything Seoul hoped it would be, and indeed, I found several South Koreans suggesting that the American military and the intelligence community knew about the North Korean submarine but failed to tell the South about it. To the best of my knowledge, that is not true.

There is also a disagreement between Washington and Seoul over the condition of the North. I described the condition of the North to be some place on a continuum between malnutrition and starvation. Some people in the South think the North Koreans are better off than we think they are, and believe that the North Koreans are nowhere near the point of starvation as we think they may be approaching. There is a belief in South Korea that the United States is much too concerned about those risks I outlined before: that our concern about war is overdrawn. They believe that it is not really that bad, that we can afford, in a sense, to kick them while they are down. They believe nothing bad will happen. As a matter of fact, a very senior South Korean official told me that they have done a study. They had done a study, and they had found that no country had ever gone to war when it knew they would lose the war. Now I know that is not true, or it is at least misleading; that worried me. Then, most bizarre of all, I found that there was a suspicion of the United States with respect to what I described earlier as an objective of U.S. foreign policy, a fundamental interest of the United States of America: the promotion of democratic market-oriented free enterprise systems around the world and in Northeast Asia. There was a suspicion that the United States did not favor reunification of North and South. I thought I was telling a terrific little anecdote to my South Korean interlocutors when I described how, when I was in Tokyo, the Japanese said they were very much in favor of unification, but they were suspicious that the Chinese really were not, and when I was in Beijing, the Chinese had said they were in favor of unification, but they thought the Japanese really were not; so I said, "How about that?" and they said, "Well, we think you

Americans really aren't in favor of unification," and I said, "How do you figure?" And they said, "Well, you know you're going to be thrown out of Okinawa and then you're going to be thrown out of Japan entirely, and then your only foothold for forward military presence is going to be in Korea. But, if Korea is not divided, you'll have no reason to be here, so you'll be without forward presence entirely and your whole Asia-Pacific strategy will go right down the drain."

Now, that is interesting. The ROK has some fundamental suspicions about our relationship. I think there is a structural reason why this is so. There are probably cultural reasons, too, but the structural reason is important. In an alliance, when there is a dependent ally, and South Korea is in a relative sense dependent on the United States for its security, that dependency leads to a dissatisfaction with the stronger party's policy, almost no matter what it is. We found great swings in South Korea. We found that when we were negotiating successfully with the North Koreans we were accused of being soft on the North Koreans and cooperating too much with an enemy. And then when we started our military buildup, when we said we were putting negotiations aside and going for sanctions, we were accused of being too provocative and too rigid. It reminded me of all those years in which I dealt with European security in which there was no way to satisfy our allies in Europe. When we said we were going to deploy various kinds of missile systems in Europe or neutron bombs in Europe, we were told we were absolutely crazy, we were going to provoke a war, and by the way, that war would not be fought in New Jersey, but in Europe, so it is irresponsible and insensitive to allied interests. But when we negotiated arms control agreements with the Russians, we were accused of pursuing condominium, negotiating over the heads of the Europeans. From the American perspective, we were never able to satisfy our allies. I think there is something structural in some alliance relationships that makes it very hard to get exactly on the same wavelength. All this was true before the Agreed Framework, but the point here is that it all has become more true after the Agreed Framework.

So, if U.S. interests have remained the same, but very important conditions have changed, what should American policy be now? I will make three points about this and then I will stop. The first point is that we should have no ambiguity about our military posture. We should be sure at every moment that we have done everything we can to present to the North Koreans a very strong deterrent posture, so that if North Koreans calculate the way Americans calculate (and by the way, I do not think they do, but if they do) they will figure out that if there is a conflict, they will lose. We must be sure that we have modernized our forces and that their readiness is what it ought to be for deterrent reasons, and then, if deterrence fails and there is a conflict, that we can shorten its duration as much as possible. That is obviously important because the length of the conflict determines the extent of the casualties. Yes, we will win, but as General Gary E. Luck, commander of the U.S. forces in Korea, said so eloquently, "I can win this one for you . . . but not right away."

The second point is that we should try to insulate the Agreed Framework from what will be inevitable disturbances between the North and the South. There will be incidents in the DMZ, there may be another submarine, there may be more defectors, but whatever it is, it is in the interest of South Korea, the United States, Japan, and everybody else. We should continue to execute the deal we made in October 1994. We should not give the North Koreans any reason to reprocess spent fuel, extract plutonium, build nuclear weapons, and leave us with the choice of either accepting nuclear weapons in North Korea or launching a military attack to do something about it. That is not smart; we need to preserve the Framework: keep nuclear weapons off the table, keep delivering heavy fuel oil, keep supporting KEDO, and get on with the LWR project.

A question, parenthetically, we should ask ourselves—those of us who believe what I just said—what happens over time if the North continues to poke its finger (metaphorically) in the eye of the South, refuses to negotiate with the South? Does the South still continue with the Agreed Framework? That, for me, is a big question and it is a difficult one. It seems to me that the answer on prudential grounds is "yes," and that the answer on political grounds is, "it is very hard." In the meantime, the answer is that we should work hard to avoid allowing the situation to develop.

The third point I want to make is that the United States should act to promote a transition in the North. That is close to saying that we should promote a soft landing for the North. That is very close to the title of Sig (Selig) Harrison's excellent article in the spring 1997 edition of *Foreign Policy*, I recommend it to you: it is an incisive analysis, and it is persuasive. That said, I disagree with most of what is in the article, including most importantly the title: "Promoting a Soft Landing in Korea." I think I have learned now, having listened to the South Korean reaction to American ideas, that we should promote a soft landing. I do not believe that we Americans, especially if you live in Washington, can afford to be soft on anything, and certainly not on North Korea. So I would look for some other way of framing this. Arguing to promote a transition in the North is probably best, and my strategy would be to recognize that the key to this is in Seoul. It is not in Washington. It is in Seoul. It behooves Americans to do their best to convince the Republic of Korea that its alliance with the United States is based on U.S. interests. Yes, it is based on trust with South Korea, and friendship, but it is also fundamentally based on interests. Alliances require credibility to work. The United States has very important alliances around the world, and as we have demonstrated over and over again, we believe there is linkage from one alliance to the other. We have a deep interest in sustaining the credibility of our alliance with South Korea. If it becomes suspect, it would do damage to our alliance with Japan. It would, more importantly, in terms of our geostrategic approach to the region, raise questions in Beijing about what the United States would tolerate, notwithstanding commitments made. It would raise questions in capitals in Southeast Asia. These are exactly the kind of questions we want to discourage. So, in addition to all the intrinsic reasons special to the Korean peninsula, the fact of alliance creates an additional important U.S. interest in defending the South. We also, I add somewhat parenthetically, have no interest in seeing South Korea have any incentive to move away from the NPT. We have in the past persuaded South Korea that nuclear weapons were not in its interest, that security was guaranteed in the context of the relationship with the United States, and that is something that we should continue to maintain.

At the same time, I would say that the United States will stay in South Korea only as long as Koreans wish us to be there: South Koreans now, and Koreans if and when the peninsula is unified. In other words, we would not seek a rationale for forward presence, and in so doing, block unification. We would not, because it would risk war by continuing indefinitely a North-South confrontation and, because it would go against our ideals. It would be counter-democratic, it would be against the free enterprise system, and I do not believe the United States of America would do that. Our goals should be to persuade Seoul that it has won its battle with the North. Its economy is twenty times that of North Korea. It has hosted the Olympics. It will host the World Cup. It has seats on the OECD and the UN Security Council. It has won. Our objective should be to get Seoul to join us, the United States, in concluding that it is better to manage a slow transition in the North than to pursue a policy that is perhaps vindictive, rigid, and aimed at provoking a catastrophic collapse. The United States should not, in trying to convince the South of this, shrink from doing what is right, politically, morally, and ethically: it should not shrink from providing food aid to North Koreans who are hungry, without political strings attached. But if, as some would suggest, we adopt our own policy independent of the South, I believe that would be a fundamental error. If we fail to bring the South along with us, our policy will, over the long term, fail.

12
No Thanks Expected:
America's Effort to Nurture a "Soft Landing"

David E. Brown

It was, arguably, a failure of communication between Washington and Seoul that turned the "nuclear issue" with North Korea into a full-scale crisis.

In mid-November 1993, Washington again turned top-level attention to the confrontation prompted by North Korea's refusal to permit "special inspections" of its nuclear facilities by the International Atomic Energy Agency. A senior inter-agency group met, pondered a recent high-level statement by North Korea (Democratic People's Republic of Korea, or DPRK), and concluded that to get the right result it would be necessary to offer the Pyongyang regime some political and economic "carrots." This was the so-called package solution that South Korean Foreign Minister Han Sung Joo had proposed two months earlier in a luncheon meeting with American officials.[1]

Policy, until then, had been to segregate security issues from political-economic issues with North Korea. That policy had been reconfirmed on many occasions in U.S.–South Korean discussions of strategy. As a matter of course, therefore, officers at the State Department responsible for Korean affairs were preparing to call in the South Korean (Republic of Korea, or ROK) ambassador, to brief our ally on the evolution of Washington's thinking, when word was passed from the Seventh Floor—the Department's top management—to hold off briefing until the president had concurred. President Clinton was already on his way to Seattle to host the first summit of Asia-Pacific Leaders. State's East Asia Bureau pleaded for authorization to tell the South Koreans that a policy shift had been put to the president for approval. "No way," came back the answer.

But, as often happened in the course of the nuclear crisis, there was a leak. This time it was not from a Korean, but from an American source, and it hit the front pages of the Seoul dailies just as President Kim Young Sam left Kimpo Airport for Seattle. The ROK Foreign Ministry was obviously in the dark. Immediately, what might have been a mildly contentious tactical debate was transformed into an evident breach of faith by the United States. The South Korean media played the news as conclusive evidence that the ROK had now been marginalized even on inter-Korean issues.

President Kim, who was to proceed to Washington for a high-profile official visit, was furious. He consulted advisors, overruled his foreign minister, and in the privacy of the Oval Office, he threw down the gauntlet. There would be no "package solution" unless the package contained North Korea's agreement to resume direct, high-level talks with South Korea *before* it engaged the United States in talks on the nuclear issue.[2]

Picking up the pieces, the State Department's designated interlocutor, Deputy Assistant Secretary Tom Hubbard, resumed meetings with a North Korean counterpart in New York. With high-level North-South talks on the "must have" list, however, the "package" would not come together. Instead, the Korea nuclear crisis inexorably deepened.

Three points are fundamental here: First, in the 1990s, the U.S. relationship with Korea has become a triangular affair. Second, the U.S.–ROK leg is the most volatile leg of the U.S.–DPRK–ROK triangle, notwithstanding an alliance that has endured for nearly five decades. The American tie with South Korea needs constant tending; there is no such thing as *too much* reassurance of American fidelity. Third, there is a powerful disposition in Seoul to see U.S. dialogue with Pyongyang as unwelcome meddling, rather than as additional leverage toward the achievement of common goals.[3]

During the eighteen tumultuous months that preceded the October 21, 1994, "Agreed Framework," and in the twenty-nine months since then that diplomats have struggled to keep the Framework process on track, the U.S.–ROK alliance has withstood great stresses. The durability of the alliance was never in doubt. Constantly in doubt, however, was whether Washington and Seoul could preserve enough common purpose to negotiate and implement a constructive resolution of the nuclear crisis.

Ironically, there has been reasonably complete accord in Seoul and Washington on the necessary elements of such a constructive resolution. First and foremost, there would not be a war. Second, North Korea would yield its presumed (but never proven) capability to produce a nuclear device.[4] Third, the mode of settlement would maximize North Korea's chances to make a "soft landing."

South Koreans have consistently judged that a sudden collapse of the DPRK would be a social and financial calamity for the South, even if fighting did not spill south of the Demilitarized Zone. The welfare burden of chaos in the North would place terrible stresses on the South's politics and set the ROK back economically for decades.[5] Thus in recent years it has been South Korean doctrine that the ROK objective is not to "absorb" the DPRK, but to draw North Korea into cooperative relations that lead to the convergence of the two systems and, ultimately, to reunification of the Korean peninsula.[6]

The South's official position flows from a logical judgment based on sound analysis and cogent analogy. American policymakers in the Bush and Clinton administrations therefore endorsed the goal of "soft landing" with considerable enthusiasm as the foundation of a step-by-step effort to convert North Korea from regional truant to a well-adjusted supporter of a stable status quo.[7] In our enthusiasm, however, we often lost sight of the fact that while South Korean *heads* drew them in one direction—toward peaceful reconciliation, their *hearts* too often drew them in the other—toward retribution, or at least away from extending the long-time foe a hand in time of need.

This emotional dimension, this constant struggle between the heads and the hearts of South Koreans, helps to explain the extraordinary inconsistency of ROK tactics as the United States and the DPRK fumbled their way toward a relationship—the missing third leg of the triangle. When U.S. politics seemed to be carrying the United States toward a showdown with North Korea—as for example, when the president talked too glibly of "not allowing" the DPRK to build a bomb,[8] or when U.S. diplomats orchestrated the UN's May 1994 call for economic sanctions on the regime in Pyongyang—our allies in Seoul were notably unenthusiastic. Conversely, when we—without giving much thought to what Seoul might think but acutely aware that the U.S.–DPRK Geneva meetings, just begun, hung by a thread—decided to send an immediate message of sympathy to "the people of North Korea" when Kim Il Sung died, the United States was flayed raw by its ally. And when against what had seemed very long odds, Ambassador Robert (Bob) Gallucci secured the Agreed Framework, Seoul could barely choke back public charges of betrayal.

An even stronger driver for Seoul's mercurial posture, however, has been South Korean resentment of a semi-independent U.S. relationship with the DPRK. Needless to say, Pyongyang has missed few opportunities to goad Seoul to a fury by its efforts to draw in the United States while giving the ROK the back of its hand. That is a tactic that has not worked in any fundamental way, nor will it work, for there is nothing the DPRK could offer that would rival the value and importance—in every dimension—of U.S. ties with South Korea. Yet it is difficult to escape the conclusion that a significant body of South Korean opinion fears that the DPRK can fool Washington into a fatal misstep, or even that Pyongyang can replace Seoul in Washington's affections. ˙

Nor, viewed in the context of a tragic century for Korea—of colonization, war, and division—are our South Korean allies entirely paranoid. Historical experience suggests to many on the peninsula that good things rarely happen when outside powers determine Korea's fate. Rather than be big power pawns, the argument goes, Seoul must do whatever is required to stay in control of inter-Korean issues. North-South détente must be on ROK terms, or not at all.

So—what can Americans do, what should we do about the dysfunctional emotional component in the ROK's management of American relations? My view is that we have to live with it. We have to accept it as a chronic, enduring feature of the relationship. Every once in a very great while, it may be necessary to let some tactical daylight show between the allies, but by and large the costs of getting out ahead of the ROK are not worth the gain.

One reason for caution is ROK political clout in Washington. As the South Koreans proved after the Agreed Framework was concluded, when they whipped up their old friends in the Congress against the Administration's alleged lack of concern for ROK interests, the ROK Embassy swings a lot of weight. Long-tended friendships between conservatives in both capitals gives extra potency to the political club that the ROKs wield.

The other reason for caution—the better one—is that while Seoul may do the right thing if it feels fully consulted and more or less in control, it surely will do something counterproductive if it senses that the United States is moving off in an uncoordinated direction.

Thus some basic rules of managing the now triangular relationship are that every gesture toward the DPRK has to be coordinated with the ROK, and that inevitably these gestures will take several times more effort to bring forth than seems possible.

The so-called "two plus two" peace talks initiative is a case in point. The initiative was Seoul's idea, a proposal made in the course of spring 1995 U.S.–ROK consultations that were designed to mend the scars of the U.S.–DPRK deal at Geneva. Without a great deal of confidence that it would bear fruit, but judging it better to have a peace initiative on the table than not, "Korea hands" in Washington cranked the policy mill to prepare support for the ROK proposal. It was to be unveiled in President Kim's August 15 National Day speech. Senior U.S. and South Korean officials had traveled to Honolulu for final coordination when, literally as the ROK group was landing, President Kim shelved the initiative. There was no explanation, and the initiative would not resurface until nine months later, when President Clinton secured Kim's consent to it in a bilateral summit on Cheju Island.

Then, of course, it took another nine months, punctuated by the submarine incident, of nudging North Korea before it would consent to sit still for a joint U.S.–ROK briefing on what has been renamed the proposed *four-party* peace talks. "Four-party" presumably because it is no longer clear on which side of the table China will sit. Dare we hope, now, that this small and grudging step signals greater pragmatism on the DPRK's part?

Particularly since the Agreed Framework was signed, Pyongyang has pursued a strategy of trying to get close to the United States and Japan, while heaping abuse on the ROK. It should be obvious by now that such a strategy will not work. Seoul is not prepared to trail in the wake of its allies, and it has the means to enforce reticence on their part. Japan is even less ready than the United States to jeopardize its extensive relations with the ROK by a dalliance with the DPRK. Although neither Japan nor the United States bears North Korea a lasting grudge, in neither country is there more than fringe support for building relations at the expense of the ROK. Considered in the context of the DPRK's continued heavy spending on military priorities, in both the United States and Japan it is hard to mobilize support even for famine relief. North Korea's survival as an independent entity thus depends on its ability to work out, through direct dialogue, a civil relationship with its larger, vastly more prosperous and, in every important respect, stronger rival to the South.

South Korea, meanwhile, awaits a government confident enough to make peace, and a president who can persuade the Northern regime that the South's purpose is not revenge and domination, but reconciliation.

Two American administrations—Bush and Clinton—have pursued a policy line that makes sense, and over time has made real progress. That progress has been the result of unceasing, mostly thankless labor by a large number of officials who have understood that our purpose has been to fashion a set of circumstances that gives North Korea the *option* of something other than Armageddon. There is no way the United States, acting alone or in concert with its allies, can ensure a "soft landing" for North Korea. The best the United States can do is create opportunities that North Korea can seize to create an alternative future, to the extent that its regime dares to risk economic opening and détente.

The nuclear crisis was a special challenge to the U.S. system of policy making. At stake were core objectives of the nonproliferation community, on one hand, and the East Asia policy people, on the other. This intersection of two first-rank policy themes provided plenty of press hooks, and too many officials were ready to give reporters their versions of what was said at Cabinet-level meetings. Nonproliferation zealots posed a palpable danger to a carefully wrought structure of deterrence in Northeast Asia. By the end of 1993, things were really out of control. The nuclear crisis had become too big, too complex, and too well-ventilated an issue to micro-manage from the NSC.

That is where the Clinton administration got smart, or maybe just lucky. It decided to try a new approach—to put a single person with a strong mandate in charge from top to bottom and across all agencies—the so-called vertical slice.[9] Perhaps intentionally, that was someone from a nonproliferation background, Bob Gallucci. His deputy was another person with strong nonproliferation credentials, Dan Poneman of the NSC. Word went around: "There goes Asia." But of course, the consequence of being put in charge of resolving the issues in their broadest dimension was that Gallucci and Poneman became quite good at navigating on the shoals of Asia policy. State and Defense Department "Asia hands" made sure of that. People who understood the Asia context and who had been prominent in the last administration gave strong support.[10] The leaks slowed, although they did not stop.

Ultimately, with some timely help from former president Carter, things began to come together. Carter, or someone else playing a similar role, was in retrospect a historic inevitability. North Korea had escalated the confrontation by defueling its small nuclear reactor in the spring of 1994, a deliberate step toward reprocessing the spent fuel into weapons-grade uranium. The United States, Japan, and the ROK had followed through by carrying out their threat of UN sanctions. Although there was little enthusiasm for an exercise so evidently risky *and* so likely futile, officials saw no better way to show Pyongyang that the United States and its allies would take action in response to direct provocation.[11] Once both sides had painted themselves into a corner, and military options were being discussed in the event that the DPRK now sought to hide the spent fuel, the situation was ripe for Carter's dramatic and successful effort to bridge a growing chasm, and put the nuclear crisis on the way to resolution.[12]

The arrangement reached five months later resolved some but not all of the concerns raised by North Korean adventurism. Other problems were "just kicked down the road,"[13] to be addressed one by one and presumably in a more trusting context than existed in October 1994. The question *now*—as Mike Mazaar asks in his excellent book on *North Korea and the Bomb*—is whether the U.S. government can sustain the "nuanced, patient engagement" needed to hold North Korea to *its* Agreed Framework commitments and exploit their potential as a tool for political and economic opening.[14]

The jury is still out. North Korea is very hungry, but still far from collapsing. It has lost its allies and its dynamism, and has fallen way behind the ROK in the things that count. Although its military capabilities remain formidable, Pyongyang knows it cannot overrun Seoul, let alone South Korea. North Korea's posture is essentially defensive, and there must now be real concern in the North that the ROK may try to do to them the sort of thing the DPRK itself would do if *it* had overwhelming superiority.[15]

The events of the past several years suggest that the North Korean regime knows that the only way to break out of an ever-descending spiral is to forge profitable relations with the outside world. I believe that if we keep hammering away on the point, eventually the DPRK will concede that it will not achieve such a breakout until it establishes a civil relationship—not necessarily a warm one—with the regime in the south.

Dialogue at the government-to-government level will proceed, inevitably, by fits and starts. To get through the bad patches, it is important to multiply and reinforce contact at other levels. The cheapest and most effective way to influence the DPRK's view of the world is to allow the multiplication of business links. Washington, Seoul, and Tokyo should not treat trade and investment as a reward for DPRK good behavior in other spheres. Holding commercial ties hostage to that standard may force the United States to back away from business ventures that can draw North Korea steadily into constructive dealings with the West and, especially, with the ROK.

American officials have stressed the importance of holding North Korea strictly to its Agreed Framework commitments. American leverage depends on strict U.S. performance of its own commitments, and in at least one respect, to date the U.S. government has failed badly. The Clinton administration undertook to remove barriers to normal commercial relations as the DPRK addressed matters of concern to the United States, such as cooperating on Korean War MIAs, canning the spent nuclear fuel, exporting missiles, and repudiating terrorism as an instrument of policy.[16] Yet, notwithstanding movement on the North Korean side, except for a trivial first step toward trade liberalization in January 1995, the United States has done nothing to carry out this commitment.

Instead, although nothing is more subversive to a closed system than private enterprise, the myth has persisted in Washington—especially on Capitol Hill—that a heavy blanket of economic sanctions serves American purposes.[17]

A priori, there seems to be no economic reason why North Korea could not revive and grow its economy by following the familiar East Asian development model. To overcome the effects of prolonged isolation, it would need to rely heavily at first on foreign partners for technology transfer, quality control, and interpretation of market signals. Were it not for political constraints, this would probably be happening already. In the interim, it ought to be politically, as well as economically, feasible to use the light-water reactor (LWR) project as a powerful driver for economic development.

The LWR project provides a proactive and depoliticized framework for North-South cooperation. A particular benefit may be practical demonstration that it is possible for DPRK and foreign—particularly including South Korean—firms to partner successfully. In a typical reactor project of this scale, local procurement would amount to well over one billion dollars in value. That would include construction materials such as concrete, structural steel, pipe and plywood, as well as labor services. There would also be considerable related work to build roads, expand airports and ports, provide housing, water and electricity, and recreational facilities.

Providing such goods and services will challenge DPRK capabilities. Northern goods and services ought to be used when it makes economic sense. The economic development impact can be maximized by encouraging formation of joint ventures that transfer construction technologies and management skills to DPRK enterprises. Executed with such a long view, the LWR project could contribute importantly to the economic reintegration of the Korean peninsula. The experience that ROK and DPRK enterprises can gain in working together on the LWR project could provide a solid platform for further steps to overcome a legacy of national division.

Particularly while politics are gridlocked in Seoul and Pyongyang, only good can come of letting the business sectors of the ROK, Japan, and the United States do more of what they do so well. Nothing is more likely to persuade North Korean elites that it is safe to follow a path of reconciliation, and so begin to repair the tragic division of the Korean nation.

Notes

1. I was, from August 1993 to August 1995, the director of the State Department's Office of Korean Affairs, often called the "Korea Desk," and then, until January 1996, member for Korea and Southeast Asia on the Department's Policy Planning Staff. I have considered it unnecessary to footnote the information in this essay that is based on first-hand information, or on direct and immediate debriefing of principals in the meetings described.

2. To show that he had dominated the White House meeting, Kim insisted that the revised approach bear a new name: "The broad and thorough approach."

3. President Kim, South Korea's first popularly elected president, is acutely sensitive to shifts in public opinion. An unintentioned consequence of the democratization of South Korean politics during the last decade seems to be greater pressure on the ROK president to demonstrate that *he* is leading the peace process, and not the American ambassador.

4. Whether or not North Korea already had a usable bomb, it was evident to Seoul, Washington, and Tokyo that the DPRK was on a course that could give it dozens of bombs in the next several years. The challenge was to persuade the Pyongyang regime that yielding its bomb-making capability would make it more, rather than less, secure.

5. Estimates made by ROK think-tanks reportedly range from US$40 billion to US$2.5 trillion—a range reportedly explained by different approaches to calculating the opportunity costs of maintaining large, combat-ready armies in North and South. (The *Korea Herald*, Seoul, April 7, 1997)

6. A policy first enunciated in the ROK's September 1989 proposal for a "Korean National Community" and restated by the Kim Young Sam administration in early 1993.

7. In January 1992 (a time of remarkable thaw in inter-Korean relations), U.S. Undersecretary of State Arnold Kanter outlined in some detail a step-by-step progression toward the establishment of U.S.–DPRK relations to a senior North Korean diplomat.

8. On NBC Television's "Meet the Press," November 7, 1993, and widely reported the next day.

9. An initiative I have heard attributed to Strobe Talbott, President Clinton's close friend, who had recently been made Deputy Secretary of State.

10. Among these were Doug Paal and Jim Kelly, who had been on the National Security Council staff, Don Gregg, who had been President Bush's ambassador to Korea, and Dick Solomon and Bill Clark, who had served as Assistant Secretary of State for East Asian Affairs.

11. Sanctions could not be airtight without China's cooperation, but Japan's readiness to clamp down on remittances from pro-DPRK Korean residents estimated at 500 million dollars or more yearly ensured that Pyongyang would feel some serious pain.

12. Mike Mazaar's account is highly accurate. See *North Korea and the Bomb* (New York: St. Martin's Press, 1995), pp. 159–163.

13. Gallucci's phrase.

14. Mazaar, *North Korea and the Bomb*, p. 180.

15. Elsewhere, I have discussed the shift in Pyongyang's military perspective in some detail: "Pyongyang moves to defensive posture," *Washington Times*, December 13, 1996.

16. A mantra that was repeated endlessly by the State Department spokesman and by officials in congressional testimony after the framework was agreed.

17. The DPRK's famine-driven decision to invite congressional delegations to visit North Korea seems to have reduced resistance to administrative steps that would enable the DPRK to buy food and pay for it with mineral commodities. See the April 11 press conference of Senator Ted Stevens (R., Alaska) and members of his fact-finding delegation (USIA transcript, published also on NAPSNET [*www.nautilus.org/napsnet/special_reports*], April 14, 1997).

13

The United States and the Future of Korea

Selig S. Harrison

Two years before the United States concluded its nuclear freeze agreement with North Korea in October, 1994, I had a revealing exchange with a retired senior U.S. diplomat at a Washington seminar. The topic discussed was how the United States should respond to Pyongyang's suspected nuclear weapons program. My argument was that carrots would work better than sticks in resolving what was a potentially dangerous problem. "They can be bought," I concluded, "if the price is right." "I don't want to buy them," was the prompt retort. "I want to destroy them."

What my interlocutor had in mind was not a military invasion of North Korea but a policy of sustained pressure based on the premise that the North Korean communist regime is economically and politically bankrupt and will collapse sooner or later. Instead of offering economic and political rewards in exchange for a nuclear settlement, he argued, the United States should seek to hasten North Korea's demise. Rejecting former South Korean President Roh Tae Woo's 1989 proposal for a loose confederation in which unification would develop gradually, he urged that the United States promote a surgical, German-style unification process, with South Korea absorbing the North.

Despite the conclusion of the nuclear freeze agreement in 1994, hopes for a collapse in Pyongyang continue to shape the debate over Korea policy in Washington, Seoul, and Tokyo in 1997. The freeze agreement implicitly recognizes North Korea as an established reality, committing the United States to a process of economic and political normalization with Pyongyang. Of particular importance, the agreement provides for the relaxation of economic sanctions. It was the need to compensate for the loss of Soviet and Chinese economic aid, with an economic opening to the West and Japan, that led Pyongyang to accept the nuclear freeze. In Washington, however, both the Clinton administration and Congress are deeply divided over whether a collapse in Pyongyang is inevitable or desirable, and if not, what steps, if any, should be taken to help North Korea ease its food shortage and other economic problems resulting from the loss of its Soviet and Chinese subsidies. As a result, the administration has attempted to carry out the freeze agreement without facing up to integrally related decisions concerning broader U.S. goals in the Korean peninsula.

There is now an urgent need for a reassessment of American interests in the context of post–Cold War changes in North Korea and of the new role played by Russia and China in the peninsula. Such a reassessment should focus on whether North Korea is, indeed, on the verge of collapse or is likely to survive by moving toward a liberalization of its economy broadly similar to what has been happening in China since the death of Mao. It should consider whether the collapse of the North and its absorption by South Korea would be desirable, or whether American interests would be better served by a "soft landing"—a gradual process of unification in which neither side is swallowed up by the other and the United States helps Pyongyang achieve a China-style economic transformation.

The widespread assumption within the administration that a collapse is inevitable was exemplified in a statement by General Gary E. Luck, the former commander of U.S. and U.N. forces in South Korea, who said in congressional testimony that "the question is not will this country disintegrate, but rather how it will disintegrate, by implosion or explosion, and when."[1] Expectations of a collapse have been strengthened by the serious food shortage resulting from two years of unprecedented flood damage and by the defection in February 1997 of Hwang Jang Yop, a former secretary of the ruling Workers Party in the North. As this chapter will argue, the food shortage could indeed have destabilizing political consequences over a period of years if it is not resolved. Hwang's defection, however, while a demoralizing psychological blow to the Workers Party, is not likely to have a significant impact on political stability in Pyongyang in the foreseeable future.

In four meetings with Hwang in 1987, 1992, and 1994, I found him to be an idealistic intellectual with wide cosmopolitan interests, but not a mover and shaker in Workers Party power struggles. As an intimate of the late Kim Il Sung, he held significant honorific and policy-making positions. Since Kim's death, he has been demoted. Among the many factors that may have led to his defection, I would emphasize first, the frustration of a leading reform advocate with the entrenched power of the party Old Guard, and second, the desire expressed in his initial post-defection statement to help promote peaceful unification. His defection is not likely to foreshadow other important defections. Indeed, Hwang declared in his statement that "I do not think there is any danger of the DPRK collapsing . . . the DPRK is experiencing some economic difficulties, but it is solidly united politically."[2]

In early 1996, alarmed by the specter of a North Korean famine, the White House initiated a review of Korea policy that was soon sputtered out as the U.S. presidential campaign approached. When the U.S. ambassador to South Korea, James Laney, made a significant but little-noticed speech in May 1996—"Beyond Deterrence"—emphasizing economic incentives in dealing with Pyongyang, it appeared that the administration might be preparing to move toward a "soft landing" policy.[3] But the Laney initiative soon foundered in the face of continuing conservative resistance in Washington and Seoul, especially after a North Korean military intelligence adventure in September that aborted when its submarine with twenty-six armed agents aboard ran aground off the South Korean coast.

The submarine fiasco, resulting in the deaths of three South Korean civilians in clashes with the fleeing North Korean agents, aroused understandable indignation in the South. This has been exploited by President Kim Young Sam to consolidate right-wing support for his governing New Korea Party in the 1997 presidential election campaign. Depicting the submarine incursion as proof that the North is planning an invasion, President Kim has adopted an increasingly hard line toward Pyongyang on a variety of issues, including the terms for implementation of the nuclear freeze. This prompted American officials to complain openly that the South is now a "bigger headache" for the United States than the North,[4] which expressed regret for the submarine incident and is making conciliatory gestures to the United States on issues of special importance to Washington, notably, missile exports to the Middle East; permission for U.S. airlines to cross North Korean airspace, and cooperation on finding the remains of American service men killed during the Korean War.

The U.S. alliance with South Korea rests on Cold War assumptions that should now be reexamined to conform to post–Cold War realities. When Washington concluded its mutual security treaty with Seoul, the Soviet Union and China had operative military alliances with Pyongyang. Now the United States finds itself committed to one side in a civil war. South Korea has much more significant economic links with Russia and China than the North does. Russia has nullified the operative clauses of its security treaty with Pyongyang and is selling its most advanced military equipment and technology to Seoul. China, while formally retaining its security commitment, has progressively diluted its relations with Pyongyang in most spheres.

Despite these changes in the geopolitical environment, the United States continues to view its relations with North Korea as a subordinate aspect of its alliance with Seoul. In addition to maintaining its 37,000 troops in the South and its commitment to intervene in the event of North Korean aggression, the administration feels compelled to seek South Korean approval for all of its behavior relating to Pyongyang. The United States has thus become a hostage to entrenched right-wing military and political leaders in the South who favor policies completely incompatible with a soft landing.

The most extreme of these elements wants to promote a quick collapse and absorption of the North. A more widespread approach favors U.S. and South Korean policies designed to debilitate North Korea gradually, by maintaining existing economic sanctions and other forms of pressure, forcing it to unify with the South on South Korean terms without a sudden breakdown—the "contained collapse" scenario. Both of these approaches are opposed by centrist and liberal leaders in the South who support the loose confederation concept long espoused by opposition leader Kim Dae Jung and adopted with modifications by former president Roh Tae Woo in his 1989 proposal for a "Korean Commonwealth." This division over unification policy is paralleled by a split in public opinion over whether South Korea should honor its commitment to provide $4 billion in financial support for the nuclear freeze agreement. The hardliners argue that the agreement only serves to delay the collapse of North Korea, pointing, in particular, to a key clause providing for a relaxation of economic sanctions.

The starting point for a reappraisal of U.S. policy in Korea should be a dispassionate examination of North Korean prospects conducted without ideological blinders. Based on five visits to North Korea since 1972 and continuing contacts with fellow North Korea watchers in Japan, China, Russia, and other countries, I will present my own assessment of the collapse issue and will then turn to a discussion of specific U.S. economic and security policy options.

Will North Korea Collapse?

While the North Korean system is not likely to "implode" or "explode" in the foreseeable future, as General Luck predicts, it could well *erode* over a period of five to ten years if the United States and its allies remain wedded to obsolete policies that exacerbate the economic problems facing the Kim Jong Il regime. In particular, if one assumes the continuance of economic sanctions and a failure to give significant support to the UN food aid program in Pyongyang, the prospects for a "soft landing" would clearly be reduced. Entrenched orthodox elements in the North Korean leadership would be strengthened. Advocates of reform, such as Hwang Jang Yop, would be isolated. Factionalism would increase, inviting South Korean, Chinese, Japanese, and Russian manipulation of competing power groups in Pyongyang. The end result could well be growing instability with incalculable consequences, including massive refugee flows to South Korea, "boat people" attempting to enter Japan, and civil strife that could spill over into North-South military encounters involving American forces. In the unlikely event of a complete breakdown in Pyongyang, the costs of economic reconstruction in an absorption scenario would be colossal, greatly exceeding those in Germany.

Since the death of Kim Il Sung in July 1994, the North Korean system has survived, with its fundamental unity intact. The quasireligious nationalist mystique associated with his memory continues to evoke broad, popular acceptance of the totalitarian discipline of the ruling Workers Party. This discipline is reinforced by powerful Confucian traditions of political centralization and obedience to authority. Facile comparisons between North Korea and East Germany ignore the critical cultural and historical factors that set the two cases apart. In East Germany, the Soviet occupation imposed a totalitarian system in a cultural environment relatively hospitable to democratic concepts. By contrast, the Confucian ethos has influenced in varying ways the political evolution of South Korea as well as North Korea, making it much easier to sustain authoritarian and totalitarian systems.

Another obvious contrast between Germany and Korea lies in the fact that the two Koreas fought a fratricidal war. West German Chancellor Willy Brandt did not have to overcome the bitter legacy of such a conflict when he initiated his *Ostpolitik*. It was the network of contacts and economic linkages between East and West Germany made possible by *Ostpolitik* over a twenty-five-year period that set the stage for the upheaval triggered in the East by Gorbachev's relaxation of the Soviet grip. By the same token, it is the absence of North-South interchange that freezes the situation on the Korean peninsula.

For all of its repression, East Germany did not achieve the Orwellian thoroughness of North Korea, where children begin to spend six days a week away from their parents at the age of three, and often earlier. Well-equipped and well-staffed, the lavish childcare centers that one sees even in rural areas are exuberant places bursting with seemingly joyous children who begin their education by learning that Kim Jong Il personifies the patriotic virtue that was exemplified by his father, Kim Il Sung. Unlike Eastern Europe, where television, short-wave radios, and cassettes have leapfrogged national frontiers, North Korea is tightly insulated from outside influences. All television and radio sets must be registered and have fixed channels. Only the top echelon of the Workers Party has more than an inkling of what the rest of the world is like. To be sure, as foreign contacts increase, the system is gradually becoming more penetrable, increasing the possibility of eventual political change.

Kim Jong Il's position as the anointed successor to his father and the principal link to his father's memory makes his presence in the forefront of leadership essential to legitimize the Workers Party regime. The North Korean ambassador to the United Nations, Kim Hyong U, tells visitors that Kim Jong Il will assume the posts of president and general secretary of the Workers Party by the end of 1997, following the third anniversary of his father's death on July 8. However, Kim Jong Il does not command the absolute authority that was exercised by Kim Il Sung and is not the charismatic, revered figure that his father was. Significant personal and interest group rivalries within the regime have become visible, leading to tortuous processes of accommodation and delays in decision making. The armed forces and the internal security services play an increasingly assertive role. Cutting across the turf rivalries and power plays within the regime is an intense policy conflict between an orthodox Old Guard and a younger generation of reform-minded pragmatists with greater cosmopolitan exposure identified with Kim Jong Il.

This policy struggle began to emerge during the last years of Kim Il

Sung and is directly attuned to American, Japanese, and South Korean policies. Thus, when the United States promised in 1994 to give North Korea economic and political rewards in return for the nuclear freeze, the pragmatists in Pyongyang were strengthened. Similarly, the failure of the United States to honor its pledge in the freeze agreement to relax economic sanctions has vindicated hardliners who were opposed to the freeze.

In setting the pace of change, the Workers Party faces political risks in going down the road of reform too rapidly that may be as great as the risks of moving too hesitantly. Most compelling, in the eyes of party leaders, is the risk of losing control. Equally important in terms of the stability of the regime would be the growth of disruptive social tensions. Until now, discontent over the food shortage and other economic hardships has been cushioned by the absence of visible economic inequities. The greatest danger to the regime would come from the type of blatant corruption that helped to trigger the Tiananmen tragedy in China. Just as corruption in China has grown in tandem with the expansion of foreign economic ties, so the emergence of a high-living North Korean comprador class could prove politically destabilizing as Pyongyang opens up to the outside world.

Economic Normalization: The Pivotal Issue

The removal of U.S. economic sanctions is a precondition for the overall liberalization of economic relations with the West and Japan that the North seeks as the key to solving its economic problems, especially its food shortage. Article Two, Section One of the freeze agreement explicitly stated that "within three months of the date of this document, both sides will reduce barriers to trade and investment." This provision was unconditional and was not linked to performance on other issues. By contrast, Section Two conditions the establishment of a liaison office on "the resolution of consular and other technical issues," and Section Three makes upgrading relations from a liaison office to the ambassadorial level contingent on "progress on issues of concern to each side." But the commitment to reducing trade and investment barriers is unqualified, although it avoids specifying precisely how far and how fast the reduction should proceed.[5]

In formal and informal meetings with North Korean leaders in September 1995, and continuing contacts with North Korean diplomats, I have found an increasingly bitter feeling that the United States has cheated the North out of the most important benefits promised under the nuclear freeze agreement. Pyongyang is not seriously threatening to break the agreement—yet—but the North Korean leaders I met[6] clearly felt that it is not working out. What they say, in effect is, "We're living up to our side of the deal. We have frozen our nuclear program and this has been verified by the International Atomic Energy Agency inspectors and by U.S. government experts. We've given up our nuclear independence, and we've done it for one reason, because we thought this would lead to friendly relations with the United States, particularly economic relations. But you have made only token reductions of trade and investment barriers. You are not living up to your part of the deal."

An objective evaluation of the sanctions issue indicates that the North Korean grievance is justified. By January 1997, all that the United States had done to implement Article Two was to lift sanctions on the exports of one commodity, magnesite, and to grant permission to American Telephone and Telegraph (AT&T) to open up telephone and fax communications. The few U.S. companies that have gone to Pyongyang and shown interest in investing cannot obtain Treasury Department licenses. General Motors, which is looking into the possible construction of an auto parts plant, is a prime example.

North Korea is aware that American trade and equity investment might not amount to much until it has begun to pay back outstanding debts to European and Japanese banks totaling $3.2 billion. But it believes that the removal of U.S. economic sanctions would have an important symbolic value, stimulating Japanese, West European, and South Korean interest in barter deals, and subcontracting arrangements that would help to jumpstart its stagnant economy. Pyongyang recognizes that some U.S. sanctions can be removed only with congressional approval, but points out that President Clinton could strike North Korea from the list of proscribed countries in the "trading with the enemy act" by executive order.

Part of the explanation for the administration's paralysis on the sanctions issue lies in domestic political concerns. When the freeze agreement was concluded on October 24, 1994, the administration had intended to move decisively on sanctions within the required three months by permitting the foreign subsidiaries of U.S. firms to deal with North Korea. This would have permitted General Motors and other firms with such subsidiaries to invest in the North. But the unexpected Republican sweep of Congress less than one month later aroused administration fears that the removal of sanctions would stir up opposition to the freeze agreement as a whole and endanger the congressional support needed to implement it. In defending its position, the administration has frequently misrepresented what the agreement provides, seeking to give the impression that it conditions the removal of sanctions on North Korean concessions on other issues. For example, a State Department official responsible for economic relations with North Korea said incorrectly that "under the agreement, the United States has said that it would ease more sanctions on North Korea as progress is made on other areas of interest to us."[7]

The continuation of sanctions imposed during a period of Cold War military tensions is increasingly anachronistic in the context of the North Korean effort to liberalize its foreign economic relations. In the new Rajin-Sonbong free trade and investment zone, foreign investors can establish fully foreign-owned enterprises, get a five-year tax holiday, and a 14 percent tax rate, and enter the zone without visas. Urging an end to the sanctions policy in April 1996, Kim Jong U, chairman of the Committee for External Economic Cooperation, acknowledged that "the world market today has been unified into a single market, the capitalist market." To join this market, he said, Pyongyang

> has launched an across-the-board introduction of business forms and modes that currently prevail in the international market, including a wide range of equity and contractual joint ventures as well as wholly foreign-owned businesses. Our main objective is the active introduction of the high technology and foreign capital investment so urgently needed by our national economy. In this regard, the State has taken a series of measures aimed at doing away with all phenomena giving rise to our poor credit rating and is prepared, among other things, to extend in-kind or cash guarantees.[8]

In addition to its sanctions policy, the United States has actively promoted the conversion of the Cold War export control regime, COCOM (Coordinating Committee on Export Controls), into a new multilateral grouping of thirty countries targeted at Iran, Iraq, Libya, and North Korea. The "Wassenaar Arrangement," named after the Dutch town where it was established in 1995, is designed to block the export of conventional weapons and dual use technology to "rogue states." A more appropriate initiative, given the end of the superpower military rivalry, would have been a universal, nondiscriminatory regime addressed to the worldwide problem of burgeoning conventional arms sales. Such an approach would have attempted to curb arms sales both to Seoul and Pyongyang. In any case, bilateral U.S. steps to liberalize economic sanctions would become meaningless if dual-use technology is defined rigidly by applying the Wassenaar Arrangement to North Korea.

The United States can properly seek to prevent Pyongyang from obtaining military hardware or technology with a direct military application but should permit all other trade and investment. As a first priority, it should remove restrictions on North Korean exports so that Pyongyang can finance food imports.

Although a "soft landing" would serve American interests, the United States and its allies cannot assure this result. American policy should steer a middle course between assuming that a collapse is inevitable and, at the other extreme, subsidizing Pyongyang, as the Soviet Union and China did during the Cold War. Thus, the United States should distinguish between bilateral economic aid, which should be limited to technical assistance, and support for multilateral assistance to viable economic development projects in North Korea, which should be encouraged. For example, the United States could increase its support for the United Nations Development Program, until now the only foreign-aid agency with permanent representation in Pyongyang. American support would open the way for North Korean admission to the Asian Development Bank, the Asia Pacific Economic Cooperation (APEC) grouping, the World Bank, and other multilateral agencies.

As closer neighbors with a much greater geopolitical stake in Korea than the United States, Japan and China should be encouraged to extend bilateral economic aid to Pyongyang. In normalizing relations with South Korea in 1965, Japan made a "reparations" or "economic cooperation" payment of $800 million. At the end of 1994, a comparable sum as part of a Japanese normalization agreement with North Korea would have been $3.76 billion, based on the Consumers Price Index at that time, but North Korean spokesmen have advanced arguments that seek to justify a minimum of $10 billion.[9]

Food Aid and Agricultural Reform

An American policy designed to promote a "soft landing" would include urgent action to help alleviate the food shortage. The United States should acknowledge that the current crisis has resulted in large part from factors beyond North Korea's control and should actively help to mobilize a short-term international humanitarian relief effort.

The impact of the 1995 and 1996 floods has been crippling because the areas most severely damaged were the "breadbasket" provinces in the south and west that normally produce the lion's share of North Korea's food grains output. Moreover, even before the floods struck, North Korean agriculture had been paralyzed by the loss of the Soviet oil that had fueled its tractors and its fertilizer factories.

North Korea is a mountainous country with only 18 percent of its land arable and has thus faced food scarcity since its inception. Despite ambitious irrigation, reclamation, and mechanization programs that have brought impressive increases in food production, Pyongyang has relied on significant food imports, especially concessional imports from China. Beginning in 1989, China toughened its terms but continued to be a reliable source of food grains, shipping 600,000 tons of corn in 1994. Then in 1995, rising domestic demand led Beijing to cut off grain shipments to North Korea abruptly as part of a global decision not to export grain, which left Pyongyang in the lurch just when the floods struck. In April 1996, China extended 120,000 tons of emergency food grains aid and signed a five-year agreement with Pyongyang to provide 500,000 tons of grain annually, half of it as a grant and half at concessional prices.[10] But this still left a projected gap in 1997 of at least one million tons in the amount of food needed to provide nine ounces of grain per person per day.

The most serious crisis is expected in isolated North Hamgyong province in the northeast corner of the country, where near-famine conditions already prevail. In North Korea's nine other provinces, malnutrition in varying degree is pervasive, with the exception of the relatively well-fed capital city of Pyongyang.

In response to the food shortage, Kim Jong Il is making announced, and unannounced, changes in agricultural policy similar to those adopted by China and Vietnam in the early stages of their movement toward market reforms. The most important announced change is an increase in production incentives. Until now, farmers in government-controlled cooperative farms have been organized in work teams made up of as many as twenty-five members. Since payment is made by the state to the team as a group, hard workers and laggards benefit equally from increases in output. Under the new system, work teams will consist of eight members, which will put pressure on the laggards to produce. Each work team will be permitted to keep up to 30 percent of what it harvests, with the amount retained dependent on the extent to which the team meets or exceeds production targets.[11]

What makes this modest reform significant is that it goes together with an unannounced decision by local authorities in some areas to permit private markets where work teams can sell or barter their surplus, and individual farmers can sell or barter food grown on their household plots.[12] This is clearly being done with the approval of Kim Jong Il but without any formal doctrinal justification that would upset the party Old Guard.

In selected experimental areas, the government has also introduced contract farming. Individuals or families get 15-year lease agreements under which they must sell a fixed amount to the state but can then dispose of the rest in private markets. When contract farming was introduced in China, the state quota was gradually whittled down under pressure from farmers. For more than a decade land contracts have been bought and sold in China without government interference.

As the Seoul-based British journal *North Korea Report* has perceptively observed, the emergence of private markets and land contracts in North Korea represents

> reform by stealth. . . . Pyongyang's reformers just aren't powerful enough to challenge the Old Guard head-on. So what do they do? They just wait—for the sheer desperation caused by two years' flooding to force the diehards to allow change on the ground. Just an emergency, you understand. But the reformers realize that once market practices are in place, there'll be no going back.[13]

The United States should not seek to condition the relaxation of sanctions or food aid on specific economic reform measures. Surrendering to direct foreign pressure would only weaken Kim Jong Il's position and complicate the process of "reform by stealth." However, in helping to mobilize international food aid, the United States should make clear that it will contribute to the UN effort only for the next two or three years as a short-term response to a humanitarian crisis, thus applying indirect pressure for reform.

In 1996 a consortium of six UN agencies appealed for $436 million in flood-related food aid and other assistance to cover "the most urgent needs" in North Korea. Only $18 million was pledged, with the United States and Japan each contributing $6 million (10,000 tons). Tokyo provided 300,000 tons in direct food aid in 1995 and was planning to give more last year until South Korea objected. Seoul gave 150,000 tons of food aid in 1995 but now wants Japan and the United States to join in denying further aid until Pyongyang agrees to a North-South dialogue on Seoul's terms. In 1997, the World Food Program issued a new appeal, leading to token U.S. and South Korean contributions of $10 million and $6 million, respectively.

Opponents of food aid in Seoul and Washington have questioned whether the crisis is genuine, despite on-the-spot assessments by experts from the United Nations, the Red Cross, and other international relief agencies who have been permitted to tour the countryside without hindrance. The United States and Japan should disregard South Korea's objections and undertake a concerted global campaign to win support for a greatly expanded UN effort including upgraded U.S. and Japanese contributions. It would be morally indefensible and politically self-defeating to apply criteria for food relief to North Korea different from the criteria applied in the past to other countries.

Replacing the Armistice

Apart from economic sanctions and food aid, the most important issue facing American policy makers in Korea is how to replace the 43-year-old armistice with more permanent arrangements that will ensure peace in the peninsula. The need for a new post–Cold War peacekeeping structure was explicitly acknowledged when the United States and South Korea made their proposal for a four-power peace conference (the United States, China, South Korea, and North Korea) on April 16, 1996.

North Korea responded predictably that the United States would have to honor Article Two of the nuclear freeze agreement as an initial precondition for its participation. Moreover, the fact that the United States made the proposal in concert with the South underlined North Korean anxieties that a four-power meeting would be used mainly to step up U.S. and South Korean pressure on the North for a bilateral North-South peace treaty that excludes the United States.

The South did not join (with the UN Command, China, and North Korea) in signing the 1953 armistice because Syngman Rhee regarded it as a U.S. sellout and wanted to march on the North to unify the country. For this reason, North Korea has opposed the idea of a peace treaty between the North and South, calling instead for a bilateral peace treaty with the United States.

Maintaining that the United States is its real adversary, North Korean leaders point to the U.S. force presence in the South and the U.S. mutual security treaty with Seoul. Above all, they emphasize that a U.S. general heads the U.S.–South Korean Combined Forces Command and that the United States would have operational control over South Korean forces in the event of a war.

The United States has properly resisted North Korean demands in earlier years for a bilateral peace treaty that excludes South Korea. But it should give careful consideration to a new North Korean proposal for a trilateral peacekeeping process in which the United States would join with Pyongyang and Seoul in shaping and implementing what the North has variously called a "new peace mechanism" and "new peace arrangements."

The underlying premise of the North Korean proposal is that the nuclear freeze agreement envisages a normalization of relations with the United States that is incompatible with the adversarial relationship enshrined in existing arrangements. As a precondition for diplomatic relations, North Korean leaders say, the United States must phase out the United Nations Command as the legal umbrella for American presence in Korea and join with North Korea in replacing the Military Armistice Commission established to monitor the 1953 ceasefire, with new arrangements reflecting post–Cold War realities.

As an afterthought, they add that a formal peace treaty with the United States is their ultimate goal, but that it can wait. Japan and Russia, they note, do not yet have a peace treaty but they do have established diplomatic relations.

In place of the current U.S. role in Korea, limited to the defense of the South against possible North Korean aggression, Pyongyang wants a broadened American role designed to stabilize the North-South status quo militarily through the participation of the United States in its proposed new peacekeeping structure. In the words of First Deputy Foreign Minister Kang Sok Ju, "the new structure will help to prevent any threat to the peace, whether from the South against the North or the North against the South."

The American force presence and the U.S.–South Korean security treaty can continue, in the North's concept, but must be accompanied by U.S. participation in the new structure.

The contents of the North Korean proposal were unveiled for the first time during a four-hour meeting I had on September 28, 1995, with Lieutenant General Ri Chan Bok, the North Korean representative at

Panmunjom, and were formally presented more recently to visiting State Department official Kenneth Quinones on July 18, 1996.

In my meeting with General Ri, I pressed him to explain precisely what the North had in mind when it spoke of "new peace arrangements." First, he said, the United States and North Korean armed forces would set up what might be called a North Korea–U.S. Mutual Security Commission. It would consist solely of military officers and would not have government representation. Immediately following establishment of the Commission, the North Korea–South Korea Joint Military Commission negotiated in 1992 would begin to operate in parallel with the North Korea–U.S. Commission. When I suggested that the two bodies should be established simultaneously, the idea was brushed aside, but a Key North Korean spokesman subsequently agreed in Washington that this would be possible.[14]

The functional role of both commissions would be to prevent incidents in the Demilitarized Zone (DMZ) that could threaten the peace and to develop arms control and confidence-building arrangements. But the idea of a strictly U.S.–North Korean entity as part of the new structure clearly points to a new U.S. role as a stabilizer and balancer for the peninsula as a whole.

General Ri said explicitly that the North would not object to the presence of U.S. forces in Korea if the armistice and the UN Command were replaced:

> The Americans think that if they join in establishing the new peace mechanism that we will raise the question of withdrawing troops from the Korean peninsula. But it's clear from the Asian strategy of the United States that the U.S. army will not pull out tomorrow. It will take a long time. Accordingly, we will set up a new peace mechanism on the basis of a mutual understanding that U.S. forces will continue to be stationed in Korea indefinitely.

Off the record, one of the key officials I met during my 1995 visit said that "Korea is surrounded by big powers: Russia, China, and Japan. We must think of the impact of the withdrawal of U.S. troops on the balance of power in the region." Another said that "if U.S. troops pull out of Korea, Japan will rearm immediately."

I went to Pyongyang with some specific proposals of my own concerning how the armistice could be replaced. My message was that I did not think the United States would terminate the UN Command as the basis for the American presence unless tensions at the thirty-eighth parallel were first reduced. I proposed a mutual pullback of offensive forces or, at the very least, significant reductions in offensive forces. I also emphasized that the North-South Military Commission would have to go into effect simultaneously with the proposed U.S.–North Korean Commission and that the two bodies should be closely coordinated within one overall trilateral structure. The North-South Commission, I said, should properly handle all military issues involving only the two Koreas, since the United States could not speak for South Korea. General Ri's answer was that the North is willing to negotiate a compromise on the modalities of a new structure and to consider arms control measures, but these issues should be discussed initially between North Korean and U.S. generals. The United States has refused to hold such discussions.

Following the capture of a U.S. helicopter pilot over North Korean territory in February 1995, the United States and North Korea did initiate contacts at the DMZ. Fourteen meetings were held at the level of colonel until South Korean protests led to their suspension in September 1995, shortly before a crucial meeting at which plans for contacts at the level of general were to be finalized.[15]

The South Korean position was that discussions on the replacement of the armistice should not be held between the United States and North Korea. Instead, Seoul argued, the South and the North should decide what role, if any, the United States, China, and other powers should play in future peacekeeping.

It was to counter North Korean pressures for direct talks with the United States on replacing the armistice that South Korea began to float trial balloons in mid-1995, suggesting a four-power peace conference including China. But Pyongyang is likely to resist Chinese participation in any future peacekeeping machinery because it fears that its giant neighbor will become a dominant influence in Korea and it wants to offset Chinese power with a U.S. presence.

Whether or not a Chinese role proves to be negotiable, American participation in peacekeeping arrangements would serve American interests, provided that it is accompanied in practice by a meaningful role for the North Korea–South Korea Joint Military Commission. The United States should work toward a compromise combining some elements of General Ri's proposal for a two-track structure with a trilateral coordinating body that would prevent the North from using the new structure to drive a wedge between the United States and the South.

The fact that the United States retains wartime operational control over South Korean forces makes it reasonable for the North to ask that some form of U.S.–North Korean dialogue be built into any new peace-keeping arrangements. The only way to avoid this would be for the United States to relinquish operational control to the South. Several retired South Korean generals have urged that the United States do this, notably Major General Lim Dong Won, who directed negotiations with the North during the Roh Tae Woo period.

"Only with the reversion of operational control will North Korea respect and fear the South," Lim declared recently. "Unless this is done the North will continue to confine its approaches to the United States alone and sidestep or bypass the South."[16] But the South Korean government suspects that the surrender of operational control might presage a U.S. withdrawal, and the United States, for its part, fears that the South might drag it into needless conflict unless the South is kept on a tight leash.

The Future of the American Presence

How long should American forces remain in Korea? At one extreme, many South Koreans and North Koreans alike argue that the United States should remain even after unification to help offset Chinese, Japanese, and Russian power in Northeast Asia. At the other extreme, Doug Bandow of the Cato Institute has called for the United States to withdraw its forces and terminate its security treaty with Seoul within four years.[17] In between are a variety of proposals that would link U.S. force reductions and an eventual disengagement with the pace of tension reduction in the peninsula. President Clinton has pledged that the United States would "keep American forces in Korea as long as they are needed and as long as the Korean people want them to remain.[18]

The idea of linking a U.S. withdrawal with tension reduction is superficially attractive but embodies a dilemma for the United States. South Korean hardliners who want to see the collapse of the North are generally opposed to the arms control measures that would be critical to a reduction of tensions, such as a mutual North-South reduction of forces and the mutual redeployment of forces along the DMZ. Thus, while it would be desirable for the United States to promote easing tensions as part of a new peacekeeping role in the peninsula, the success of such efforts would be problematical. A commitment to remain until tensions are reduced could become a commitment to stay indefinitely.

In calling for a phased withdrawal of American forces, Doug Bandow does not envisage a role for the United States in promoting tension reduction. By contrast, I believe that the United States would be uniquely situated to play a mediating role in Korea if it adopted a more balanced posture in dealing with Seoul and Pyongyang. It is for this reason that I would support a continued American presence while efforts are made to establish new peacekeeping arrangements and for a designated period thereafter not longer than ten years. During this transition period, U.S. ground forces would be reduced and repositioned so that South Korean forces would bear the brunt of any fighting, and U.S. forces would become involved only if it should become essential. This would radically alter the existing strategy, in which U.S. forces are designed to serve as a "tripwire." However, the reduction and withdrawal of U.S. forces should not affect the security treaty commitment, as Bandow proposes, unless China ends its security treaty with Pyongyang and Russia pledges not to restore its former commitment.

The fundamental reason for setting a deadline such as ten years is that the economic subsidy represented by U.S. forces and U.S. bases enables the South to have a maximum of security with a minimum of sacrifice. Although the direct cost of stationing U.S. forces in the South at present is $3 billion annually, creating and sustaining the relevant units costs substantially more—at least $10.5 billion to $12.7 billion per year. Moreover, in order to measure the full extent of the cost, it is necessary to take into account the expense of maintaining all of the U.S. military units in the Pacific that are earmarked for a Korean conflict, which would add another $16 billion or more to the total.[19]

The South's upper- and middle-income minority, in particular, has acquired a vested interest in the status quo. As long as the South has the U.S. military presence as an economic cushion, it is under no compulsion to explore a modus vivendi with the North.

Opponents of disengagement have argued that the South would react to a U.S. withdrawal by accelerating its defense buildup and that its accompanying anxieties would foreclose meaningful dialogue with the North. But this line of analysis is not borne out by the South's approach to North-South dialogue in recent years. For example, far from exploring mutual force reductions, the South has been moving in the opposite direction, expanding its defense budgets and its military-industrial complex.

The United States should do what it can to set in motion a process of tension reduction before completing the withdrawal of its forces. But it should be prepared for failure and should stick to its disengagement timetable come what may. In the final analysis, an open-ended presence is more likely to result in continued tension than would a U.S. departure preceded by ample notice and a serious mediation effort. It is only in the absence of U.S. forces that Seoul would have to face up to post–Cold War realities, choosing between the sacrifices required to match the level of defense strength now provided by the United States and an accommodation with the North based on a loose confederation and the coexistence of differing systems.

Putting the Pieces Back Together

In moving toward a more balanced posture in Korea, the United States should consciously seek to redefine the U.S.–South Korean alliance as a military alliance that does not necessarily extend to diplomatic, political and economic issues. As long as the security treaty remains in force and the U.S. capability for effective intervention in Korea is maintained, such a redefinition need not and should not vitiate the credibility of the U.S. commitment to defend the South against any North Korean aggression. But even with the most skillful diplomacy, the United States will have to be prepared for a rocky period of readjustment in its relations with Seoul.

The key to avoiding needless strains in what will inevitably be a difficult transition lies in handling the issue of unification with clarity and sensitivity. Until three years ago, the United States was not explicitly committed to the goal of unification. Then president George Bush told the South Korean National Assembly on January 6, 1992, that the American people favored "peaceful unification on terms acceptable to the Korean people." This deliberately vague statement insulated the United States from criticism as an outright enemy of unification but conveyed a sanguine attitude toward the prospect of indefinite division.

What makes many South Koreans so bitter about the normalization of U.S. relations with Pyongyang is the fear that this will freeze a "two Korea" division of the peninsula. By contrast, collapse scenarios offer the hope of a quick, albeit costly, route to unification.

For this reason, a "soft landing" policy should include more explicit declarations of support for unification as an essential component of stability in Northeast Asia. The United States should make clear that it favors structured progress toward unification through the type of co-equal North-South institutions envisaged in Roh Tae Woo's "Korean Commonwealth" proposal and Kim Dae Jung's plan for a loose confederation. Such an American policy would be a logical concomitant to participation in a new trilateral peacekeeping structure.

In North and South alike, it is an article of faith that the United States was partly to blame for the division of the peninsula after World War II—if not as the principal culprit—and thus has a responsibility to help in putting the pieces back together. Linked to this historical grievance is the belief that the United States has reinforced the division by using the South as a pawn in pursuing Cold War strategic objectives related primarily to Japan. Anti-American nationalism is surprisingly virulent in the South, where military dependence on the United States has generated strong undercurrents of xenophobia that are sweeping aside the gratitude felt by the older generation for the American role in the Korean War. The legacy of bitterness left by four decades of American involvement in Korea is likely to increase on both sides of the thirty-eighth parallel unless Washington can find a graceful way to extricate itself.

The United States should actively prepare the way for its disengagement, not only by moving to a new role as an honest broker between North and South, but also by inviting China, Japan, and Russia to join with it in an agreement to keep out of the peninsula militarily. Stable progress toward unification and enduring peace in Northeast Asia will be a realistic possibility only if Korea can be insulated from the historic rivalries of its powerful neighbors.

Notes

1. Testimony before the House Committee on National Security, March 28, 1996.

2. A statement attributed to Hwang Jang Yop was issued in Korean by the South Korean Embassy in Beijing following his defection and was translated by the U.S. Foreign Broadcast Information Service. This excerpt is based on an examination of both versions.

3. This address was first delivered before the Asia Society, Seoul, April 10, 1996, and later before the National Press Club in Washington, May 12, 1996.

4. Nicholas Kristof, "How a Stalled Submarine Sank North Korea's Hopes," *New York Times*, November 16, 1996, p. 2.

5. "Agreed Framework Between the United States of America and the Democratic People's Republic of Korea," *The Arms Control Reporter*, January 1995.

6. For example, Deputy Prime Minister and Foreign Minister Kim Yong Nam; First Deputy Foreign Minister Kang Sok Ju; and Lieutenant General Ri Chan Bok, then the North Korean representative at Panmunjom.

7. Stephanie Eshelman, "Problems and Prospects for North Korea–U.S. Trade and Economic Relations," a paper presented at a conference on "Korea: Prospects for Economic Development," sponsored by the Gaston Sigur Center for East Asian Studies, George Washington University, April 22, 1996, p. 5.

8. Kim Jong U, "Some Issues of North Korea's External Economic Policy," a paper prepared for a conference on "Korea: Prospects for Economic Development," sponsored by the Gaston Sigur Center, George Washington University, April 22, 1996, pp. 3, 4, 6.

9. In addressing a Carnegie Endowment Seminar in Washington on May 1, 1996, Ri Jong Hyok, vice-chairman, Korea Asia-Pacific Peace Committee, said "nothing less than $10 billion" would be equitable.

10. Taobing Wei, director of China Studies, China Institute of International Affairs, disclosed this agreement at a seminar on "The North Korea Policies of the United States, China, Russia, and Japan" sponsored by the Kim Dae Jung Peace Foundation, Seoul, November 26, 1996.

11. *Economic Studies*, Pyongyang, January, 1996.

12. Ibid. See also *Kyonghyang Shinmun*, Seoul, September 11, 1996. The author has also verified this information from a variety of other sources, including North Korean sources.

13. *North Korea Report*, Seoul, December, 1996, p. 13.

14. Ri Jong Hyok, Carnegie Endowment Seminar.

15. Interviews with General Ri Chan Bok, September 28, 1995, and officials of the UN Command in Seoul, October 1, 1995.

16. Lim Dong Won, "A policy toward North Korea for Peace and Unification in the Korean Peninsula," Keynote Address at a conference on "The North Korea Policies of the United States, China, Russia, and Japan" sponsored by the Kim Dae Jung Peace Foundation, Seoul. November 26, 1996, p. 9.

17. Doug Bandow, *Tripwire: Korea and U.S. Policy in a Changed World*, Cato Institute, Washington 1996.

18. News Conference, Seoul, July 27, 1995 (In *Administration of William J. Clinton*, 1995, July 27, p. 1312).

19. Doug Bandow, *Tripwire*, p. 62.

14
The Korean Peninsula at the Crossroads: Which Way?

William J. Taylor, Jr.

Introduction

The end of the Cold War was clearly a turning point in the balance of power on the Korean peninsula. Most notably, it spelled doom for Pyongyang. Virtually abandoned by the Soviet Union and kept at arm's length by China, North Korea lost its fundamental political, economic, and security relationships in its struggle against the South. Isolated by its economic partners and burdened by its inefficient command economy, North Korea's economy became unsustainable. Economic deterioration accelerated in 1995 and 1996 as waves of torrential rain battered the North Korean countryside, destroying crops, infrastructure, and homes. North Korea is facing a severe economic crisis that is undoubtedly undermining the uncertain leadership of Kim Jong Il. Political and economic change is inevitable; it is a question of how this transformation will occur—reform, soft-landing, peaceful unification, sudden collapse, coup d'état, revolution, and/or war.

With the rapidly developing events and changing conditions on the Korean peninsula, analysts and policymakers in Seoul and Washington realize that the parameters of the Korean problem have changed—we are no longer facing a strong, stable North Korea with a menacing military, but an unstable, starving, and increasingly desperate country with a "loaded gun"—a large military establishment and a potential nuclear threat. Conditions on the Korean peninsula are now more volatile than they were during the Cold War.

As of this writing, it appears that the Democratic People's Republic of Korea (DPRK, or North Korea) is falling apart at the seams and that implosion will occur a lot sooner than most observers think. Almost everything is going wrong in the North:

- There is an apparent generational power struggle as Kim Jong Il purges the Old Guard who have lost any confidence they may ever have had in his leadership ability. Although we cannot be certain about this until the defector, Hwang Jang Yop, is taken to Seoul, it appears that Kim Jong Il is trying to consolidate his power by elevating to higher rank some of the junior military officers and other party officials he thinks he can trust.
- There is a rapidly growing number of defections, including chief *juche* ideologist Hwang Jang Yop.
- There is an approaching famine that $16 million in grain from the United States and the Republic of Korea (ROK, or South Korea) cannot forestall for very long.
- North Korea's industrial sector has been crumbling, operating at less than 30 percent capacity because of mismanagement, lack of technological expertise, and lack of fuel.
- The Korean People's Army (KPA) lacks the fuel required for adequate training.
- There is a lack of capital that cannot be borrowed because the DPRK has defaulted on many large foreign loans. The Special Economic Zone concept in the Rajin-Sonbong area will not be productive unless South Korea invests heavily there.

When implosion comes, no one can predict whether it will take the form of a coup or a revolution. In either case, tensions along the DMZ will be so high that a North-South war could occur by accident or miscalculation, or, the North could lash out in final desperation with a limited attack on the South to envelop and seize Seoul, then seek to negotiate a settlement with Washington.

Juche Under Siege

The key question in North Korea at this juncture is when or whether Kim Jong Il can consolidate his power and whether the political and ideological institutions that sustain the *juche*-based system will remain viable. Although Kim Jong Il has not officially received the titles of president and general secretary of the Korean Worker's Party (KWP), the general opinion among analysts who focus on North Korea is that Kim Jong Il is recognized as the de facto leader. Kim Il Sung and Kim Jong Il's meticulous effort to build the foundation for political succession has paid off for the time being. But, does Kim Jong Il have unfettered power and control over the country that his father had? His legitimacy as ruler is closely linked to the legacy of his father, and how he sustains this legacy and the *juche* system will have major influence on the support of key constituents.

Some analysts believe that the anointment of Kim Jong Il was born out of Kim Il Sung's fear that, after his death, the political and ideological kingdom that he built would meet the same dismal fate of other authoritarian leaders such as Mao, Stalin, and Ho Chi Minh—the demystification and criticism of the Great Leader and revision of the revolutionary movement. The senior Kim trusted that his "revolutionary cause [would] be pushed forward by his son whose loyalty he trusts above all others."[1]

The speeches of senior North Korean leaders and the DPRK media commentaries make it appear that Kim Jong Il will be held to this father-son trust. He has been touted as the "eminent theorist and ideologist who embodies the *juche* ideology" as well as "a tested revolutionary who embodies perfectly and is realizing brilliantly the distinguished leadership art of the Great Leader."[2] Therefore, not only does Kim Jong Il possess the "brilliance, wisdom, and leadership" exemplified by the "Great Leader," but he is also the only one qualified to carry out the revolutionary struggle and socialist construction instituted by his father "through the generations until its completion."[3] Kim Jong Il may or may not be the next official living ruler of North Korea, but his dead father has been setting the parameters of his authority. In brief, Kim Il Sung—embalmed for all to see—has been "ruling from the grave." If the son clearly is purging the Great Leader's Old Guard and is seen within the KWP as inept, trouble is on the way.

In addition to moral obligation, we must consider the institutions that have been created to protect and perpetuate the *juche* ideology since Kim Il Sung's first enunciation of the homegrown, Marxist-Leninist ideology in 1955. Every aspect of North Korean society has been slowly shaped into a monolithic system of authority under the Great Leader's exclusive leadership.[4] Over the years *juche* evolved from a political slogan into a complex ideological system that mobilized the entire country under the rule of one person, Kim Il Sung. In 1986, a significant advancement was made in the *juche* ideology with the institution of the doctrine of "sociopolitical life." This doctrine captured the anthropocentric nature of *juche* that argues that mass is the primary force of sociopolitical development but that the masses need the party and the leader for guidance.[5] Moreover, it also systematized the idea, contrary to Marxism, that "human behavior is guided not by conditions and relations of production but by the direct guidance of the leader."[6] The relationship between the leader, the party, and the masses was compared to the human body. The leader is the brain that gives guidance and the masses serve as the various body parts that follow directions as well as give feedback. The party serves as the nervous system that mediates and conveys important information between the brain and the various organs.[7] *Juche* is a "corporate philosophy" under which the human being is conceptualized as a cell in a living organism (corpus). The individual has meaning only as a part of the healthy body.

What is important to highlight here is the vital role of the party and the interdependence between the leader and the party in maintaining control over the country—and the military. The party draws its authority or direction from the leader while the leader cannot exercise his authority and execute policies without the party.[8] Kim Jong Il himself explains:

> The most important thing to the revolutionary movement is for the party leadership to make a scientific analysis of situation created at each stage and to forward a correct line and policies, strategy and tactics and thus clarify the road of struggle. . . . Another important thing in party guidance to the revolutionary movement is to strengthen its kindred ties with the masses and organize them to implement the line and policy set forth by the leader.[9]

The party and its leadership has just as much at stake in the maintenance of the current political-ideological structure to ensure authority and control over the system—including their lavish lifestyle and perquisites. I know; I have seen them.

In 1987, the *juche* Academy of Science was established to protect, develop, and promote Kim Il Sung's *juche* system. The *juche* theoreticians of this academy took the ideology a step further by developing it into a systematized quasitheology. Hwang Jang Yop, one of the architects of *juche* and its former leading theoretician, and who recently defected, pointed out that *"juche* will not be perfected as a philosophical system without being 'religionized.'"[10] Borrowing from and distorting Christian doctrines such as eternal life and the trinity, *juche* ideology attempts to instill absolute loyalty to the system. For example, one can obtain immortal life by relinquishing selfishness and individualism and by integrating one's existence into the society. By sacrificing to serve the betterment of society, one becomes a part of society and will be remembered for his contribution both in the present and to come. Through the deification of the *juche* system, the loyalty of its followers to a demised leader will be assured.[11]

In this light, we can see the difficulty of introducing liberal economic policies that may change and undermine one or more pillars of the *juche* belief system. True reform within North Korea would have to involve fundamental reforms of the economic planning mechanism and the introduction of market principles in decision making, production, and allocation of resources.

Economists argue that North Korea cannot follow a gradualist reform strategy similar to those implemented in China and Vietnam. The economies of China and Vietnam were primarily agrarian, and the size of their heavy industrial sectors were small when the two governments began their reforms. The growth and increased standard of living that resulted from initial agricultural reforms provided a cushion to absorb some of the political shockwaves of reform and countered the erosion of political legitimacy.[12] However, for more industrialized, centrally planned economies, such as those of some Eastern European countries and North Korea, gradual reform is not an option.

Marcus Noland explains the necessity of comprehensive reform for more industrialized, centrally planned economies than a piecemeal reform strategy: "The more highly interdependent nature of industrial enterprises means that a whole host of reforms (such as macroeconomic stabilization, introduction of rational pricing, liberalization of international trade, and introduction of a convertible currency, tax bankruptcy, and social safety net reforms) are a seamless web and must be done simultaneously for reform to be successful economically, and politically sustainable."[13] In other words, the complex nature and the interconnected institutions of an industrial complex require the implementation of a series of reforms to successfully break the socialist pattern of the economy and to be able to replace the socialist structure with a market-oriented economy. Some analysts argue that fast institutional change in the economy and political structure is important for industrialized, centrally planned economies, if economic transformation is to avoid the danger that reforms will become bogged down and carried out only in part to lessen the social disruption of protracted economic structural crisis."[14]

Introducing real economic reform in North Korea would require basic changes in the theopolitical belief system that shapes and drives the economic system. In the eyes of those who work to protect *juche*, reform may be considered as "treason," "blasphemy," or even a direct attack on the embalmed Kim Il Sung himself. A second problem with reforming the economic system is that it would cost party authorities directly. Economic reforms, such as decentralization of bureaucratic planning or permitting self-management of factories, to free industries from unproductive intervention and allow the market to control production, would either weaken or sever the links between the party-government bureaucracy and the masses. In other words, bureaucrats and party cadres who manage and control economic production from the planning level to the factory floor would have to relinquish their power and authority to external market forces.

As Chalmers Johnson argues, the bureaucracy in a totalitarian society is a rigid, self-preserving institution that will resist any change that threatens to rearrange the patterns of power relationships within the government, particularly in the form of efforts to ease party-government control over the functions of state and allowing the market to control the economy.[15] As has been learned from other transitional socialist economies, to eliminate economic interference of the bureaucracy is to dissolve the bureaucratic command structure altogether.[16]

Then, one must consider certain groups' dependence on *juche* in North Korean society for leadership and livelihood. As mentioned above, the unique role of the party gives members a high level of authority as the Great Leader's messengers. With this status, the three million members of the Korean Workers' Party are given privileges and special treatment. North Korean society is categorized into three general groups: (1) the core, (2) the unstable, and (3) the hostile classes. The core class (about 30 percent of the population) consists of party members and North Korea's elite. The upper class children are allowed to attend privileged schools. High cadres live in luxurious residences, possess high quality, foreign goods, attend extravagant parties at "the dear leader's Pleasure Palace" and have telephones, television sets and radios capable of receiving foreign broadcasts. Most of them live in Pyongyang or within major cities and are recruited for influential positions in the military, party, or the government.[17] A weakening or the destruction of the *juche* system would threaten these privileges. Consequently, those with the greatest political influence are also the least likely to accept reform.

Beyond protecting the power and perquisites of the elite, the *juche* system is needed to maintain order among the masses. *Juche* provides the justification of the sacrifice the common people must make within an oppressive system. The North Korean masses are told that their sacrifices today will guarantee their independence and the eventual reunification of the Korean people."[18] As a *Rodong shinmun* article on the second anniversary of Kim Il Sung's death explains:

> Even though our struggle for succession to and perfection of the *juche* revolutionary cause is painful and difficult, we will surely triumph someday and live a happy and rewarding life looking back upon the pain and difficulties of today. If we are to bring the *juche* revolutionary cause to perfection under the respected Comrade Kim Jong Il's leadership, we have to restrengthen the Party, the People's Army, and the League of Kim Il Sung Socialist Youth. . . . With a strong Party, a strong army, and a strong youth league, there is nothing we cannot achieve and there is no enemy we cannot beat.[19]

Given such declarations, it is difficult to foresee any deliberate and meaningful reforms by the Kim Jong Il regime.

For the time being, the plan of the North Korean leadership appears to be twofold. The first answer to the current economic situation is intensifying campaigns, mobilization, and terror. As the above quote illustrates, the masses are increasingly called to sacrifice for the *juche* revolutionary movement and to invest in tomorrow's happiness. Besides ideological campaigning, South Korean intelligence reports indicate that security agencies in the DPRK government have been empowered to enforce stability and instill fear among the general public.[20] Recent defectors have testified that the growing demoralization of the general populace has led to increased public executions to deal with increased crime.[21] The question becomes, how long will ideological campaigns and coercion be effective in keeping people in line before it begins to ring hollow in the ears of starving North Korean citizens and an increasingly deprived military? As B.C. Koh argues: "Coercive power alone cannot maintain the regime indefinitely and it is particularly deficient as a means of ensuring a smooth transition in the political arena. Normative power . . . may well have reached the point of diminishing returns. What remains, then, is utilitarian power—the use of material incentives.[22]

Second, Pyongyang is depending on the anxiety and generosity of the international community to address the immediate problems of hunger and lack of fuel in North Korea. Anxiety stems from the risks associated with repeated North Korean brinkmanship and the North's leadership knows this. At present, the generosity accorded Pyongyang flows from the humanitarian impulses of an America generally unprepared to link food aid to policy objectives and from the Clinton administration's misguided belief that "constructive engagement" will lead to DPRK reform and a "soft-landing" for North Korea.

Flawed Policy of Engagement

Engaging North Korea is akin to hugging a rattlesnake. The question is not whether Pyongyang will go to the brink again, but when, over what issue, and how.

It is clear that the DPRK's economy is in crisis and that, without significant external assistance, collapse is inevitable. The possibility of the North Korean military lashing out toward the South, a violent regime collapsing by coup, a revolution or civil war accompanied by heavy outflows of refugees to neighboring countries, are among the many scenarios that analysts and policymakers fear might be initiated by an economic crash. As a result, Seoul and Washington agreed, some time ago, that delaying an economic crash and promoting a soft-landing is important. But, given the near-disastrous internal problems of the DPRK and continuing North-South tensions in the wake of the September submarine infiltration, and the defection of Hwang, the proper direction toward a soft-landing and gradual and peaceful unification is unclear.

What is clear is that a soft-landing scenario must include certain key components: (1) dialogue between Seoul and Pyongyang; (2) substantial investment in and trade with the DPRK by South Korea and its allies; and (3) the adoption of substantial economic reform by North Korea. For these factors to materialize, two basic features are required: (1) a concerted decision by Seoul, Washington, and Tokyo, to provide massive assistance to help North Korea out of its current crisis, and (2) a deliberate decision by Pyongyang to reform its system and accept outside assistance.

However, it is highly unlikely that Pyongyang will cooperate with a soft-landing policy for three reasons. First, the notion of soft-landing or hard-landing is moot for Pyongyang's leadership because, ultimately, the conclusion is the same—the eventual termination of the current *juche* system of North Korea. The soft-landing approach serves only the self-interest of South Korea and the United States, not the DPRK; a soft-landing would make it less costly for South Korea to pick up the pieces after the current DPRK regime has crumbled.

Second, the DPRK leadership is aware of the fate of other leaders who chose to reform their Leninist states. For the Soviet Union, the institution of reforms led to the eventual collapse of the regime and the communist system. For China, although economically prospering, reforms also caused political disruption, evident by the Tiananmen Square riots, which seriously challenged the leadership and stability of the country. Perhaps most sobering are the trials and sentencing of former ROK Presidents Chun and Roh.

Third, Kim Jong Il's legitimacy as the next preeminent leader of North Korea is directly linked to his ability to protect the *juche* ideology that the "Great Leader" Kim Il Sung established as the basis of the entire DPRK political system. Introducing substantive reforms and eliminating *juche* would result in Kim Jong Il's own end. There are institutions within the DPRK society, such as the 3–million-member Korea's Workers Party, that exist to ensure the viability and the integrity of *juche*. The party and its leadership has just as much at stake in the maintenance of the current political-ideological structure as has Kim Jong Il, to preserve their authority and the privileges that they enjoy.[23]

Again, Kim Jong Il is faced with a "catch-22" situation in which the two pillars of his legitimacy are mutually destabilizing. *Juche* requires him to maintain a strong, centralized, and controlled economic system, while economic tensions, logically, would pressure him to loosen the government's grip over production and to introduce a free market system. Either way, the younger Kim may ultimately undermine his own authority and break the link of legitimacy from his father—and *juche* may fall.

Pyongyang's inability and, thus, its unwillingness to reform its society suggests that the Clinton administration's policy of engagement, dialogue, and unconditional aid will not work. Rather, aid must be coordinated among the United States, ROK, and Japan, and tied tightly to conditions that Pyongyang must accept, such as the reactivation of

North-South dialogue. Does this means carrot and sticks? Yes, but in a different formula. Right now, Pyongyang is using all the sticks and Washington all the carrots! Without laid-out conditions, we are only rewarding North Korea's belligerence and propping up Kim Jong Il's dictatorial regime, which has no interest in reforming its system and helping its people. Meanwhile, what we think we know about horrible human rights abuses in North Korea continue.

DPRK's Deadly Games

The government of Kim Jong Il seeks its survival and unification of the Korean peninsula on DPRK terms. To survive, Pyongyang needs the assistance of Washington to provide food aid and oil, to remove trade and sanctions, and to take the lead in leveraging others, primarily Seoul and Tokyo, to follow suit. To achieve unification on its terms, Pyongyang needs a separate peace treaty with Washington, a normalization of DPRK–U.S. diplomatic relations, and the withdrawal of U.S. troops from the South. Meanwhile, Pyongyang contemplates waiting for the contradictions of capitalism's economic forces to take hold; producing chaos in the South; and providing greater opportunity for terrorism, subversion, and military intimidation, orchestrated by the Central Committee in guiding the march of socialism to cause the collapse of the ROK and the possibility of unification.

Pyongyang continues to believe that the U.S.–ROK relationship can be destroyed and that both Washington and Seoul can be intimidated through continuing cycles of brinkmanship. After all, the recent nuclear brinkmanship of 1993 gained an advantageous deal in the form of the nuclear Agreed Framework. Next, the brinkmanship over Chief Warrant Officer Bobby Hall's downed helicopter in December 1994 brought further progress in direct dialogue with the United States. In April 1996, placing armed KPA troops in the DMZ in violation of the 1953 armistice agreement resulted in the four-party talks proposal, which Pyongyang still believes will provide a direct U.S.–DPRK peace agreement that excludes Seoul. In August 1996 the submarine brinkmanship caused severe strains in U.S.–ROK relations when Secretary of State Warren Christopher and Secretary of Defense William Perry called on South Korea and North Korea to "cool it." How could such an ailing DPRK get away with brinkmanship with the "world's sole superpower"?

The Political-Military Facts of Life

The last unclassified version of the JCS *Joint Military Net Assessment* was published in 1991. That assessment concluded that the U.S.–ROK Combined Forces Command (CFC) would win a second Korean War in about four months of mid-to-high intensity conflict. In our own assessment in the Political-Military Studies Program at CSIS (Centre for Strategic and International Studies), we would now win such a war in two months or less. Why the discrepancy?

Recall that the U.S.-led coalition quickly defeated Saddam Hussein's forces in Desert Storm. Saddam's forces were about the same size as North Korea's present forces and were armed with much of the same Soviet-type equipment. They were also trained in Soviet-type battlefield tactics, as are North Korea's forces.

Since the Gulf War in 1991, a great deal has happened to improve U.S. and ROK capabilities for joint and combined operations in both the Persian Gulf region and around the Korean peninsula. The improvements are across the board, but mainly in technology. The U.S.–ROK CFC can witness the entire battlefield via satellite, Airborne Warning and Control Systems (AWACS), and the Joint Surveillance Target Attack Radar System (JSTARS). What we can see, we can destroy. The KPA lacks such sophisticated assets.

Many analysts talk about the strength of KPA units stationed underground beyond sight and strike of the CFC. But, dug in and immobile, they are of little threat to South Korea. If and when they come out in the open to attack, we can see and destroy them.

Given the rugged, mountainous terrain of the Korean peninsula, there are very few valleys (corridors) through which the KPA could attack. The two main corridors are the Chorwon corridor and the Munsan corridor. Both are located near Seoul. If the North were to attack through either or both, the CFC would enjoy a "turkey shoot" reminiscent of the 100–hour war against the Iraqis. In short, after absorbing the brunt of a massive, DPRK short-warning attack, we would win decisively and quickly.

So, why worry about the DPRK military threat? First, even though the CFC would win in two months or less (there are some important considerations here about how much the Japanese would do to help us), under present circumstances, the KPA may destroy Seoul in the first 2–4 days. Why? How? The three-part answer to this is: First, Seoul has no missile defense, and the DPRK has an estimated eighty-five surface-to-surface missiles that carry high-explosive, chemical and, perhaps, biological munitions. Second, the adequacy of the air defense system around Seoul is questionable in the event of a very short warning attack. Some KPA aircraft armed with such munitions could get through. No one knows how many aircraft could get through, but the fact that even Seoul's air defense warning system failed in May 1996 to sound the alarm when a defecting North Korean pilot penetrated the ROK airspace with a MIG fighter is not reassuring. Third, although the number of counter-battery radar units around Seoul (designed to quickly identify incoming artillery rounds, trace back the source to the DPRK firing units, and destroy them) has increased, there are not enough of these radars nor are there sufficient CFC long range artillery and multiple rocket launchers. Thus, rapid responses to the massive number of DPRK artillery and rocket launchers deployed near the DMZ within striking range of Seoul is problematic. The bottom line is that Seoul is defenseless and vulnerable!

How can this be? Seoul is the jewel in the ROK crown. Depending on the definition of "Seoul's boundaries" after years of urban sprawl, about 11 million Koreans live there and Seoul represents about 25 percent of the total ROK economy. In addition, roughly 59,000 Americans live and work in South Korea (about 37,000 troops, approximately 10,000 business people and roughly 12,000 dependents of both), mostly in or around Seoul.

How can Seoul and Washington accept such risks from North Korea? Simple. The reason has been about who will pay for missile defense, upgrading air defense, and many other aspects of military capability. With a booming economy until recently, the ROK government has wanted Seoul's defense to be paid for in large part by the United States. Washington, on the other hand, has thought that the ROK government should bear the financial burden for Seoul's defense. Until now, little has happened.

None of the ROK or U.S. diplomatic initiatives, including the nuclear Agreed Framework, rice giveaways, or four-party talks proposal have moved the United States closer to peaceful North-South unification. Even if the North's leadership were to accept the four-party talks, they will not enter them as envisioned in the Clinton-Kim Cheju Island proposal. They will have their own formulation, which will not produce the results sought by Washington and Seoul. Unification as a strategic objective is lost in the shuffle, although both sides pay lip service to it.

Juche ideology notwithstanding, the DPRK leadership knows that unification means their own demise and absorption by the South. Signing up for unification means signing their own death warrants. Seoul knows this, too, but worries mightily about the costs of DPRK "implosion."

The North's leaders surely are watching, and probably misreading, the political situation in the South (i.e., recent student riots and arrests, two former presidents in jail, mass labor strikes, a ruling party in serious political trouble over the Hanbo Steel scandal, and charges and counter-charges of corruption) and are calculating how they can take advantage of the situation. We can be certain, too, that they are observing the major U.S. military commitments in the Persian Gulf and Bosnia and reading the debates in the American media about declining U.S. military capa-bilities. If they believe that the U.S. is militarily overstretched, and if their typical pattern of diplomacy holds, we should anticipate some form or other of typical DPRK brinkmanship again, soon, based on Mao's dictum—"When you meet steel, retreat, when you meet mush, advance."

Peaceful unification and even peaceful coexistence remain elusive. Both Pyongyang and Seoul have domestic problems, although of very different magnitudes, and are focused on priorities other than unification. Seoul is intent on its struggle to keep the democratic process working. Pyongyang is intent on maintaining the *juche* dictatorship. In the meantime, given all the uncertainties of the day, Seoul and Washington should redouble their vigilance and look to our common security interests.

Where Should We Go from Here?

The United States has vital national interests in the regional stability of Northeast Asia, in the security of our ROK ally, in the security of about 59,000 American military and business people and their dependents, and in billions of dollars of U.S. private capital investment and trade.

Given that we know so little about the inner workings of the *juche* government and the motivations of its leaders; considering that the pat-tern of DPRK brinkmanship creates repeated situations of high tensions along the DMZ; understanding that wars occur more often than not by accident or miscalculation during times of high tension; and recogniz-ing the damage that the DPRK could inflict on Seoul if war were to break out by either accident or miscalculation, there are a number of policy changes that should be made in consensus among Washington, Seoul, and Tokyo:

1 . Get an agreement quickly with our ROK ally on shared costs for the systems required to protect or limit damage to Seoul—in particular

missile defense, air defense, and defense against DPRK long-range artillery and mortars. The production of new systems takes too long, so decide what risks we can take elsewhere in the world by shifting required U.S. military systems to the ROK now. Recent increases in the ROK defense budget by 12.9 percent over five years and plans to purchase Patriots and MLRs (and to accept some Russian S-300 SAMs as partial debt repayment) are all good signs, but the impact in limiting damage to Seoul will not come fast enough.

2. Give Pyongyang a set date certain for the resumption of North-South dialogue on two existing agreements—Denuclearization of the Korean peninsula and the Agreement on Non-Aggression, Cooperation, Reconciliation, and Exchanges.

3. Make the continuation of funding to the DPRK for light-water reactors and infrastructure development, future supplies of oil, and humanitarian food supplies contingent on initiation and continuation of North-South dialogue. The approach should be: the DPRK enters talks; we and our allies supply. They stop talks; we and our allies stop the supply.

4. Stop playing around with the notion of representative offices in Pyongyang and Washington and with removal of U.S. sanctions; link progress in both areas to items (2) and (3) above.

5. Refuse to participate in North Korea's Special Economic Zone without substantial ROK involvement there.

6. Get our policy straight on human rights; if this is an important interest in East Asia and the Pacific, then apply the same standards across the board, including North Korea.

The bottom line is that if the United States is to remain the "world's sole superpower"—which much of the world expects—then Washington must get back to "realpolitik."

International politics, like all politics, is a struggle for power. This is the one thing that the DPRK leadership understands.

Conclusion

A "constructive engagement" of Pyongyang will not lead to a soft-landing for North Korea or further the cause of North-South reunification. We are watching North Korea on the move toward a train wreck. Kim Jong Il and company are in a "catch-22" situation. They must preserve *juche* or they fall by coup d'état, a revolution, or both. *Juche* is a theoretical seamless web that cannot be "reformed" in political terms because such a stifling command economy cannot be reformed. Without reform, the DPRK implodes. Implosion in North Korea carries great uncertainties and risks. A North-South war could break out by accident or miscalculation. Washington and Seoul should move now to protect or limit damage to Seoul in the event of war, then sit back and watch the demise of yet another communist dictatorship.

Notes

1. Chong-Sik Lee, "Evolution of the Korean Workers' Party and the Rise of Kim Jong-Il," *Asian Survey*, vol. 22 (1982): pp. 435–447.

2. Mark Clippinger, "Kim Jong Il in the North Korean Mass Media: A Study of Semi-esoteric Communication," *Asian Survey*, vol. 21, no. 3 (March 1981), p. 302.

3. Sung-Chul Yang, *The North and South Korean Political Systems: A Comparative Analysis* (Boulder, CO: Westview Press, 1994), p. 676.

4. Pan-Suk Kim, "Government and Politics," in Andrea Matles Savada, *North Korea: A Country Study* (Washington, DC: Library of Congress, 1994), pp. 165–208.

5. Unattributed, "The Theory of Socio-Political Organism," *Vantage Point*, vol. 19, no. 3 (March 1996), p. 37.

6. Han S. Park, "The Nature and Evolution of *Juche* Ideology," in Han S. Park, ed., *North Korea: Ideology, Politics and Economics* (Englewood Cliffs, NJ: Prentice Hall, 1996), p. 15.

7. Ibid., p. 13.

8. Chan-Yong Bang, "Chuch'esasangkwa yuilchitoch'ekyeul bonchilkwa hankye," vol.2, [The essence and limitations of the Chuch'e Ideology and the Single Leadership System], (in Korean) unpublished report (I 995), p. 24.

9. Kim Jong Il, "The Workers' Party of Korea is a *juche*-type Revolutionary Party which Inherited the Glorious Tradition of the DIU," in Kim Jong Il, *On Enhancing the Party's Leading Role* (Pyongyang: Pyongyang Foreign Publishing House, 1988), pp. 94,95.

10. Han S. Park, p. 16.

11. Ibid., p. 15.

12. Minxin Pei, *From Reform to Revolution: The Demise of Communism in China and the Soviet Union* (Cambridge: Harvard University Press, 1994), p. 21.

13. Marcus Noland, "The North Korean Economy," in M. W. Robert Warne et al., eds., *Economic and Regional Cooperation* (Washington, D.C.: Korean Economic Institute of America, 1995), pp. 160–161. See also Jeffrey Sachs and Wing-Thye Woo, "Structural Factors in the Economic Reforms of China, Eastern Europe and the Former Soviet Union," *Economic Policy*, vol. 18 (1994), pp. 401–422; Maftin Raiser, "Lessons for Whom, from Whom? The Transition from Socialism in China and Central Eastem Europe Compared," *Communist Economies and Economic Transformation*, vol. 7, no. 2 (Juile 1995), pp. 133–157.

14. Unattributed, "Gradual Economic Integration of South–North Korea Superior to Shock Therapy," *Korea Times*, March 14, 1996.

15. Chalmers Johnson, "Comparing Communist Nations," in Chalmers Johnson, ed., *Change in Communist Systems* (Palo Alto: Stanford University Press, 1970), p. 17.

16. Robert Campbell, *The Socialist Economies in Transition* (Bloomington: Indiana University Press, 1991), p. 167.

17. Unattributed, "Human Rights Violation through Discrimination by Degree of Loyalty," in Tae Hwan Ok, ed., *White Paper on Human Rights in North Korea* (Seoul, Korea: Research Institute of National Unification, 1996), pp. 78–80.

18. Stephen Linton, "North Korea Under the Son," *Washington Quarterly*, vol. 19, no. 2 (Spring 1996) p. 7.

19. Unattributed, "Let Us Continuously Bring Glory to the Great Comrade Kim Il-Sung's Cause under the Party Leadership," *Rodong shinmun*, July 8, 1996.

20. Unattributed, "Seoul Says North Korea Using 'Terror Politics,'" *Reuters*, July 25, 1996.

21. Unattributed, "Kim Jong Il Believes He Can Conquer South Korea in One Week," *Vantage Point*, vol. 19, no. 6 (June 1996), pp. 28, 29.

22. B.C. Koh, "Political Institutionalization in Asian Communist Societies: China, North Korea and Vietnam," in Robert Scalapino and Dalchoong Kim, eds., *Asian Communism: Continuity and Transition* (Berkeley: IJC Berkeley, 1988), p. 89.

23. For more detail, read: William J. Taylor, "Is Peaceful Unification Possible?" Conference paper presented at The Seventh Annual KLDA International Defense Conference on *The Prospects for Peace and Reunification on the Korean Peninsula Toward the 21st Century* (Seoul, Korea), November 4–6, 1996.

15

North Korean Crises and American Choices: Managing U.S. Policy Toward the Korean Peninsula

Scott Snyder

Is there a crisis in North Korea today? Is it an economic crisis or a political crisis, or both? Could such a crisis have military ramifications? If so, what are the consequences for neighbors such as South Korea, Japan, and China, who could be affected directly by such a crisis? Is the United States prepared to manage a new crisis on the Korean peninsula? If there really is a crisis in North Korea today, is the situation being treated as though there is a crisis?

All of these difficult questions might be usefully explored by applying rigorous analysis and forecasting of North Korea's current political and economic downslide and its possible consequences. These difficult questions are of direct concern to policy analysts, where information gaps and unverified data have been sources of continual frustration for those who are trying to predict and to manage the consequences of North Korea's decline. Presumably, the goals of policymakers are to define policy options that might effectively manage the avoidance of and defuse the potential for crisis by (a) stabilizing the short-term situation while (b) fashioning some means by which to reduce and eventually eliminate the risks posed by the current environment of confrontation.

As one attempts to understand the role and significance of crisis in politics and policy on the Korean peninsula—especially as it has affected and is likely to affect American policy options—it is useful to consider what is meant by "crisis" in the context of the Korean situation and how these "crises" have been applied to American understanding and knowledge of the situation in North Korea. In addition, it is necessary to examine the history of crisis and the manipulation of it in recent inter-Korean relations and American dealings with Korea. Such analysis should help us to understand more clearly the current situation on the Korean peninsula as perceived by Washington and how "crisis" in North Korea might affect the future American policy-making environment and process in several key areas.

The Normalcy of "Crisis" on the Korean Peninsula

Before examining specific instances of crisis involving North Korea and implications for American policy, it is necessary to acknowledge that the crisis situation on the Korean peninsula is not abnormal. The Korean peninsula is locked in a historical and structural state of dysfunction stemming from a continuing state of division and confrontation. "Crisis" has become the "normal" state of affairs in Korea. At another level, "crisis" appears to have become a characteristic element defining South Korean political and social interaction within society, brought about by the stresses of modernization, institutional change, political transition from authoritarianism to democracy, interest group competition, and transformation accompanying industrialization. Many of these stresses extend to and are reflected in the context of inter-Korean relations.

Historically, the institutionalization of national division over two generations creates an abnormal situation on the Korean peninsula. Korea's division was preceded by four decades of subjugation by a colonial power. This situation contrasts with the prior millennium during which Korea enjoyed its status as a unified, independent state. This historical state of division will remain unresolved until conditions exist under which reunification can occur, or at least until reconciliation and normalization of ties between Koreans in the North and the South has made porous the almost impermeable boundary that currently exists between two parts of the Korean peninsula.

Korea's division resulted from a structural dysfunction of two states contending for legitimacy. The seeming permanence of bureaucratic and institutional interests in both North and South Korea are obstacles that perpetuate national division. These structures will be required to sacrifice power and influence in order to accommodate new governing structures that define national interests in terms that cut across current national divisions.

The emergence of new generations, who do not share with their ancestors the historical memory of a Korea without dividing lines, may reinforce the structures of national division. New generations may balance a rhetorical desire for reunification with practical concerns about the sacrifice called for in terms of their own personal living standards, in effect, narrowing the conditions under which Korean reunification might be acceptable or possible.

Not only is the Korean peninsula in a historical and structural state of dysfunction, but the instigation and escalation of "crisis" also seems to have become an essential element in the process of managing and resolving conflict among individuals and institutions in South Korea. As one examines the frequency and nature of "crises" either within the context of rapid industrialization and democratic transition in South Korean society or in the context of negotiations between the governments of North and South Korea, crisis appears to be a necessary part of the process of negotiation and management of inevitable conflicts between two opposing parties. For instance, the nature of competition between South Korean political parties (both over issues and in competition between regions), the tradition of student protest and the democratization process, attempts over time to deal with the Kwangju incident, or labor management conflicts, reflect a pattern of crisis escalation and its management as an essential element of conflict resolution. In the inter-Korean context, the zero-sum approach of negotiations and the role of crisis in spurring stimulating inter-Korean contact necessarily connects crisis with negotiations.[1]

An Operational Definition of "Crisis"

What makes a situation a crisis? Among the many definitions available, William L. Ury and Richard Smoke describe a crisis situation as one in which (1) high stakes are involved, (2) there is a perception that little time is available in which to make decisions, (3) there is high uncertainty about what is happening and how to respond, and (4) there is a sense of narrowing options for managing the crisis.[2] For the policymaker, these factors seem essential, regardless of whether they are applied in Ury and Smoke's case to a crisis accompanying a negotiation or whether it is a crisis that involves the management of complex humanitarian emergencies resulting from systemic breakdowns in failed states.

An atmosphere of crisis, therefore, immediately involves a complex array of factors that introduce unpredictability into the analysis of events and the actors in international negotiations. The neatness of rational choice models for decision making may be challenged by less predictable factors, such as psycho-social variables of personality in handling stresses resulting from time pressure and growing stakes accompanying a crisis; the problem of decision making without sufficient facts available for analysis; and dangers that parties might lose control in an escalation of tensions leading to unintended or unmanageable conflict. Thus, the complexities of crisis and its management in international relations pose rich but far from settled challenges for political scientific theory. From a policy-making perspective, the recognition of the dangers that accompany crisis and its potential escalation has led to a growing experimentation since the end of the Cold War with the development of both institutional structures and procedures by which to carry out "preventive diplomacy"—the diplomatic equivalent of deterrence—as a means of managing conflict.[3]

The definition of crisis presented above requires an understanding of a complex mixture of perception and reality on the part of all parties concerned. Tensions in a crisis are often manipulated by the parties involved to attain their objectives. The possibility remains that a crisis may occur due to unintentional factors beyond the control of either party. In the North Korean case, I will examine factors in the escalation of two types of crises: (1) the willful instigation or manipulation of crisis by the North Korean leadership for potential gain in the context of a negotiation, and (2) the potential consequences of unexpected crises in North Korea, which may or may not be beyond the control of all parties concerned. Before examining these topics, I will briefly explore the effects of one common factor in both types of crisis: the effects of high uncertainty in analytical understanding of North Korea's intentions and stability.

The Singularity of North Korea and American Perceptions

High uncertainty about North Korea's real situation and intentions has been the dominant factor in instigating a crisis atmosphere in the formulation of policy toward North Korea. Assistant Secretary of State for East Asia and the Pacific Winston Lord has repeatedly said that the title "North Korea expert" is an oxymoron, and ambassador to Japan Walter Mondale has said, "If anyone claims to be an expert on North Korea, watch out." Ambassador Robert Gallucci, expressing his frustrations with U.S. intelligence on North Korea and the opaqueness of North Korea as an intelligence target, said of his preparations for his first negotiation with North Korea in June of 1993: "It was the thinnest briefing book" he had ever received in preparation for a negotiation.[4] In many respects, the dominant perceptions of American policymakers have seemed to project North Korea as akin to a quantum singularity in the universe of international relations, otherwise known as a black hole. Four general characteristics are attributed to North Korea that are similar to those of black holes:

- North Korea is perceived as an unknown, opaque singularity in the international environment; the internal workings are unseen, but it is still part of reality that must be coped with.
- North Korea is perceived as a kind of vacuum cleaner that sucks in material goods and resources from the outside for its own unknown, internal uses.[5]
- North Korea appears to have high potential for instability that might spread to the area around it, with highly negative consequences.
- North Korea appears as a failed shadow of its former self, a collapsed star, a dwarf.

Many current analyses project the opaqueness of North Korea as though it were a mirror, reflecting more about the analyst than about the object of study; or as a prism in which the indiscernible object of analysis is divided into visible components, but the sum of the whole remains unrevealed. The primary effects of currently available information on North Korea are refractory, revealing in stark contrast differing assessments of North Korea's situation. These differences originate with the vast gap between image and reality projected in North Korea's own official media statements versus the actual situation. Individual North Koreans who communicate with the outside world perpetuate the paradox, putting forward North Korean propaganda in the face of an empirical reality with which they are familiar, but are not in a position to articulate in public. Such a gap must put enormous stress on these individuals who are forced both to live in the world of illusion and to cope with North Korea's reality.

The refractory quality of our analysis of North Korea is further reinforced by South Korea's politics and policy, which is perpetually and irreconcilably divided on the issue of how to deal with North Korea. The result is widely varying assessments that often manipulate or obscure—both intentionally and unintentionally—the small database of existing facts available for analysis. In an environment in which any information from North Korea is unverifiable, rumors contend with the facts, with little regard for whatever truths might be gleaned about the actual situation in North Korea.

Nonetheless, careful long-term analysis and hard experience have yielded a growing body of evidence that has added to understanding the significance of North Korean actions to induce crisis as part of its negotiating strategy. A growing body of analysts in the United States has argued that our relative lack of knowledge of North Korea is no longer inhibited by a shortage of information, but rather by a failure to systematically organize and interpret available information. Less clear evidence is available to determine the likelihood of major instability in North Korea, but the likely shapes of potential instability are clear and require adequate preparations and consultation by the governments affected to reduce the risks that accompany high uncertainty.

North Korean Crisis Diplomacy and Crisis Manipulation

North Korea has successfully used crisis diplomacy to facilitate direct negotiations with the United States on two occasions during the past five years, both in the context of negotiations over North Korea's nuclear weapons program. In addition to uncertain American analysis of North Korean intentions, the instigation of a crisis in each instance was over an issue that involved high stakes, creating the perception that little time was available for American negotiators to make decisions. In addition, there was a perception of narrowing options as North Korea manipulated the perceived costs of alternatives to a negotiated settlement.

William Mark Habeeb has shown that weak states can increase their leverage in issue-specific negotiations relative to their aggregate power by preserving or expanding alternatives to a negotiated settlement, demonstrating commitment to achieving the identified negotiating goal, and maintaining control of the negotiating process.[6] Throughout nuclear negotiations with the United States, North Korea masterfully used crisis diplomacy as a means by which to demand the attention of the United States and to manufacture negotiating leverage, as well as to manipulate the atmosphere of negotiations so that it reflects more positively in favor of North Korean objectives.[7]

When the International Atomic Energy Agency (IAEA) called for special inspections to verify discrepancies in information North Korea had provided on its nuclear program, Pyongyang responded by creating a crisis that would clearly focus attention in both Washington and Seoul. North Korea announced on March 12, 1993, that it would withdraw from the Nuclear Non-Proliferation Treaty (NPT) effective in ninety days (in accordance with the provisions of the treaty). It already had the opportunity to discern the high priority placed on nuclear issues in Washington based on the message delivered by Arnold Kanter at the January 1992 high-level meeting with the United States. It would have been a reasonable calculation on the part of Pyongyang that instigating a crisis over its nuclear program and setting a deadline for its resolution might be an effective way to use crisis diplomacy to draw the attention of U.S. officials at the highest levels. This would make direct dialogue with the United States unavoidable and shape the agenda for discussion away from North Korea's alleged IAEA violations and toward the issue of whether North Korea should remain a part of the international system for countering nuclear proliferation.

North Korea had taken the initiative, defined the alternative costs of not negotiating a resolution to the issue in terms of the survival of the global nonproliferation regime, and used a time deadline of June 12, 1993, to control the negotiations. The remarkable success of this crisis diplomacy was revealed when the United Nations, faced with a sense of the narrowing options available to avoid confrontation (again, North Korea narrowed perceived options and raised the costs of alternatives to negotiation by declaring that international sanctions would be perceived as tantamount to a declaration of war), allowed a last-ditch option for settling the issue. It postponed consideration of an international economic sanctions regime for North Korea—instead it called for international negotiations with North Korea to resolve the issue. The payoff came when the United States—faced with no viable alternative but to change its decades-old policy (with the acquiescence of Seoul) of not negotiating with North Korea—came to the negotiating table.

The use of crisis diplomacy to threaten North Korea's nuclear withdrawal proved to be a master stroke. It set the stage for negotiations with the United States on North Korean terms. Despite having been cornered by the IAEA's discovery of discrepancies in information North Korea had provided regarding its own nuclear facilities, North Korea defined the issue and agenda not as IAEA violations, but as the price the international community was willing to pay to keep North Korea in the regime. And it forced the United States to the negotiating table to allow what many analysts had said was North Korea's primary goal: the achievement of direct talks with the United States at the expense of South Korea. Without instigating a crisis that challenged a major global goal of the United States, North Korea would not possibly have achieved its goal of a dialogue with the United States. When it had sought dialogue under normal circumstances, the United States seemed to signal that, without fundamental (and possibly regime-threatening) change in North Korean policies, the best North Korea could hope for was a one-time, one-way discussion—not a dialogue in which mutual interests might be explored on a "level playing field."

The second major use of crisis diplomacy by North Korea is well known. The May 1994 decision by North Korea to unload fuel rods from its 5-megawatt reactor directly contradicted U.S. stipulations that such an action would constitute crossing a "red line," which would end prospects for dialogue and result in an international economic sanctions campaign. The decision to create a crisis over the unloading of the fuel rods turned out to hold considerable risk, not because of the immediate danger from Pyongyang, which had considerable experience in managing reactions to crises of their own making, but rather from the United States, where some in the nonproliferation community and other senior policymakers took this provocation as grounds that made preemptive military action in response to the provocation seem justifiable.[8]

This crisis followed an earlier failed attempt to return to the negotiating table through working-level channels. In late November of 1993, Presidents Kim Young Sam and Bill Clinton agreed at their Washington summit to pursue a "broad and thorough" approach to North Korea, in effect responding to North Korean diplomatic signals that Pyongyang was ready to negotiate a "package solution" to the nuclear standoff with the United States. Almost three months of working-level contacts between North Korea and the United States resulted in an "Agreed Conclusion," a four-point plan to get U.S.–North Korean negotiations back on track through pledges to resume IAEA inspections and to hold working-level meetings to prepare for an exchange of special envoys between Seoul and Pyongyang. That deal fell through when a North Korean negotiator threatened to turn Seoul into a "sea of fire" in a heated exchange over mechanisms for resuming inter-Korean dialogue, torpedoing possibilities for resumption of U.S.–North Korean negotiations in Geneva.

Following this failure to renew talks, Pyongyang again created a crisis, this time by flouting U.S. conditions for holding a political dialogue that had already been stalled by North Korea's problems with the IAEA and unwillingness to submit to demands for direct North-South dialogue.

The crisis atmosphere again provided Pyongyang with an opportunity to manipulate the agenda and return to the negotiating table under conditions that North Korea perceived to be more advantageous than was the case in earlier circumstances, when the alternatives of waiting or walking away might have seemed more attractive to the United States. But by creating a crisis that could be defused only through communication at the highest levels, Kim Il Sung had put himself in the driver's seat—if only he could find a channel through which to establish top-level communication with the United States before the crisis escalated out of control. No more attractive channel could have fixed the attention of Kim Il Sung and others in the North Korean leadership than the opportunity to have a dialogue with former president Jimmy Carter, who activated an old invitation to visit North Korea for discussions to defuse the crisis.

While Jimmy Carter's historic visit to Pyongyang had the virtue of saving the newly formed Clinton administration from taking steps to further escalate the crisis, Kim Il Sung used this opportunity to achieve a number of objectives to seek a return to the negotiating table with the United States. First, it provided an opportunity to create the conditions necessary for a resumption of negotiations between the United States and North Korea, so that the "package solution" that had been signaled by North Korean diplomats nine months earlier could finally be discussed.

Second, crisis diplomacy effectively allowed North Korea to reshape the agenda, unilaterally diminishing the focus in negotiations on questions of the history of North Korea's nuclear program while offering prospects for a deal on future cooperation to cap and dismantle the nuclear facilities in return for energy assistance, a long-term joint project to induce cooperation with the United States, and gain exposure to new technology.

Third, crisis diplomacy allowed North Korea to signal its ability as an independent actor outside the context of negotiations. This psychological and symbolic action, demonstrating self-reliance, served to reinforce carefully cultivated North Korean images of independence through the act of having defied the only remaining superpower.

In both cases, North Korea's instigation or escalation of crises appeared to be tied to its larger objectives in the context of a negotiation:

as an apparently weak state with few alternatives, the instigation of crisis on specific issues has served as a necessary part of North Korea's negotiating strategy. However, when used as a recurring tactic, crisis diplomacy appears to have diminished effectiveness, as was the case with North Korea's continual threats to refuel its reactor in negotiations on the type of light-water reactor to be provided subsequent to the signing of the Geneva Agreed Framework.

"Beyond Deterrence"—Implications of and Responses to North Korea's Institutional Decline

Aside from crisis induced as part of a strategy to attain or influence negotiations with the United States, there exists the possibility that an unexpected—as opposed to an induced—crisis might occur as a result of factors external to the influence of the North Korean government. This type of crisis may come in one of two forms: (1) an unexpected crisis to which the North Korean government is able to react with a coherent policy response, or (2) an unexpected crisis affecting North Korea in which the necessary policy response may be beyond the control of the North Korean government. Although the most likely determinant of crisis in North Korea will be a series of unexpected events to which the current leadership finds itself unable to respond, it is useful to briefly consider the past effects of unexpected crises that have induced the North Korean government to formulate coherent policy responses.

First, the Nixon opening to China and the signing of the Shanghai Communiqué in 1972 shocked the Northeast Asian region and changed the context of the confrontation on the Korean peninsula. The initial North Korean response included seeking a dialogue with South Korea, which resulted in the negotiation of three principles for pursuing national reunification, signed on July 4, 1972. After a period of adjustment and reassessment by North Korea, further progress in inter-Korean negotiations stalled.

Second, the failed Soviet coup and subsequent breakup of the Soviet Union in 1991, which undoubtedly came as a serious shock to North Korea, appeared to breathe new potential for progress into high-level talks at the prime-ministerial level between North and South Korea. The historic result was the signing of the Agreement for Reconciliation, Nonaggression, Exchanges, and Cooperation between North and South Korea (known as the Basic Agreement) in December 1991. Again, after further time had passed during which North Korea presumably engaged in some reassessment, implementation of that agreement was indefinitely suspended.

Third, the submarine incident in September 1996 appeared to catch the North Korean government by surprise. It can safely be said that it was not part of the North Korean government's plan for the submarine to run aground, creating a highly charged political standoff between North and South Korea. The North Koreans sought indirect negotiations with South Korea through a third party—the United States—to lessen tensions, and issued a statement of regret, which was hailed as unprecedented in many quarters.

Fourth, the U.S. and South Korean responses to the United Nations World Food Programme (UNWFP) appeal in the context of the food crisis (combined with the recent defection of Secretary Hwang Jang Yop) might have played some role in bringing North Korea to the table for a joint briefing with South Korea and the United States on the substance of the Four Party Talks Proposal issued by Presidents Clinton and Kim Young Sam in April 1996. But it remains to be seen at this writing whether subsequent progress will result, or even whether the defection and other recent events in the North Korean leadership might be described as a major shock or "crisis" that might induce progress in negotiations.

The most serious crisis on the Korean peninsula—and one that has captured the most attention and concern among Korea analysts and policymakers—has been the possibility of an unanticipated internal crisis in North Korea, which the North Korean leadership does not have the capacity to manage. In essence, this crisis is one that might result from the continued decline in North Korea's economic and energy capabilities, combined with a presumable loss of cohesion, disintegration, or inability by the top leadership to impose central political control within the ruling apparatus. Such an event, or series of events, might have the following effects: (1) It might trigger a desperate and destructive policy response by North Korea's top leadership; (2) it might result in the temporary loss of control by central political authorities; (3) it might result in a transition in political power from the current regime to a new leadership; and (4) it might even result in the collapse of the North Korean system, following the example of East Germany and other former communist countries.

Although questions regarding the possibility of regime collapse had surfaced among administration officials in various forms since the Geneva Agreed Framework,[9] the first extensive public statement by an American official to address these possibilities directly was delivered by James Laney in a speech entitled "Beyond Deterrence" at an Asia Society conference in May 1996. In this speech, Laney spoke about the important role of deterrence in guaranteeing four decades of stability on the Korean peninsula, but he raised questions about whether North Korea's continued economic decline and political isolation might present new challenges to regional stability that could express themselves through North Korean military option. "Warnings only work when deterrence is effective. It is the erosion of the effectiveness of our warnings that requires us now to look for new ways of communication and interaction between North and South, and to convince Pyongyang that it has better options than its military one."[10]

North Korea's food problems, its economic decline, and its political instability constitute challenges to North Korea's leadership that remain unresolved and are potential catalysts for a new crisis. A report by the U.S. Institute of Peace (USIP) in October 1996 called for contingency planning to meet such challenges, stating that "prudence requires preparedness for the possibility of a sudden, crisis-induced change on the Korean peninsula," and calling for a two-track approach that continues to pursue possibilities for dialogue to reduce tensions on the peninsula while engaging in multilateral consultation and coordination to prepare for the consequences of potential instability.[11] Among the contingencies explored were the North Korean food crisis and possibilities for either a "silent famine" or massive refugee flows—indicators of economic collapse—including the continued downward trend of North Korea's trade volumes, its continued energy and food shortages, and desperate behavior and economic "freelancing" by local officials; and political-military challenges posed by North Korean instability. This includes the possibility of a military strike or that a factional struggle might tempt various types of interference from South Korea or China.

Deputy Assistant Secretary of Defense for International Security Affairs Kurt Campbell stated in recent testimony before the House International Relations Subcommittee on Asia that consultations between the United States and South Korea on contingency planning for such scenarios is underway, although he provided no specifics in open session regarding the nature, progress, or goals of such planning.[12] However, some American analysts express private doubts about the quality of coordination between the United States and South Korea on contingency planning. Others criticize South Korean planners for not taking seriously the real possibility of contingencies and possible collapse; a third group suspects that South Korea has already developed its own independent plans for handling North Korean instability, which it is reluctant to share with the United States.

A number of constructive suggestions have surfaced regarding specific policy options needed to properly prepare for the effects of negative contingencies and the possibility of collapse in North Korea. Marcus Noland has suggested that in order to discourage migration from North to South, South Korea should maintain the Demilitarized Zone (DMZ) to control population influx; it should also encourage capital investment in the North in order to lessen incentives for emigration. He additionally suggests that South Korea tap international public capital through the World Bank (and outstanding post-colonial claims on Japan) to manage the exorbitant economic costs of a transition to Korean unification (Noland predicts the cost of Korean reunification could be as much as $1 trillion).[13] Nick Eberstadt's policy recommendations to the South Korean government in the most recent issue of *Foreign Affairs* include hastening South Korea's economic transition to a fully open market economy, the improvement of ties between Seoul and Tokyo, commitment to a policy of "malice toward none" following Korean unification by guaranteeing full civil and political rights to North Koreans, and expanding people-to-people contacts between the two Koreas.[14]

The Korean Crisis and Dilemmas for U.S. Policy

Due to the presence of U.S. troops and U.S. commitments to South Korea under the U.S.–Republic of Korea (ROK or South Korea) Mutual Defense Treaty of 1954, South Korea is arguably the only area in the world (aside from Bosnia) where conflict or instability would automatically involve U.S. troops. Therefore, a crisis on the Korean peninsula inevitably will require the attention of American policymakers at the highest levels. There is no high-level official in the U.S. government whose primary expertise has focused on the Korean peninsula, and few cabinet-level officials in the Clinton administration have even had that much experience with Asia. Absent a crisis in Korea, American attention to Korean issues at the highest levels is sporadic and inconsistent, although capable officials with long experience working in Korea provide good analysis at lower levels, and President Clinton has outlined the Geneva Agreed Framework and Four Party Talks proposal as the principal elements of a guiding policy in Korean affairs.

Until the Hwang defection and Secretary Madeleine Albright's visit to Korea in mid February 1997, there was a growing mismatch between projections by intelligence officials that North Korea was one of the top three areas of potential instability in the world and the long-term priorities of the Clinton administration. Even if top-level interest in Korea existed in the U.S. government, the fact of the matter is that U.S. national priorities would place other issues above Korea. This would create a structural asymmetry of interests and priorities between the United States and South Korea, which would inevitably engender feelings in South Korea that the United States is not paying sufficient attention to the Korean peninsula. Ironically, it is only during a crisis on the Korean peninsula that such an asymmetry of interests is temporarily resolved, but the lack of direct experience with Korea at the highest levels may also render a less sure-footed response than might be the case with European or other issues.[15] A second challenge for U.S. policy in responding to crisis on the Korean peninsula stems from the near-permanent dysfunctionality that exists as part of the Korean confrontation. This dysfunctional state, represented by the fact that North Korea is still technically at war with the United Nations Command and South Korea, serves to desensitize U.S. policymakers to the dangers inherent in the stability of the Korean peninsula amid crisis. The state of crisis has become normalcy, numbing American policymakers not only to the possibility that one could easily recur at any time, but also raising questions about whether one indeed exists. Alternatively, media "discoveries" of evolving and seemingly shocking new developments in Korean affairs often makes Korea into the "crisis du jour," in which an event taken out of context becomes a defining moment, often with no clearly defined relationship to its true significance in the context of Korean affairs.

A second aspect of the permanency of crisis derives from the tactics of brinkmanship and zero-sum approach that can be discerned to varying degrees on both sides of the Korean peninsula. One result of Korean brinkmanship and tit-for-tat relations is the "Boy Who Cried Wolf" syndrome: there have been so many false alarms on the Korean peninsula in which the decibel level between the two Koreas has risen sharply that

U.S. policymakers either may have become immune to calls for crisis or have failed to discern between a real crisis and tactical attempts to create an atmosphere of crisis.

Having noted these dilemmas in U.S. policy created by crises on the Korean peninsula, I turn to a discussion of specific issues where crises continue to pose difficult choices for U.S. policymakers:

1. Soft Landing Versus Collapse

Many of the difficulties between the United States and South Korea in managing policy toward the Korean peninsula in recent years have stemmed from the differing priorities placed on maintaining stability versus achieving conditions that might facilitate Korean reunification. Although U.S. policy has been to support a peaceful reunification of the Korean peninsula according to the desires of the Korean people, policymakers have been slow to realize that the process of managing stabilization and tension reduction on the peninsula has an inevitable impact on shaping of Korean reunification. Americans often reassure their South Korean allies that they have won the Cold War because of their towering economic, political, and even military advantages in many areas over North Korea, yet North-South confrontation remains unresolved. Despite being named the winners by acclamation, South Koreans feel that they are not in a position to step into the winner's circle or to celebrate until after having received the long-awaited victor's prize of reunification.

It is part of North Korea's strategy to separate the issues of security and reunification, an issue that everyone agrees must be settled by Koreans themselves. However, just as North Korea must realize that the primary interlocutor on reduction of tensions and establishment of a secure peace on the Korean peninsula must be South Korea, American policymakers should recognize that because of U.S. involvement in the tension-reduction process and because of American influence on the Korean peninsula, it is impossible for the United States to abstain from playing a role in shaping the context for the process of reunification.

The inadvertent and confused secondary signals given by U.S. policymakers on the issue of Korean reunification are reflected most clearly in an examination of statements on the possibility, likelihood, and desirability of a North Korean collapse versus a soft landing. The U.S. debate on this issue has, in many respects, mirrored the South Korean debate, but with less intensity and from a more distanced perspective.

Although the Geneva Agreed Framework has proved to be more successful than anticipated in addressing the threat posed by North Korea's nuclear weapons program (some of the harshest critics of the Agreed Framework believed that North Korea would never trade away such a powerful card), the Framework itself—a product of unprecedented direct negotiations between the United States and North Korea—is the unintended source of much of this confusion. The agreement confers legitimacy on North Korea as a negotiating partner over the long-term, providing vague promises of steadily improving U.S.–North Korean relations over the decade during which the Korean Peninsula Energy Development Organization (KEDO) will build LWRs in Korea. Ironically, U.S. negotiators offered private justifications for the Agreed Framework that it was unlikely that the project would ever reach completion because of North Korea's possible collapse within that time frame. Jim Hoagland wrote, in the *Washington Post* a year after the Agreed Framework was completed, that American negotiators privately described the project as a Trojan Horse that might even facilitate North Korea's collapse.[16] The practical implications of the Agreed Framework from the perspective of the issue of Korean reunification, however, have aroused the suspicions of those who might interpret U.S. policy as opposing reunification. They argue that North Korea has used provisions in the Agreed Framework allowing improved U.S.–North Korean relations in an attempt to change its international situation so as to assure regime survival. North Korea has also gained material benefits through the Agreed Framework that critics argue have served to prop up and strengthen its regime. And perhaps most significant, the Clinton administration has increasingly demonstrated its own vested interest in perpetuating the Agreed Framework in order to avoid the prospect of a widespread crisis on the Korean peninsula, precisely the opposite view of the welcome for North Korea's collapse that was presented by those who were part of the negotiations.

The major side effect of the Clinton administration's commitment to the Agreed Framework has been the interpretation among some South Korean analysts that the United States is pursuing a status quo policy in support of the continued existence of North Korea and the perpetuation of Korea's division. The juxtaposition of these contrasting themes suggests one of two equally unsettling possibilities from the perspective of those who believe that the likelihood of reunification has grown more imminent: either the guiding U.S. policy on how or when Korean reunification is desired to occur is too ambiguous to meet the concrete challenges of imminent reunification, or this issue is a secondary priority for U.S. policymakers who are focused primarily on maintaining stability and have simply given little, if any, thought to the implications for reunification.

Although many Korea specialists in the American policy community accept the Clinton administration's desire to see a "soft landing" for North Korea—in which current problems are managed in such a way that gradual economic reforms can result in a peaceful transition and eventual Korean reunification—the perception that the North Korean government continues to be unwilling to engage in reform has recently raised voices of skepticism regarding the attainability of a soft-landing policy. Jim Mann has characterized the debate as between "Hawks," who believe that the United States and its allies should not bail out North Korea; the "Doves," who are supporters of the "soft landing" policy; and the "Hummingbirds," who think North Korea is still strong enough to survive without far-reaching changes.[17] Most notable is the recent resurgence of hawkish views that has accompanied North Korea's continued downward decline.

Karen Elliott House argues that "for a terminal regime there are no miracle cures," so the Clinton administration would be wise not to attempt to save North Korea's leaders from collapsing under the weight of its own failed policies. Protection from the enhanced risk of military instability caused by any suicidal "lashing out" by North Korea "doesn't lie in more appeasement . . . the diplomacy is theater of the absurd: Pyongyang promises, then procrastinates, then provokes, then pauses. After a prolonged pause come new promises, and the cycle starts anew." Enhanced deterrence is the answer, according to House: the United States should cease propping up Pyongyang and let its inevitable collapse come sooner rather than later.[18]

Although House presents a compelling moral argument for not standing in the way of North Korea's demise, her argument makes three dangerous assumptions: (1) that the collapse of North Korea is imminent and inevitable; (2) that outside actors such as China or Japan will not use North Korea's vulnerability to increase their own leverage in ways that may undercut U.S. interests; and (3) that the United States, or other external parties, have the capacity to influence North Korea's future, which lies primarily in the hands of its own leadership. She dismisses options for American diplomacy to manage inter-Korean tensions while failing to underscore the need for contingency planning to prepare for the scenario of collapse, which she paints as inevitable.

As the title suggests, Nicholas Eberstadt's provocative argument in favor of "hastening Korean reunification" is more forward-leaning than Karen Elliott House's editorial, but this argument also founders in several key areas. Like House, Eberstadt overemphasizes the likely influence of U.S. policy in determining whether or not North Korea is able to survive. However, if the United States attempts to hasten Korean reunification but does not have the capacity to succeed, such a policy would be perceived as provocative and would heighten the likelihood of confrontation and conflict.

Eberstadt argues that the risks of delaying reunification may outweigh whatever costs are involved in seeking early reunification. The potential economic and military costs accompanying the likely implosion of North Korea, in his view, should give Western nations pause as they "classify the Korean question as a problem that can be postponed and then muddled through."[19] He argues that the costs of Korea's reunification will only grow as the economic levels of North and South grow further apart, and the North Korean military grows more lethal as reunification is delayed. Eberstadt paints a rather optimistic picture of a "free and united Korea" that "would be a force for stability and prosperity."[20] According to Eberstadt, "A united Korea's foreign policy would likely be moderate and pragmatic,"[21] voluntarily giving up a nuclear weapons option and setting aside decades-old feelings of hostility for Japan.

Although the exercise of considering the possibility of hastening Korean reunification is worth thinking through, Eberstadt provides in the course of his own argument a lengthy list of the major "constraints" that will likely give policymakers pause in applying his policy to the current situation in Asia: "Neither China nor Russia can be counted on to cooperate"; "South Korea, Japan, and the United States have already restricted their freedom of movement through the Agreed Framework"; "China in particular has reason to appreciate the status quo"; "South Korea's transition from a dirigiste system to a fully open market economy is not yet complete"; "The 1996 squabble over the disputed Tokdo-Takeshima islands, which culminated in a South Korean military landing on those barren rocks, is exactly the sort of distraction that a defense policy for South Korea cannot afford"; "With regard to South Korea, the South must begin to think not only about deterrence but about reconciliation."[22] In the unlikely event that these matters are all resolved, Eberstadt's policy recommendation becomes salient. In the meantime, given the weakening economy of the North, in which gas shortages are an obstacle to timely delivery of food shipments, it does not make sense to assume that the military has simultaneously been able to squirrel away amounts of money sufficient to fund a continuing covert nuclear weapons program and a missile program.

Although both Eberstadt's and House's arguments are not ultimately convincing, they provide a useful service in drawing attention to the fact that security and reunification issues—inextricable elements of U.S. and South Korean policy that are in dire need of comprehensive coordination—have been neglected. While North Korea's leadership has bound itself by its own rope, it has also shown an extraordinary instinct for survival, and in an era in which no external power will actively intervene in North Korea's domestic affairs, the leadership continues to hold its fate in its own hands.

2. Food Crisis

A related area in which a potential crisis poses difficult choices for American foreign policy is the issue of how to respond to North Korea's food situation. North Korea's invitation to the UNWFP to enter the country following major floods in fall 1995 marked a departure in practice from its traditional focus on self-reliance. It was the first time that the reclusive North Korean leadership was willing to accept the assistance and involvement of international organizations, and it showed desperation of the situation caused by a mismanaged agricultural system unable to provide self-sufficiency in food without aid formerly received from China and the Soviet Union.

A second year of more minor flooding in 1996 has perpetuated the involvement of the UNWFP and expanded opportunities for long-term involvement by international and nongovernmental organizations (NGOs) in meeting North Korea's agricultural needs. The North Korean government found a new constituency in the support of donations to meet North Korean food needs that could not be met through its own failing resources.

The issue of how food aid should be handled and whether it is necessary to forestall the prospect either of a "silent famine" or movement by millions of starving North Korean refugees—a major humanitarian crisis-in-the-making—has become a serious debate in policy circles. That debate has intensified as the crop damage from floods no longer becomes a rationale for North Korea's agricultural failings and the bankruptcy of North Korea's system. Sporadic pressure from a South Korean government, skeptical of the extent of North Korean food needs and fostering suspicions that grain reserves continue to be held by the military, has further complicated and politicized the debate over whether and how food aid should be provided to North Korea.

For policymakers, the debate contains several central components. First, is a decision to give food aid separate from political considerations or is it an inherently political decision? Andrew Natsios castigated the U.S. government for failing to resist external political pressures; he called on the Clinton administration to maintain past practice of separating the food issue from political considerations, citing the Reagan-era doctrine, "a hungry child knows no politics."[23] In contrast, Bob Manning and Jim Przystup responded in an opinion column entitled "Feed Me Or I'll Kill You" that without military and agricultural reforms in North Korea, requests for food assistance were little more than a North Korean hold-up and shakedown of the international community.[24] James Lilley has charged that the North Korean government's malfeasance in its spending priorities, which provide for self-aggrandizement (through the completion of a large pedestrian mall in front of the building where the body of Kim Il Sung lies in state) and for continued military priorities that take up over one-quarter of national GDP, should raise serious questions about North Korean government's qualifications to receive food aid without helping itself.[25]

Second, should the food issue be approached as a security and a humanitarian issue or should provision of food to North Korea be used as a policy tool, a "carrot" to induce desired North Korean behavior in exchange for certain types of fundamental reform? If provision of food is both a humanitarian and a security issue, the minimal conditions for delivery might include monitoring to ensure that food is not diverted to the North Korean military or for other unauthorized uses. Provision of food with minimal conditions may also be desirable as a moral choice since the North Korean government is failing to meet the needs of its own people; however, unconditional or minimally conditional food aid runs the risk of being perceived as indirect support or the propping up of a despotic regime.

The use of food aid as a "carrot," or tool to gain policy leverage, carries its own dilemmas. Regardless of whether food aid is linked to participation in negotiations such as the Four Party Talks proposal for peace talks made by Presidents Clinton and Kim Young Sam in April

1996, the perception of linkage may be used by North Korea to create leverage or to attempt to gain undeserved rewards simply for showing up at negotiations in which it has no real intention to engage substantively. On the other hand, using North Korean participation in such negotiations as a condition for provision of food aid may end up being self-defeating or unwittingly create conditions of gridlock in achieving diplomatic objectives—since North Korea has steadfastly rejected talks when it is perceived as being "pressured" into making concessions. The issue of leverage may carry additional ramifications if food aid can be used to increase external influence on the North Korean leadership, as some have suggested in the context of North Korea's increased dependence on China for food aid.

The difficulty in coming to grips with a proper policy response to North Korea's food situation lies in the overlap between the humanitarian, economic, and political components of the problem. The food crisis in North Korea is a classic example of a food shortage caused by politics; however, unlike in Africa where failed state structures or civil wars have been the source of political obstacles to food distribution, North Korea's food shortages arise not from systemic breakdown, but rather from the continued existence of institutional structures of Cold War confrontation combined with the North Korean leadership's inability to adapt its political system to new circumstances. The result is that North Korea failed to develop alternative political and economic relationships with new trading partners following collapse of support from traditional allies in Russia and China.

The international community's invitation to assist North Korea on a humanitarian basis following the floods of 1995 and 1996 was a proper response to the hardship caused by a natural disaster affecting North Korea's food production capacity, but there are practical limits to the capacity of the UNWFP to meet all of North Korea's needs. Since UNWFP's primary contributions are from governments, a decision to extend assistance beyond the immediate humanitarian need caused by the floods is beyond its mandate. The expansion of the UNWFP's latest appeal to 200,000 tons of grain—targeting children in flood affected areas aged six or younger—approaches the limits of humanitarian response to damage. Even with the expansion of this appeal, the international response to the humanitarian component of North Korea's food crisis has been woefully inadequate.

To an unusual extent, the UNWFP has received support from NGOs who have attempted to respond to the appeal. Efforts by South Korean grass-roots organizations and church group coalitions such as the Korean Sharing Movement have been particularly notable for such efforts. Although the North Korean leadership has continued to limit NGO access, responses by these organizations should be encouraged. If possible, direct NGO access to North Korea should be expanded, although the UNWFP remains a suitable conduit for provision of nongovernmental aid in response to North Korean appeals. The South Korean government and other governments should encourage, not oppose, grass-roots NGO efforts to respond to North Korea's humanitarian crisis. A truly nongovernmental response organized through South Korean grass-roots NGO and civic groups should not be limited by politics; in fact, their access to North Korean counterparts on a people-to-people basis should be encouraged.

Unfortunately, any humanitarian response to the massive food shortfall caused by North Korea's agricultural inefficiencies will serve only as a "band-aid" approach unless fundamental political and economic obstacles are also addressed. It should be clear that North Korea's food crisis is not an agricultural problem, but rather an economic and political one. Economic reforms on the part of the North Korean government are a necessary and inevitable part of a comprehensive response to solve the food problem, but the leadership in Pyongyang has little motivation to embark on a course of reform without assurances of the benefits that come with economic integration. One approach might be to link the economic integration of North Korea into the international economic system. Such an approach might involve negotiations with international financial institutions such as the World Bank and Asian Development Bank to provide steadily expanding food credits and technical assistance in agricultural production methods in response to North Korean economic transparency and other reforms.

Although linking food aid to Four Party Talks is a less desirable approach and one that is uncomfortable for American policymakers who might prefer to avoid the perception that food is being used as a negotiating tool, President Kim Young Sam's government has clearly established a linkage between food aid and North Korea's response to the Four Party Talks proposal in his August 1996 Liberation Day speech. The South Korean Ministry of National Unification has offered periodic public statements that the South's response to North Korea's difficulties would be "generous," if only North Korea would come to the negotiating table. Indeed, in negotiations held in April 1997, at which North Korea was to respond to the Four Party Talks, the major sticking points were not whether North Korea would come or the agenda and protocol for the talks, but how much food aid South Korea would give and when it would be delivered.

Indeed, there are several difficulties with linking food aid to the Four Party Peace Talks on the Korean peninsula. First, it has become clear that for political reasons, South Korea's provision of food aid must be linked to substantive progress in such talks, not simply to process, that is, whether the North Koreans show up. The North Koreans recognize and are wary of the vagaries of South Korea's domestic opinion and, as a result, require concrete assurances from the South Korean government. Second, the agenda for Four Party Talks may take years to negotiate because substantive progress on tension reduction and military draw-downs is necessary to achieve lasting peace on the Korean peninsula. All this could conceivably take place in the absence of economic re-form, leaving South Korea in the position of effectively subsidizing a substantial North Korean food bill without addressing the core of the problem. Third, a long-term program of food aid to North Korea is not politically sustainable even in South Korea, where the generosity of South Korean citizens to their Northern neighbors may prove short-lived if it appears that South Korea trades negotiations on political issues for a North Korean "welfare" program.

Finally, given the dire reports of the UNWFP and others that North Korea faced a food shortfall of 1–2 million tons in 1997, the parameters of the food debate might easily change if there are more visible manifes-tations of crisis, in which high uncertainty and narrowing options might tempt the United States and others to push food aid as a means by which to prevent the spread of instability beyond North Korean borders. In this event, the "carrot" of food aid may turn out to be a dwindling asset, or even a liability, either as a negotiating chit or as a smoke screen that prevents the settlement of the more fundamental issue of North Korea's structural reform.

3. Managing U.S.–South Korean Relations

A third challenge for U.S. policy that might result from a crisis on the Korean peninsula is the task of managing U.S.–South Korean relations. Despite close coordination between the United States and South Korean

governments and the existence of clearly defined, shared national interests that are at the foundation of a decades-long security relationship
between the two countries, public perceptions of major political differences have surfaced repeatedly on aspects of policy coordination on
North Korea. To a certain extent, friction over policy nuances may actually be a reflection of the closeness of policy coordination between the
two governments; frictions may also result from the magnitude of the
challenges presented in managing the changes that accompany North
Korea's extreme vulnerability. In recent years, crises have brought tensions to the surface as the United States and South Korea attempted to
reconcile differences in their relative priorities.

Frustrations on either side have been reflected in a variety of ways.
First, unresolvable internal differences within the South Korean policy
community on how to deal with North Korea have occasionally spilled
over to create sensitivities on aspects of U.S. policy toward North Korea. Despite rhetorical support for a shared policy of pursuing a "soft
landing" for North Korea, actions and statements by some South Korean
policymakers, even President Kim Young Sam, have appeared to deviate
from this position, suggesting policy inconsistency, division, and disarray, which reflects the fragility of policy consensus in South Korea on
how to deal with the North.

The frustrations of individual American officials with the fluctuations
in South Korean policy and its extraordinary attentiveness to even minor
changes in the political mood of the South Korean public have occasionally been reflected in accurate but impolitic comments to American media. The *New York Times* quoted an unnamed U.S. official as calling South
Korea a "headache" to deal with,[26] and the *Washington Post* recently reported that North Korean counterparts are sometimes easier to deal with
than South Korean allies.[27] A *New York Times* editorial recently emphasized the need to work closely with the South Korean government on
major policy toward the North, but then proceeded to skewer South Korea
for not being more cooperative in dealings with the North.[28] United States
official concerns over the possibility that the South Korean military could
be tempted to go North in the event of instability or suspicions that South
Korea has not shared contingency plans with the United States are concrete manifestations of fraying at the edges, as are persistent and unfounded
South Korean fears that the United States may seek to cut a special deal
with North Korea behind Seoul's back. The USIP's latest special report
underscored the need for close policy coordination at the highest levels to

forestall perceptions that there may be gaps in U.S.–South Korean cooperation and to cope with the potentially vast challenges resulting from any potential crisis in North Korea.[29]

The issue of managing an improved relationship between the United States and North Korea, while also facilitating improved North-South relations, will remain the biggest challenge for U.S.–South Korean relations. It is clear that North-South dialogue is a practical requirement both for improving U.S.–North Korean relations and for maintaining harmony in U.S.–South Korean relations. In this respect, the diplomatic challenge for the United States is to balance the roles of ally and facilitator of tension reduction on the Korean peninsula. One analogy might be the situation the United States faces as both a friend of Israel and as a guarantor of peace arrangements between Israel and the Palestinian authorities. The Middle East analogy, however, suggests that caution, skill, and sustained high-level attention to a negotiation process are prerequisites for the U.S. role in facilitating the success of a peace process on the Korean peninsula.

In a foreign policy article entitled "Promoting a Soft Landing in Korea,"[30] Selig Harrison suggested the following: that the United States has failed to meet its commitments to lessen the economic embargo against North Korea in the Geneva Agreed Framework; that the United States should take more seriously North Korean proposals for an interim peace arrangement; that the United States establish a date certain for U.S. troop withdrawal from South Korea within ten years; and that the United States play an "honest broker" role in negotiating a peace between North and South Korea. Assessing the utility of each of these recommendations requires an examination of U.S. interests in the context of U.S.–South Korean relations. While such an approach shows due appreciation for shared interests and values developed over five decades between Washington and Seoul, such a perspective should not be construed as meaning that Seoul holds a veto over U.S. policy toward the Korean peninsula.

The Clinton administration appears to have overestimated the extent to which lessening the economic embargo under the Agreed Framework would be sensitive on Capitol Hill or in Seoul; however, a complete lifting of the economic embargo is politically impossible without major changes in the security environment on the Korean peninsula. It may also be a miscalculation to believe that the possibility of lifting the economic embargo is a strong inducement for positive action to a North

Korean leadership, which believes that political benefits must accrue before economic changes are possible.

An honest broker role for the United States is not necessarily helpful in establishing North-South dialogue if the United States is perceived as standing *between* Seoul and Pyongyang; rather, the United States must stand *aside* and push both parties toward each other if the necessary political conditions are to be created for real progress in tension reduction between the two Koreas.

The Four Party Talks proposal by President Clinton and President Kim Young Sam has provided a useful political context for U.S.–South Korean consultation on how to engage North Korea in a substantive dialogue on security issues; it also provides North Korea with an opportunity to present its concerns regarding security issues to both the United States and South Korea. If the Four Party Talks are realized, tactical differences between the United States and South Korea in negotiating with North Korea might provide additional challenges for U.S.–South Korean coordination. Such challenges will require political attention at the highest levels if the Four Party Talks are to move forward substantively.

Finally, the issue of troop reductions is important for the United States and South Korea, but it is a future issue that must be evaluated in the context of reduced tensions on the Korean peninsula and pragmatic assessments of how respective national interests are affected by changes in the regional security environment in Northeast Asia following a successful management of the North Korean threat, not as the result of an artificial deadline. The process of tension reduction and possible reunification will shape the context for a debate on the future of the U.S.–South Korean security alliance in Northeast Asia. It is difficult to imagine that given the possibility of tensions among other powers in the region Korea will want to terminate a security alliance with the United States following reunification, although the structure of such a relationship remains difficult to predict without a clearer picture of specific circumstances.

The immediate challenge of managing U.S.–South Korean relations and of insulating shared core interests from the effects of potential crisis in the North will be even more important given the political competition in the South Korean presidential campaign during the rest of 1997. During the political season in Seoul, the best that policymakers can hope for is that it will be possible to contain fallout from the presidential campaign and prevent the possibility of a negative cycle or downward spiral in inter-Korean relations and in U.S.–South Korean relations in the event of renewed crisis on the Korean peninsula.

Coordination between the United States and South Korea on a long-term basis is necessary to manage the process of tension reduction and peaceful Korean reunification. The quality and nature of U.S.–South Korean consultation to manage periods of crisis on the Korean peninsula in the coming years will be the major determinant in shaping the nature and will form the basis for a continuing relationship consistent with shared national interests in the post-reunification era.

Conclusion

The task of managing U.S. policy toward the Korean peninsula has been full of "drama and catastrophe,"[31] as the United States and South Korea have moved from crisis to crisis in dealings with North Korea in recent years. In fact, the periodic escalation and management of crisis turns out to be characteristic of a regular state of affairs in dealing with North Korea. As such, "crisis" has become a necessary and even integral part of U.S.–Korean relations, and can even be constructive if it is anticipated and carefully managed. Although the opaque nature of North Korean society increases the uncertainty of policymakers and induces a greater sense of urgency in responding to North Korean actions, there is sufficient information available from this experience to draw some preliminary conclusions regarding crisis and North Korean behavior.

The North Korean leadership has used crisis diplomacy as an instrument of negotiation in order to limit the perceived alternatives of the negotiating counterpart and to force the counterpart to give in to its demands. A proper response to North Korea's crisis-driven policies requires a forward-looking, proactive policy and the foresight to take the initiative rather than simply to react. Unexpected changes, or crises, have brought North Korea to the negotiating table and have created, at least temporarily, an atmosphere in which North Korean concessions or agreements are possible; however, once the atmosphere has stabilized North Korea has returned to an uncompromising political stance. As conditions in North Korea continue to decline, the possibility grows that North Korea may for the first time face a crisis that is beyond the capability of its leadership to manage, possibly resulting in the disintegration or destabilization of the leadership's ability to face the difficult challenges leading to a regime transition and even toward a collapse of the North Korean system.

The prospects of instability resulting from such a collapse are a relatively new factor for consideration in American policy toward Korea, which for almost five decades has focused primarily on deterrence to prevent instability resulting from North Korean aggression. Such a possibility requires contingency planning on a wide variety of fronts. The rhythms and rituals of a "crisis"-driven process on the Korean peninsula carry a major risk: they may lull policymakers into a false sense of comfort, requiring parties that apparently need a sense of crisis in order to engage in diplomatic efforts to take even more dangerous risks before coming to grips with problems. The dilemmas of setting the relative priorities of maintaining stability on the Korean peninsula versus achieving reunification, managing the North Korean food crisis, and maintaining U.S.–South Korean relations are the primary areas in which a crisis might force American policymakers to face up to difficult choices.

In the meantime, the North Korean government remains as the primary authority in North Korea and the entity with which the United States and South Korea must work to manage tensions and reduce the risk of war. The job of a mixed strategy of diplomacy and military deterrence—if properly implemented—is to influence the process of change, where possible, by making the choices of the North Korean leadership more complex. This can be done by fashioning both a more strict and more generous policy. Such U.S.–South Korean joint policy might explicitly embrace simultaneous steps toward cooperation on fundamental issues such as the need to promote inter-Korean reconciliation and exchange in return for economic transparency and conventional arms drawdowns. At the same time, the United States and South Korea must maintain deterrence and prepare for contingencies resulting from crises that are beyond the control of the North Korean leadership.

Notes

1. These conclusions are presented in my book, *Negotiating on the Edge: North Korean Negotiating Behavior* (Washington, D.C.: United States Institute of Peace Press, 1994).

2. William L. Ury and Richard Smoke, "Anatomy of a Crisis," in J. William Breslin and Jeffrey Z. Rubin, eds., *Negotiation Theory and Practice* (Cambridge: Program on Negotiation Books, 1991), pp. 37–47.

3. Michael Lund, *Preventing Violent Conflicts: A Strategy for Preventive Diplomacy* (Washington, D.C.: United States Institute of Peace Press, 1996).

4. Author interview with Ambassador Gallucci, December 1996.

5. James Lilley, Congressional Testimony Before the House Committee on International Relations, Subcommittee on East Asia and the Pacific, February 26, 1997, and "Underwriting a Dictatorship; North Korea Has Become a Black Hole Down Which U.S. Taxpayer Dollars Disappear." *Washington Post*, July 19, 1996, p. A27.

6. William Mark Habeeb, *Power and Tactics in International Negotiation: How Weak Nations Bargain With Strong Nations* (Johns Hopkins University Press, 1988).

7. Available analysis of North Korea's nuclear standoff as a case study for Habeeb's thesis include Samuel Kim, "Explaining North Korea's Negotiating Behavior" in Taehwan Kwak, ed., *The Negotiation Strategy of North Korea and Relations between North and South Korea* (forthcoming); Yong-Ho Kim, "A Comparison of Communist Countries' Negotiation Styles: North Korea, People's Republic of China, Union of Socialist Soviet Republics," in *Social Science and Policy Research*, vol. 17, no. 2, 1995, p. 10. Seoul: Seoul National University Press, pp. 277–300, and unpublished manuscript given to the author in June of 1996.

8. Arnold Kanter and Scowcroft, *Washington Post*, June 1994.

9. Larry A. Niksch, "U.S. Policy Towards North Korea: The Collapse Theory and Its Influence," paper prepared for the Annual International Symposium of Korea National Defense University, August 22, 1996, provides the various impacts on policy of concerns among American officials regarding the possible collapse of North Korea.

10. Ambassador James T. Laney, "North and South Korea: Beyond Deterrence." Speech delivered to Asia Society conference, May 11, 1996.

11. Scott Snyder, "A Coming Crisis on the Korean Peninsula? The Food Crisis, Economic Decline, and Political Considerations." Special Report of the U.S. Institute of Peace, October 1996, p. 2.

12. Kurt Campbell, "Hearing on U.S. Policy Toward the Korean Peninsula." House Committee on International Relations, Subcommittee on East Asia and the Pacific, February 26, 1997.

13. Marcus Noland, "Why North Korea Will Muddle Through." *Foreign Affairs,* July/August 1997, pp. 105–118.

14. Nicholas Eberstadt, "Hastening Korean Reunification." *Foreign Affairs*, March/April 1997, pp. 77–92.

15. Robert Manning and others have called for the appointment of a "Dennis Ross"–type of special envoy for the Korean peninsula in recent testimony before the House Committee on International Relations, Subcommittee for East Asia and the Pacific, "Hearing on U.S. Policy Toward the Korean Peninsula," February 26, 1997.

16. Larry A. Niksch, "U.S. Policy Towards North Korea: The Collapse Theory and Its Influence," paper prepared for the Annual International Symposium of Korea National Defense University, August 22, 1996.

17. Jim Mann, "Future of North Korea May Become Clinton's Biggest Foreign Policy Test," *Los Angeles Times*, December 30, 1996.

18. Karen Elliott House, "Let North Korea Collapse," *The Wall Street Journal*, February 21, 1997, p. A14.

19. Eberstadt, *Foreign Affairs*, p. 80.

20. Ibid., p. 85.

21. Ibid., p. 86.

22. Ibid., pp. 87–90.

23. Andrew Natsios, "Feed North Korea: Don't Play Politics With Hunger," *Washington Post*, February 9, 1997, p. C01.

24. Robert A. Manning and James Przystup, "Feed Me Or I'll Kill You," *Washington Post*, February 20, 1997.

25. James Lilley, Congressional Testimony Before the House Committee on International Relations, Subcommittee on East Asia and the Pacific, February 26, 1997.

26. Nicholas D. Kristoff, "How A Stalled Submarine Sank North Korea's Hopes," *New York Times*, November 17, 1996.

27. Jeffrey Smith, "Korean Talks Jeopardized by New Tensions: U.S. Opening to North Strains Relations With South." *Washington Post*, February 17,1997.

28. "Korea: Friend or Foe?" *New York Times*, February 21, 1997.

29. Scott Snyder, "A Coming Crisis on the Korean Peninsula? The Food Crisis, Economic Decline, and Political Considerations," Special Report of the U.S. Institute of Peace, October 1996.

30. Selig S. Harrison, "Promoting a Soft Landing in Korea," *Foreign Policy*, no. 106, Spring 1997, pp. 57–76.

31. Author interview with U.S. government official, December 1996.

Part V
Looking Toward the Next Century

16
Resolving the North Korean Crisis: What Should Be Done by the Business Community?

P.H. Koo

The Crisis as Opportunity

There is an unmistakable consensus among North Korea watchers that North Korea (Democratic People's Republic of Korea, or DPRK) is indeed in dire straits. With its economic difficulties, dramatized by recent food shortages, some form of collapse seems almost inevitable. A sudden collapse would not only bring enormous costs to South Korea, but also would cause instability in the region resulting from, for example, a massive refugee problem or, even worse, a desperate lash-out against South Korea by the North Korean military. All of us know this. All of us agree that something must be done to prevent such a scenario.

I would like to take this opportunity to discuss what the business communities of both the United States and Korea can do about the situation in North Korea. As a practitioner in trade, I believe that while the problem we face may be quite serious, we can always find some pragmatic solution if we are determined to find one.

We must first examine whether the conditions in North Korea really make the situation hopeless, or whether there still is room to maneuver. I have little doubt that there is a crisis. There is no need to reiterate all the specific figures and details of the conditions in North Korea. We all agree that the fundamentals are not good.

With the end of the Cold War, North Korea lost an important economic relationship with the USSR and China. While North Korean trade with Russia consisted of 50 percent in the 1980s, now it consists of only about 10 percent. While its trade with China has recently increased in the form of "friendship trade," it is insignificant when compared with China's trade with South Korea. Because of this and other factors, the North Korean economy has contracted by 5 percent for six consecutive years. Fundamentally, North Korea's food shortages are not just a consequence of the summer floods that hit North Korea in recent years, but rather the result of a nonfunctioning and failing economy.

While there is a crisis, the situation is not hopeless. The Chinese translation of the word "crisis" consists of two words: "Wei" and "Ji." The word "Wei" means danger, but the word "Ji" means opportunity. Thus, according to the ancient wisdom of Asia, we can look at a crisis situation as one that not only entails danger but presents opportunity as well. Although the North Korean crisis situation is dire, I believe that there are ways in which we may be able to survive the crisis and turn danger into an opportunity.

Hopeful Signs

There are some signs that opportunity still exists in relation to resolving the North Korea crisis. One such sign has come in recent days. The way that North Korea quickly wrote off Hwang Jang Yop's defection is significantly different from the old North Korean way of confrontation. North Korea knew that a prolonged confrontation would only expose its weakness and, instead, declared that they would "let cowards leave the country." In addition, North Korea has recently shown a willingness to engage in discussions that has been shunned thus far. Also, its recent decision to participate in the three-party talks with South Korea and the United States to prepare for the four-party talks between South Korea, North Korea, China, and the United States, seems to demonstrate this willingness. Further, it should be noted that North Korea has shown sincerity and business-like manner throughout the KEDO negotiations.

While North Korea's recent willingness to engage with the outside world may be caused by hunger-driven pragmatism, such willingness still reflects a change in North Korea's thinking, and provides reasons for hope that disaster can be averted.

There is also hope in the realm of economics. If North Korea's fundamentally unsound economy is willing to change, there are several factors it can use to its advantage.

First, the Asia-Pacific region's overall prosperity: the entire region has been economically successful except for North Korea. The Asia-Pacific can be a source for investment and a market for North Korean goods, thus helping it to share in the region's economic success. "A rising tide can raise all ships" and North Korea should not be an exception.

Paradoxically speaking, low expectations by the international business community of North Korea's willingness and ability to change can actually turn out to be an advantage. Because of these low expectations, even small changes may be welcomed by the international community. The Rajin-Sonbong region can be a good example of this point. Even cosmetic changes can help address the problem of North Korea's image as a hostile state of political repression, and draw much needed international funds.

Finally, there is South Korea, which is willing to aid the North if it shows sincerity in its dealings with South Korea. Only South Korea can provide friendly terms and significant investment to North Korea compared with other countries. Of course, the United States, Japan, and China are willing to help keep North Korea afloat in order to avoid the impacts of collapse, and these countries can be used by North Korea to help it survive economically and recover. But the truth is: their contributions are not enough to finance North Korea.

Seizing the Opportunity

I am not pretending that I have all the answers to the problem of how to deal with North Korea. Instead, I would like to suggest certain essential steps the governments and the business community should take to help prevent a messy situation in the Korean peninsula.

First, I urge both the United States and South Korean governments to agree quickly upon a strategy in dealing with North Korea. In the past few years, a lack of agreement has led to unnecessary frictions and confusions. Goals need to be clearly defined: Should we strive for a "soft-landing" scenario, or must we settle for a "soft-collapse" scenario if a soft landing is not possible? Measures need to be outlined to deal with possible contingencies, such as a refugee crisis or military reaction. Strategy and steps should be fully agreed upon if we are to avoid a policy of "knee-jerk reactions" in response to headlines and events. If the government does not have a concrete plan, businesses cannot assess the situation to make long-term commitments. I do not mean that businesses should have complete free rein. The government should be consulted by the business community in order to avoid any possible mishap that may oppose strategic interest. In any case, there needs to be a firm strategy so that the business community and the government can work together in defusing the crisis. Business communities should not be shy in telling the policymakers about this basic requirement.

Second, the South Korean business community should commit itself to pushing for reform within the Korean economy to free it from distortion. While the government has said that liberalization and deregulation are major goals, Korea still has many miles to go. Winston Churchill once said that "war is too important to be left to generals." The economy is too important to leave to government officials and bureaucrats. The business community should not be satisfied in playing the role of a passive partner, but should take an active lead in prodding the government to act by setting examples and offering suggestions. A strong South Korean economy that operates in accordance with the international standards of free-market competition will be needed to help finance unification. South Korea's ability to finance such an undertaking is limited by its size, thus it needs to attract international capital by making it one of the best places for foreign direct investment.

In order to discuss issues and coordinate efforts, bilateral U.S.–Korea business forums or panels should be initiated. These channels would be the mechanism to discuss the business communities' strategies toward North Korea, as well as the division of labor between the United States and the South in dealing with North Korea. Such efforts should be in close communication with the governments to provide an overall strategy to both public and private sector endeavors.

While I honestly believe that even though what eventually will happen in North Korea is largely determined by dynamics within North Korea itself and its willingness to reform, outside influences such as those from the international business community can greatly influence the process. What we need is a leadership from both the government and the business community that can clearly see what is lying before us and mobilize all the resources we have, including our willpower, to defuse the current crisis and to pave the road for Korean unification.

17
Korea and the United States:
Looking to the Twenty-First Century

Robert A. Scalapino

A new century is less than three years away. When one surveys the promises and challenges of the twenty-first century, both seem awesome. The acceleration of the scientific–technological revolution shows no signs of abating, and through it, the lives of most individuals will be dramatically altered. Material gains for the majority of the world's population will continue to advance. The Internet and similar developments will render available information massive. All borders will be porous; all individuals reachable.

Yet serious challenges face those who must deal with, or live, in the decades ahead. Some lie in the field of demography and resources—the rising populations and the corresponding pressures upon energy, food, and water, as well as increased pollution. Some lie in the realm of violence. As the risk of global war involving the major powers declines, the potential of local violence connected with failing states, communal strife, and fanaticism will rise, with powerful weapons more readily available to those who seek them. Further, in the midst of dizzying change, many will lose their moorings, asking the questions, "Who am I?" and "What do I believe?"

In this context, how should we view the future of the U.S.–Korea relationship? First, let us briefly review the past and present, emphasizing interpretation rather than extensive data. More than one hundred years ago, Americans were interacting with Korea and Koreans in the fields of religion, education, and medicine, and their mark is still visible. Yet the United States as a government was generally reluctant to become involved or committed. Most Korean leaders, starting with King Kojong, saw advantages in getting a distant power involved so as to counterbalance neighboring powers, but Washington doubted that this remote peninsula, affixed to the Asian mainland, was important to its national interest.

Even after World War II, such a doubt remained, with tragic results. Presumably no one needs to be reminded that U.S. actions in withdrawing our military forces and pronouncements to the effect that Korea did not lie within our defense perimeter gave the Communists good reason to believe that they could "liberate" the South without facing American power.

Some individuals blame Russia and America for the initial division of Korea in 1945. It is true that Korea could have emerged from Japanese colonialism as a single unit. But Korea would have been under Russian aegis. The Russians were in a position to dominate the peninsula in mid-1945, and only because the Cold War had not yet begun and because they had other global objectives requiring U.S. support did they permit American access to the South.

Today, two Koreas still exist, with the prospects for unification in the near future very uncertain. And while these two Koreas share certain commonalities, including language, it is difficult to think of other culturally linked societies so different in economic, political, and social terms. South Korea today can be defined as a society that has successfully entered modernization—and now faces the problems connected with that fact. North Korea is a failing society, having pursued a flawed economic strategy and a strongly traditional political course. Modernization lies ahead.

Let me amplify those generalizations. The economic advances of South Korea (Republic of Korea, or ROK) in the past thirty-five years are common knowledge. This is now a society where per capita income exceeds $10,000 per annum, and with relatively few citizens falling into the poverty category. To be sure, there are regional variations, helping to bolster political regionalism, but as a nation, South Korea has enjoyed extraordinary economic success, and in the course of its recent development, projected itself into the region and the world with great vigor.

At the same time, South Korea, along with Japan, illustrates the fact that no economic strategy is permanently valid. The need for structural reform to permit greater flexibility is strongly evident , and the difficulties in achieving that reform are equally clear. The ROK finds itself in between the low-labor-cost societies and the high-tech leaders, with the need both to sharpen its competitive capacities and to race toward the high-tech service sector fields. Yet, whether the issue is new labor laws or greater foreign access to the economy, domestic interest groups are prepared to do battle.

In the political field also, the sky is not without clouds. In the course of a few decades, South Korea moved from authoritarian-pluralism to democracy. Under the former structure, stability was maintained while rapid economic growth took place, with politics controlled but a civil society apart from the state gradually permitted, and a mixed economy cultivated. The private sector was encouraged, although staunch mercantilist policies were pursued.

Today, South Korea is a democracy, yet while institutions are democratic, personalities often remain authoritarian. Moreover, a series of scandals involving public officials testifies to the fact that money-politics plagues this democracy, as it does many others. Such problems are by no means unknown in the West, as is commonly recognized. Yet in broad terms, Western politics is based upon legalism; Asian politics is based upon personalism and reciprocity. The difference is important, and while many Asian societies are moving toward legalism, the task is a difficult one. Thus, the distinction between formal and informal politics in a society like South Korea remains significant. Yet the problems of South Korean democracy do not seem regime-threatening, at least not at present.

Meanwhile, North Korea (Democratic People's Republic of Korea, or DPRK) presents a very different picture. Everyone, including the North Korean leaders, acknowledges the seriousness of the economic situation. Pyongyang blames the problems on the collapse of the USSR—the North's chief economic trading partner and source of support—and the serious floods of 1995 and 1996. Unquestionably, these factors are important. Yet the more critical problems lie in the economic strategy pursued. While that strategy paid initial dividends, increasingly, the autarky promoted separated the North from the scientific-technological revolution taking place around it, and extreme collectivism produced over-bureaucratization, minimal incentives, and a highly conservative approach to development. Further, excessive militarization drained resources, and limited attention to the needs of the consumer.

On the political front, the DPRK should also be portrayed not as a revolutionary society, but one strongly interlaced with traditionalism, as noted earlier. The hermit kingdom lives on, and with it, a near-religious aura surrounding the leader, promoting his presumed omnipotence and omnipresence. Mobility has been strictly controlled, at least for the common citizen, and life in all respects has remained simple. Yet some elements of modernism have been adapted in the political order: cradle-to-grave indoctrination and mass mobilization among them, along with the insistence that the government is a "people-centered" system and that this is a people's democracy.

In reality, the people have little voice in the DPRK political system. Indeed, even the political institutions long established, such as the Supreme People's Assembly and the Korean Workers Party Congress, have not met in recent times. The decision-making process is obscure. It is assumed that the military have a powerful voice, but are generally integrated with civilians in the top party organs. The image presented publicly is that of all decisions requiring the imprimatur of the new Great Leader, Kim Jong Il, and funneled to him by a group of close-in advisors. Clearly, the older generation of Kim Il Sung's confidants are passing from the scene, and younger individuals—both military and civilian—are being elevated to top positions. Moreover, there is some evidence of differences over policies, as might be expected, given the political hazards of embarking on a new course of economic reform. There are also clear signs of rivalry at the horizontal level between groups representing different organizations. Yet the precise decision-making process, and the degree of unity or disunity among central leaders remain unclear.

What is the future of this society in terms of economic and political system? No question is more crucial in seeking to envisage the future of relations between the two Koreas, and between them and the United States. At the outset, let me express the view that any answer that posits a single definitive outcome is unwise. The variables, both domestic and foreign, are many, and some defy prediction at this time. Thus, it is essential to consider various scenarios, and in considering policies, prepare for each.

One scenario involves the early, rapid collapse of the DPRK government. A number of observers, both in the ROK and elsewhere, argue that the economic changes now being undertaken or contemplated will be too little and too late. They see the collapse of the North as inevitable, and likely to come swiftly.

Should that occur, the premium for South Korea would be maximum preparedness for the gigantic tasks that would befall it. Large refugee flows might occur, especially if the economy ceased to function and/or violence unfolded. In any case, the burden of absorbing some 23 million people whose living standard is scarcely one-tenth that of the South would require multibillion dollars. Certainly, some external assistance would be essential, and the United States should be prepared to do its share.

More awesome would be imposing these people, accustomed only to a hard authoritarian system, on a fledgling democracy. At a minimum, this would produce intensive pressures, even if some form of federation were possible in the initial stage. Certain South Koreans treat these burdens lightly, arguing that early reunification via this route can be borne willingly by the South Korean people. In my opinion, their views are a product of their policy preferences, namely, bring the North down now— but these views bear scant relation to reality. Nonetheless, the collapse scenario is sufficiently possible to warrant more preparation on the part of both the ROK and the United States than has currently taken place. And that preparation should involve extensive discussions with China, as well as with Japan and Russia.

Another scenario, possibly more likely, is that of the gradual disintegration of the North over time, the product of insufficient economic improvements, faltering leadership, and rising factionalism among the top echelons of leadership. This scenario also carries dangers, and possibly even greater ones than those involved in rapid collapse. It would be signaled by increasing defections and refugee flows, the possibility of assassinations or street violence, and the likelihood of one or more factions turning to external sources for support. The latter possibility would signal the regionalization of what was initially a domestic crisis, a common phenomenon in our times.

Once again, preparation for such an eventuality, however difficult, is warranted. South Korea needs to improve its approach to defector integration, develop refugee facilities without encouraging refugee flows, and keep in close touch with others, especially the North's near neighbors. Once again, close cooperation between the ROK and the United States, including preparations that extend into the security realm, is essential.

Yet another scenario advanced by some outside observers is that of a North Korean attack on the South, generally defined as a product of desperation. The view is that Northern leaders, feeling themselves encircled and without hope of extrication, would launch an attack, hoping to mobilize their people and play upon the South's pluralism and problems.

This scenario, in my opinion, has very limited possibility. Few leaders knowingly commit suicide on behalf of themselves and their society. Most wars are started by individuals who believe they can win, as was the case in the North's strike against the South in 1950. Today, the U.S. commitment to ROK defense is fully credible, and while the DPRK could exact heavy damage on the South in the early stages of a conflict, in the end, it would be pulverized by a combination of air, sea and ground power—a fact that its leaders know. Nonetheless, it behooves the South to improve its infiltration detection capacities even as it seeks longer-range agreements relating to troop withdrawals from the demilitarized zone (DMZ) and a comprehensive peace treaty.

Yet another scenario can be labeled the "hunkering down" scenario. It is sometimes argued that the North Korean people are inured to hardship and that a tightly controlled political system can preserve order for a protracted period despite hardships. Examples such as Soviet-era Albania are cited. If this scenario were to materialize, the premium for the ROK would be upon combining vigilance with the type of overtures to lessen the hardships of their Northern brethren that might eventually solicit favorable responses. The United States should be encouraged to follow a similar course in concert with Seoul.

A final scenario is customarily described as that of a "soft landing," namely, a gradual transformation of the North, centering initially upon economic reform, that brings the DPRK out of isolation and into greater contact with its region and the world. Over time, this makes possible a greater compatibility—both economic and political—with the South, thereby advancing the cause of genuine reunification.

It is this scenario upon which the current policies of both the ROK and the United States are based, with the acknowledgment that external policies, whatever their objectives, cannot guarantee success. Let me now turn to those policies and possible adjustments for the future, starting with the ROK.

In the final analysis, peace and development on the Korean peninsula are in the hands of North and South Korea. In the past, both parties have put forth certain proposals toward the other. Generally speaking, the North's proposals have been for more immediate, sweeping moves supposedly leading to unification; those of the South, more incremental, and many would argue, more realistic.

As we have noted, however, there are sharp divisions of opinion in the South regarding proper policies. Thus, economic overtures have been recurrently advanced and put on hold, as responses to bilateral developments unfold. This is an important matter because, given its relative lack of competitiveness (poor infrastructure, weak legal guarantees, uncertain political order), the DPRK faces serious problems in attracting major foreign investment at this point. The ROK is the most logical source of such investment, given its common language and culture, geographic proximity, and quotient of patriotism. Trade has been increasing modestly, and some joint ventures have been permitted, but much in the economic sphere remains restricted by an ROK government uncertain of the consequences of a more open policy and awaiting more flexibility on key issues by the North.

Similarly, political and security dialogues at the bilateral level are largely on hold, despite the promises held forth in the Agreements of December, 1991. It is clear that the primary responsibility for this retreat lies with the North. Its recent foreign policy has centered upon establishing closer relations with the United States, secondarily with Japan, emulating the *Nordpolitik* policies of Roh Tae-Woo, who succeeded in establishing diplomatic relations with Russia and China. The DPRK strategy has been to keep the ROK government at arm's length while pursuing united front tactics toward the South.

While this strategy has had modest success, including the periodic widening of differences between the United States and the ROK over policies toward the North, it has its limits. The United States continuously makes it clear that the resumption of a meaningful North-South dialogue ranging widely over diverse issues must be an integral part of the full normalization of U.S.–DPRK relations. Moreover, in such concrete actions as the Korean Peninsula Energy Development (KEDO) program, the ROK has been prominently involved despite the North's objections, and similarly, in the preliminary phases of the yet unsettled proposal for a four-party dialogue.

It seems clear that when a suitable combination of carrots and sticks is advanced, the United States and the ROK—working in harmony— can achieve some positive results. In these respects, the coming months may be crucial, given the serious food situation in the North. At present, there are signs that the DPRK wants to broaden its contacts with Americans, working at the nonofficial as well as at official levels. It also seems clear that Kim Jong Il's assumption of civilian office will take place in the not-too-distant future, opening the way for political intercourse. Political changes in the ROK lie ahead at the end of the year, an additional impetus for new approaches.

What are the appropriate near-term policies for the ROK and the United States under these circumstances? First, consultation between these two parties must continue to be extensive, with every effort made to secure agreement.

Economic measures are likely to be crucial in the short term. Food is likely to be the most important consideration for Pyongyang, and some type of food-for-peace formula may well be advanced. The United States and ROK should give serious consideration to tiding over the North in exchange for serious negotiations on political-security matters in the crucial months that lie immediately ahead. Further, assuming some progress on the latter fronts, carefully phased relaxation with regard to broader economic sanctions should be undertaken. Such measures can serve to strengthen those in the North who are carrying the brief for economic reform—and the evidence now indicates that such individuals exist, with their numbers possibly growing, but with their policies still contested.

Meanwhile, encouragement should be given to a wide range of nonofficial contacts at both the bilateral and multilateral levels. In the recent past, the North has been reluctant to participate in such ventures, a few regularized dialogues excepted. As noted earlier, however, there are now some signs of a change in attitude. This should be met positively. The wider the contacts, the more some degree of understanding can be advanced.

It is understandable that the ROK has exhibited reluctance on this front. North Korea's policies stressing united front tactics have featured efforts to interact with the South's small "radical" elements, notably students. Thus, these efforts have been deemed subversive, and subject to severe restraint. Yet one wonders whether such students—for the most part who are naive and idealistic—would be bolstered in their sentiments by seeing the North, providing they could go beyond strictly guided tours and contacts. With respect to religious figures, the South has been somewhat more permissive. Also, a resumption of efforts to make possible visits of those coming from divided families should be promoted. The total absence of trust between North and South can only be ameliorated as contacts are broadened at every level.

Meanwhile, the KEDO project should go forward, as is now planned. It is sometimes argued that the United States made too many concessions in achieving the October 1994 Accord. Unquestionably, the DPRK played its nuclear card well. However, when the general U.S. concerns about nuclear proliferation are taken into account, and the degree to which the KEDO project brings the ROK, the United States, and others, including Japan, into a common program, with its course favorable to the South, whatever may transpire in the North, the Accord warrants support and implementation.

At the same time, every effort should be made to advance either trilateral or quadrilateral negotiations leading to a legal end to the Korean War, and to arms reductions on the Korean peninsula. In these respects, the United States and the ROK have signal advantages. The military burden being carried by the North is huge, and despite that and its quantitative advantages, the DPRK military is increasingly saddled with obsolete equipment. On the other hand, the ROK military is acquiring modern equipment regularly.

It has been logical to include the People's Republic of China in negotiations relating to a formal end of the Korean War because it has been an active participant in the war, despite the fiction of "Chinese volunteers." Similarly, the South was centrally involved, although the Rhee government refused to sign the armistice agreement. In addition, China is vitally interested in the political-strategic outcome on the Korean peninsula, and despite its claim that it has limited influence on the North today (a claim partially correct), it is the only quasi-ally of the DPRK now existing.

Nonetheless, if the North should elect trilateral negotiations, this should be given serious consideration by the ROK and the United States. In any case, means can be found to have some ongoing parts of the dialogue, whether trilateral or quadrilateral, subdivided into bilateral dialogues without damaging the basic requirement that the ROK be fully involved in peace and security negotiations. At a later point, it might be useful to expand the dialogue relating to Northeast Asian security beyond the four parties to include Japan and Russia—two parties having a direct interest in any security agreement reached. Ultimately, we need some permanent multilateral institution devoted to Northeast Asian security issues rather than dependence solely on bilateral alliance and on coalitions in the region.

As has been made clear, no one can predict at this point how and under what conditions Korean unification will take place. It is clear, however, that unification taking place under conditions where the North has undergone some economic and sociopolitical evolution and where some degree of North-South understanding and trust has been established, is desirable. Let me reiterate that much depends upon the North, and no one can guarantee the success of efforts for a so-called soft landing. Preparations should be advanced to cope with the other scenarios set forth earlier. Further, it would be unwise to abandon all "sticks" and rely wholly upon "carrots." Such a move would not be conducive to effective advances. However, under current circumstances, both the ROK and the United States can afford to be flexible, and offer new opportunities for those in the DPRK who are genuinely interested in more engaged, cooperative policies.

One other matter warrants attention, namely, the U.S. security commitment. Some Americans have advocated an immediate reduction or removal of U.S. military forces from Korea, or even from East Asia generally. Nothing would be less conducive to progress in North-South relations or relations between the United States and the two Koreas. Let us not repeat the atmosphere of 1949–50. The firmness of the American commitment to South Korean security is a vital element in any peace settlement or other steps toward peninsula stability.

After reunification, the issue of the U.S.–Korean alliance can be reconsidered, depending upon circumstances. If a unified Korea desires a more nonaligned position, that should obviously be accepted. The more complex problem may be the American attitude in the aftermath of unification. If the Korean government wishes to continue security alliance, what will be the position of the American people and government?

Some sources assert that even the Northern leaders would not be anxious for a total American withdrawal after unification, given the presence of nearby big powers. They assert that history would repeat itself, with Korea wanting the protection of a distant power. But whether the American public would support continued guarantees would no doubt depend upon the general circumstances in Asia—and in the United States.

The enormous changes taking place in military technology, including the new informational techniques, long-range weaponry, and rapid deployment capabilities, also will have a future impact. Stationary American troops in foreign bases may be less necessary in the coming decades. Yet the timing of change, if it is to come, is vital—and now is not the time.

Thus, as we approach the twenty-first century, the chances of peace on the Korean peninsula seem better than at certain points in the recent past, notwithstanding the difficulties and uncertainties. The ROK and the United States must work together to enhance those chances, hopefully with the increasing cooperation of the DPRK. And at all times, policies must be made clear to our respective publics to be better understood. This is a task of democratic leaders—one not always adequately fulfilled. Our leaders must not be immobilized by conflicting domestic pressures.

Finally, under the conditions now prevailing on the Korean peninsula, all policies must be subject to reconsideration when changing circumstances warrant it. At the same time, however, clarity and continuity in the broad objectives, and the strategy to be employed in attaining these, is equally important. Critical tests relating to these matters lie immediately ahead.

The Contributors

Evgeniy P. Bazhanov is vice-president for Research and International Relations and director of the Institute for Contemporary International Studies, Russian Foreign Ministry. Dr. Bazhanov has a doctorate degree in history from the Institute of Oriental Studies in Moscow. He has authored nine books and numerous scholarly articles on Korean, Chinese, Southeast Asian, Asian-Pacific, and U.S. affairs. Dr. Bazhanov is former political counselor at the USSR Embassy, Beijing, and political officer, Asian Affairs, USSR Ministry of Foreign Affairs, Moscow.

David E. Brown is a veteran American diplomat, manager, and energy policy strategist. He joined the Stanton Group, Boston, in 1996 after retiring from the U.S. Foreign Service. Mr. Brown is former director of the Office of Korean Affairs ("Korea Desk") and director of the Office of International Energy Policy at the State Department and Counselor for Economic Affairs at the U.S. Embassy in Tokyo.

Victor D. Cha is assistant professor of Government at Georgetown University. He is the recipient of numerous academic awards, including the Fulbright and MacArthur Foundations fellowships. Dr. Cha has a Ph.D. from Columbia University, and has published on Korea and East-Asia security-related topics in various scholarly journals, including *Asian Survey* and *Korean Studies*. His most recent publication is "Bridging the Gap: The Strategic Context of Japan-Korea Normalization," *Korean Studies* (1996).

Wonmo Dong (Ph.D., Georgetown University) was the convener and executive-director of the SMU–Dallas Forum on Asian Affairs from 1996 to 1998. A member of the Political Science faculty at SMU since 1968, Professor Dong is also former director of the Asian Studies Program at the university. He has authored or coauthored three books and more than ninety articles and research papers on Korean and East Asian affairs. A three-time recipient of the Social Science Research council postdoctoral fellowship, Dong was a national fellow of the Hoover Institution at Stanford and a Center for Korean Studies Fellow at the University of California, Berkeley. He is currently president of the Association of Korean Political Studies in North America.

Robert L. Gallucci (Ph.D., Brandeis University) is dean of the Walsh School of Foreign Service at Georgetown University. Ambassador Gallucci completed twenty-one years of service with the U.S. Foreign Service, having served in 1994–96 as Ambassador-at-Large, and successfully concluded the U.S.–North Korea Agreed Framework at Geneva. He has authored a number of publications on political-military issues, including *Neither Peace nor Honor: The Politics of American Military Policy* (1975). He received the Department of the Army's Outstanding Civilian Award in 1991.

Donald P. Gregg is currently chairman of the board of the Korea Society, New York. Ambassador Gregg is former U.S. ambassador to the Republic of Korea and a national security advisor for former vice-president George Bush. After receiving a BA cum laude in philosophy from Williams College in 1951, he joined the Central Intelligence Agency and over the next quarter century was assigned to Japan, Burma, Vietnam, and Korea. Ambassador Gregg has been awarded the Distinguished Intelligence Medal, the Department of Defense medal for Distinguished Public Service, a decoration of the prime minister of Korea, and an honorary doctoral degree from Sogang University.

Selig S. Harrison is guest scholar at the Woodrow Wilson International Center for Scholars. He was previously a senior associate of the Carnegie Endowment for International Peace. Mr. Harrison has specialized in South and East Asian affairs for forty-four years as a journalist and scholar, and is the author of numerous articles on Asia and U.S. relations with Asia. Mr. Harrison has authored four books, including *The Widening Gulf: Asian Nationalism and American Policy* (1978).

Kwang Woong Kim is professor at the Graduate School of Public Administration, Seoul National University. In 1992–94 he served as dean of the school. Dr. Kim was educated at Seoul National University and the University of Hawaii, from which he received a Ph.D. in Political Science. He has authored many books in the fields of public bureaucracy, democracy, political development, elections, and cybergovernment. His recent publications include *Lecture on Research Methods* (1996) and *Practical Opinion Survey* (coauthored, 1996).

Samuel Soonki Kim is associate director of the Center for Korean Studies, East Asian Institute, and adjunct professor of political science at Columbia University. Dr. Kim received his masters degree in International Affairs and a Ph.D. from Columbia University. He has authored or edited fifteen books on East Asia, including *China and the World* (1994) and *China's Quest for National Identity* (1994). Dr. Kim has written articles in *World Politics*, *China Quarterly*, and other journals of international affairs.

P.H. Koo is former chairman of the Korea International Trade Association and an advisory board member of the Lucky-Goldstar Group. A political science graduate of Seoul National University, Mr. Koo began his business career as a manager of the Lucky Chemical Group in 1951. He subsequently served as director of Goldstar Company, president of Honam Oil Refinery Co., and chairman of the Lucky-Goldstar Group. A recipient of Korea's highest civilian honor for service to national development, Mr. Koo has been active in many economic and social organizations. He is currently chairman of both the Korea–U.S. Economic Council and the Korea–U.S. Business Council.

Marcus Noland is senior fellow at the Institute of International Economics and a visiting associate professor at Johns Hopkins University. He completed his undergraduate work at Swarthmore College and received a Ph.D. degree from Johns Hopkins University. His publications, which were published by the Institute of International Economy, include *Pacific Basin Developing Countries: Prospects for the Future* and *Pacific Dynamism and the International Economic System* (coedited with

C. Fred Bergsten). Dr. Noland has served as a consultant to the World Bank and the New York Stock Exchange.

Masao Okonogi is professor of political science at Keio University, from which he received his BA, MA, and Ph.D. degrees. He studied at Yonsei University in 1972–74. A leading Korea specialist in Japan, Professor Okonogi has visited North and South Korea numerous times. Also a director of the Center for Area Studies at Keio University, Dr. Okonogi has been a member of the board of directors of the Association for Political and Economic Studies on Asia and the Japan Association for International Relations.

Dae-Sook Suh is Korea Foundation Professor of Policy Studies at the University of Hawaii at Manoa. He received his Ph.D. in public law and government from Columbia University. Dr. Suh has authored a number of books on Korean communism and North Korean Affairs, including The *Korean Communist Movement, 1918–1948* (1967) and *Kim Il Sung, the North Korean Leader* (1988). His articles on North and South Korean politics have appeared in leading journals in the United States, Japan, and Korea. Dr. Suh is the former director of the Center for Korean Studies at the University of Hawaii at Manoa.

Robert A. Scalapino is Robson Research Professor Emeritus of Government, University of California at Berkeley. He received his MA and Ph.D. degrees from Harvard University. A member of the political science faculty at Berkeley from 1949 to 1990, Dr. Scalapino was chairman of the Political Science Department, founding director of the Institute of East Asian Studies, and Robson Research Professor of Government at the university. Dr. Scalapino has published some 470 articles and 40 books or monographs on Asian politics and U.S. Asian policy. He is a fellow of the American Academy of Arts and Sciences, and a member of the Board of the Atlantic Council, the National Bureau of Asian Research, and numerous other boards and committees for educational and governmental agencies.

Scott Snyder is program officer in the Research and Studies Program of the U.S. Institute of Peace. He received his BA from Rice University and an MA in regional studies and East Asian program from Harvard University. Mr. Snyder is author of several articles and chapters on Korean affairs, including a 1996 special report of the U.S. Peace Institute, entitled *A Coming Crisis on the Korean Peninsula?* and "Beyond the Geneva Agreed Framework: A Road Map for Normalizing Relations with North Korea" in *Peace and Security in Northeast Asia* (1997).

David I. Steinberg is director of the Asian Studies Program at Georgetown University. A former member of the Senior Foreign Service and the Agency for International Development with the Department of State, Mr. Steinberg worked extensively on development in Asia and the Middle East. Before joining AID, he was representative of the Asia Foundation in Korea and Washington, and assistant representative in Burma and Hong Kong. Mr. Steinberg is the author of ten books and over sixty articles on Korean affairs and international development. Mr. Steinberg was educated at Dartmouth College, Lingnan University (Canton, China), Harvard University, and the University of London.

William J. Taylor, Jr. is senior vice president for International Security and Affairs and director of Political-Military Studies at the Center for Strategic and International Studies in Washington, D.C. He holds a Ph.D. from the American University and has done post-doctoral work at the American University of Beirut. He is the author, coauthor, or editor of 17 books and over 350 publications on national security affairs.

Quansheng Zhao is associate professor and Asia Coordinator at the School of International Service of American University, and Associate-in-Research at the Fairbank Center for East Asian Research at Harvard University. He holds a Ph.D. from the University of California, Berkeley. Dr. Zhao is the author of *Interpreting Chinese Foreign Policy* (1996), *Japanese Policymaking* (1993), and coeditor *of Politics of Divided Nations: China, Korea, Germany, and Vietnam* (1991).

Index

Kim, Junki, 61–73
Kim, Kwang Woong, xvi-xvii, 61–73
Kim Kwang Yop, 16
Kim, Samuel Soonki, xv-xvi, 32–54
Kim Tal Hyon, 17n.13
Kim Yong Nam, 9–10
Kim Yong Sun, 17n.13
Kim Young Sam
  authoritarianism of, 64–67, 71, 107–
    108
  in China, 141–142, 143
  decline in popularity, 73, 106, 112n.3
  democratic reforms of, 62–64
  economic reforms of, xvi
  and food aid, 255
  and Hanbo Steel scandal, 61, 62, 107
  and inter-Korean relations, xvii, xviii,
    68–71, 72, 95, 171, 191, 199,
    241, 257, 259
  labor law of, 61, 66–67, 107
  and nuclear issue, 188
  in Russia, 156
  unification principles of, 79
King Kojong, 272
Koh, B.C., 224–225
Koo, P.H., xxvii-xviii, 267–270
Korea
  and China, 134, 142–143
  crisis situation in, 234–237
  division of, 20, 216, 235–236, 272
  economy, 19–20
  Japanese rule of, 19, 134
  and Russia, 147
  and Soviet Union, 147–148
  See also North Korea; South Korea;
    Unification
Korean Airlines (KAL 007), downing
  of, xxiii, 155
Korean Peninsula Energy Development
  Organization (KEDO), xxv, 14, 96,
    123, 181, 249, 277, 278–279
Korean People's Army, 4
Koreans in China, 143
Korean Sharing Movement, 255
Korean War, 20, 134, 147–148, 158, 279

Kozyrev, 157–158
Kwangju uprising of 1980, 102

Laney, James, 58n.48, 170, 199, 245
Lee Hoi Chang, 70
Lee Hong Koo, 81
Liberal-Democratic party (Russia), 161,
  163
Liberal Justice Party (South Korea), 63
Lieberthal, Kenneth, 13
Light-water reactors (LWRs), 14, 96,
  178, 181, 182, 194
Lilley, James, 170, 253
Lim Dong Won, 213
Li Peng, 130, 140–142
Li Xiannian, 137
Lord, Winston, 237
Luck, Gary E., 184, 198

Mann, Jim, 250
Manning, Bob, 253
Mao Zedong, 131, 132
"March in distress," 4–5
Mazaar, Mike, 193
Minjung (people's) movement, xix,
  103–104
Mitrofanov, 161
Mondale, Walter, 19, 237–238
Morgan, Patrick, 83

Nationalism
  anti-American, in South, 102–105, 216
  Chinese, 133
National Security Planning Agency
  (South Korea), 69
Natsios, Andrew, 253
New Korea Party (South Korea), 63, 199
Nixon, Richard, 24
Nixon (Guam) Doctrine, 100, 112n.4
Noland, Marcus, xv, 19–30, 222, 246
North Korea
  comparison to East Germany, 201–202
  foreign relations of, 9–11, *See also*
    specific countries (China-North
    Korea relations)